# HEARINGS ON THE HILL

Good public policy in a democracy relies on efficient and accurate information flows between individuals with firsthand, substantive expertise and elected legislators. While legislators are tasked with the job of making and passing policy, they are politicians and not substantive experts. To make well-informed policy, they must rely on the expertise of others. *Hearings on the Hill* argues that partisanship and close competition for control of government shape the information that legislators collect, providing opportunities for party leaders and interest groups to control information flows and influence policy. It reveals how legislators strategically use committees, a central institution of Congress, and their hearings for information acquisition and dissemination, ultimately impacting policy development in American democracy. Marshaling extensive new data on hearings and witnesses from 1960 to 2018, this book offers the first comprehensive analysis of how partisan incentives determine how and from whom members of Congress seek information.

Pamela Ban is an assistant professor of political science at the University of California San Diego. Her research focuses on legislative politics, interest groups, information in policymaking, and the interbranch relationship between Congress and the bureaucracy. Her research has received the Congressional Quarterly Press Award and has been used by policymakers at the state and federal levels.

Ju Yeon Park is an assistant professor of political science at the Ohio State University. Her research examines legislators' competing incentives and how they shape their legislative activities and public speeches. Her research on congressional hearings won the Congressional Quarterly Press Award and received media attention from Bloomberg, FiveThirtyEight, *Roll Call*, and the *Washington Post*.

Hye Young You is an associate professor of the Department of Politics and the School of Public and International Affairs at Princeton University. Her research focuses on how interest groups influence democratic representation in the US. She has been recognized by five discipline-wide Best Paper awards from the American Political Science Association.

POLITICAL ECONOMY OF INSTITUTIONS AND DECISIONS

*Series Editors*

Jeffry Frieden, *Harvard University*
John Patty, *Emory University*
Elizabeth Maggie Penn, *Emory University*

**Founding Editors**

James E. Alt, *Harvard University*
Douglass C. North, *Washington University of St. Louis*

## Other books in the series

Faisal Ahmed, *Conquests and Rents: A Political Economy of Dictatorship and Violence in Muslim Societies*
Alberto Alesina and Howard Rosenthal, *Partisan Politics, Divided Government and the Economy*
Lee J. Alston, Thrainn Eggertsson and Douglass C. North, eds., *Empirical Studies in Institutional Change*
Lee J. Alston and Joseph P. Ferrie, *Southern Paternalism and the Rise of the American Welfare State: Economics, Politics, and Institutions, 1865–1965*
James E. Alt and Kenneth Shepsle, eds., *Perspectives on Positive Political Economy*
Josephine T. Andrews, *When Majorities Fail: The Russian Parliament, 1990–1993*
Jeffrey S. Banks and Eric A. Hanushek, eds., *Modern Political Economy: Old Topics, New Directions*
Yoram Barzel, *Economic Analysis of Property Rights*, 2nd edition
Yoram Barzel, *A Theory of the State: Economic Rights, Legal Rights, and the Scope of the State*
Robert Bates, *Beyond the Miracle of the Market: The Political Economy of Agrarian Development in Kenya*
Jenna Bednar, *The Robust Federation: Principles of Design*
Adam Bonica and Maya Sen, *The Judicial Tug of War: How Lawyers, Politicians, and Ideological Incentives Shape the American Judiciary*
Charles M. Cameron, *Veto Bargaining: Presidents and the Politics of Negative Power*
Erin Baggott Carter and Brett L. Carter, *Propaganda in Autocracies: Institutions, Information, and the Politics of Belief*
Kelly H. Chang, *Appointing Central Bankers: The Politics of Monetary Policy in the United States and the European Monetary Union*
Tom S. Clark, *The Supreme Court: An Analytical History of Constitutional Decision Making*
Mark Copelovitch and David A. Singer, *Banks on the Brink: Global Capital, Securities Markets, and the Political Roots of Financial Crises*
Peter Cowhey and Mathew McCubbins, eds., *Structure and Policy in Japan and the United States: An Institutionalist Approach*

Gary W. Cox, *The Efficient Secret: The Cabinet and the Development of Political Parties in Victorian England*
Gary W. Cox, *Making Votes Count: Strategic Coordination in the World's Electoral System*
Gary W. Cox, *Marketing Sovereign Promises: Monopoly Brokerage and the Growth of the English State*
Gary W. Cox and Jonathan N. Katz, *Elbridge Gerry's Salamander: The Electoral Consequences of the Reapportionment Revolution*
Adam Dean, *Opening Up by Cracking Down: Labor Repression and Trade Liberalization in Democratic Developing Countries*
Tine De Moore, *The Dilemma of the Commoners: Understanding the Use of Common-Pool Resources in Long-Term Perspective*
Adam Dean, *From Conflict to Coalition: Profit-Sharing Institutions and the Political Economy of Trade*
Mark Dincecco, *Political Transformations and Public Finances: Europe, 1650–1913*
Mark Dincecco and Massimiliano Gaetano Onorato, *From Warfare to Wealth: The Military Origins of Urban Prosperity in Europe*
Raymond M. Duch and Randolph T. Stevenson, *The Economic Vote: How Political and Economic Institutions Condition Election Results*
Jean Ensminger, *Making a Market: The Institutional Transformation of an African Society*
David Epstein and Sharyn O'Halloran, *Delegating Powers: A Transaction Cost Politics Approach to Policy Making under Separate Powers*
Kathryn Firmin-Sellers, *The Transformation of Property Rights in the Gold Coast: An Empirical Study Applying Rational Choice Theory*
Sean Gailmard, *Agents of Empire: English Imperial Governance and the Making of American Political Institutions*
Clark C. Gibson, *Politicians and Poachers: The Political Economy of Wildlife Policy in Africa*
Daniel W. Gingerich, *Political Institutions and Party-Directed Corruption in South America*
Avner Greif, *Institutions and the Path to the Modern Economy: Lessons from Medieval Trade*
Jeffrey D. Grynaviski, *Partisan Bonds: Political Reputations and Legislative Accountability*
Stephen Haber, Armando Razo and Noel Maurer, *The Politics of Property Rights: Political Instability, Credible Commitments, and Economic Growth in Mexico, 1876–1929*
Ron Harris, *Industrializing English Law: Entrepreneurship and Business Organization, 1720–1844*
Anna L. Harvey, *Votes Without Leverage: Women in American Electoral Politics, 1920–1970*
Seth J. Hill, *Frustrated Majorities: How Issue Intensity Enables Smaller Groups of Voters to Get What They Want*
Shigeo Hirano and James M. Snyder, Jr., *Primary Elections in the United States*
Murray Horn, *The Political Economy of Public Administration: Institutional Choice in the Public Sector*

John D. Huber, *Rationalizing Parliament: Legislative Institutions and Party Politics in France* Jack Knight, *Institutions and Social Conflict*
Sean Ingham, *Rule of Multiple Majorities: A New Theory of Popular Control*
John E. Jackson, Jacek Klich and Krystyna Poznanska, *The Political Economy of Poland's Transition: New Firms and Reform Governments*
Jack Knight, *Institutions and Social Conflict*
Michael Laver and Kenneth Shepsle, eds., *Cabinet Ministers and Parliamentary Government*
Michael Laver and Kenneth Shepsle, eds., *Making and Breaking Governments: Cabinets and Legislatures in Parliamentary Democracies*
Michael Laver and Kenneth Shepsle, eds., *Cabinet Ministers and Parliamentary Government*
Margaret Levi, *Consent, Dissent, and Patriotism*
Brian Levy and Pablo T. Spiller, eds., *Regulations, Institutions, and Commitment: Comparative Studies of Telecommunications*
Leif Lewin, Ideology and Strategy: *A Century of Swedish Politics (English Edition)*
Gary Libecap, *Contracting for Property Rights*
John Londregan, *Legislative Institutions and Ideology in Chile*
Arthur Lupia and Mathew D. McCubbins, *The Democratic Dilemma: Can Citizens Learn What They Need to Know?*
C. Mantzavinos, *Individuals, Institutions, and Markets*
Mathew D. McCubbins and Terry Sullivan, eds., *Congress: Structure and Policy*
Anne Meng, *Constraining Dictatorship: From Personalized Rule to Institutionalized Regimes*
Gary J. Miller, *Above Politics: Bureaucratic Discretion and Credible Commitment*
Gary J. Miller, *Managerial Dilemmas: The Political Economy of Hierarchy*
Ilia Murtazashvili, *The Political Economy of the American Frontier*
Monika Nalepa, *After Authoritarianism: Transitional Justice and Democratic Stability*
Douglass C. North, *Institutions, Institutional Change, and Economic Performance*
Elinor Ostrom, *Governing the Commons: The Evolution of Institutions for Collective Action*
Sonal S. Pandya, *Trading Spaces: Foreign Direct Investment Regulation, 1970–2000*
John W. Patty and Elizabeth Maggie Penn, *Social Choice and Legitimacy*
Daniel N. Posner, *Institutions and Ethnic Politics in Africa*
J. Mark Ramseyer, *Odd Markets in Japanese History: Law and Economic Growth*
J. Mark Ramseyer and Frances Rosenbluth, *The Politics of Oligarchy: Institutional Choice in Imperial Japan*
Stephanie J. Rickard, *Spending to Win: Political Institutions, Economic Geography, and Government Subsidies*
Jean-Laurent Rosenthal, *The Fruits of Revolution: Property Rights, Litigation, and French Agriculture, 1700–1860*
Michael L. Ross, *Timber Booms and Institutional Breakdown in Southeast Asia*
Meredith Rolfe, *Voter Turnout: A Social Theory of Political Participation*

Shanker Satyanath, *Globalization, Politics, and Financial Turmoil: Asia's Banking Crisis*

Alberto Simpser, *Why Governments and Parties Manipulate Elections: Theory, Practice, and Implications*

Norman Schofield, *Architects of Political Change: Constitutional Quandaries and Social Choice Theory*

Norman Schofield and Itai Sened, *Multiparty Democracy: Elections and Legislative Politics*

Alastair Smith, *Election Timing*

Pablo T. Spiller and Mariano Tommasi, *The Institutional Foundations of Public Policy in Argentina: A Transactions Cost Approach*

David Stasavage, *Public Debt and the Birth of the Democratic State: France and Great Britain, 1688–1789*

Charles Stewart III, *Budget Reform Politics: The Design of the Appropriations Process in the House of Representatives, 1865–1921*

George Tsebelis and Jeannette Money, *Bicameralism*

Georg Vanberg, *The Politics of Constitutional Review in Germany*

Nicolas van de Walle, *African Economies and the Politics of Permanent Crisis, 1979–1999*

Stefanie Walter, *Financial Crises and the Politics of Macroeconomic Adjustments*

John Waterbury, *Exposed to Innumerable Delusions: Public Enterprise and State Power in Egypt, India, Mexico, and Turkey*

David L. Weimer, ed., *The Political Economy of Property Rights Institutional Change and Credibility in the Reform of Centrally Planned Economies*

# HEARINGS ON THE HILL

*The Politics of Informing Congress*

**PAMELA BAN**
University of California San Diego

**JU YEON PARK**
Ohio State University

**HYE YOUNG YOU**
Princeton University

Shaftesbury Road, Cambridge CB2 8EA, United Kingdom

One Liberty Plaza, 20th Floor, New York, NY 10006, USA

477 Williamstown Road, Port Melbourne, VIC 3207, Australia

314–321, 3rd Floor, Plot 3, Splendor Forum, Jasola District Centre, New Delhi – 110025, India

103 Penang Road, #05–06/07, Visioncrest Commercial, Singapore 238467

Cambridge University Press is part of Cambridge University Press & Assessment, a department of the University of Cambridge.

We share the University's mission to contribute to society through the pursuit of education, learning and research at the highest international levels of excellence.

www.cambridge.org
Information on this title: www.cambridge.org/9781009534093

DOI: 10.1017/9781009534048

© Pamela Ban, Ju Yeon Park and Hye Young You 2024

This publication is in copyright. Subject to statutory exception and to the provisions of relevant collective licensing agreements, no reproduction of any part may take place without the written permission of Cambridge University Press & Assessment.

When citing this work, please include a reference to the DOI 10.1017/9781009534048

First published 2024

*A catalogue record for this publication is available from the British Library*

Library of Congress Cataloging-in-Publication Data
Names: Ban, Pamela, author. | Park, Ju Yeon, author. | You, Hye Young, author.
Title: Hearings on the Hill : the politics of informing Congress / Pamela Ban, University of California, San Diego; Ju Yeon Park, Ohio State University; Hye Young You Princeton University, New Jersey.
Description: Cambridge, United Kingdom ; New York, NY : Cambridge University Press, 2024. | Series: Political economy of institutions and decisions | Includes bibliographical references and index.
Identifiers: LCCN 2024020387 | ISBN 9781009534093 (hardback) | ISBN 9781009534048 (ebook)
Subjects: LCSH: Legislative hearings – United States. | Legislative process – United States. | United States. Congress Senate – Committees. | United States. Congress House – Committees.
Classification: LCC KF4935 .B36 2024 | DDC 328.73/0765–dc23/eng/20240729
LC record available at https://lccn.loc.gov/2024020387

ISBN 978-1-009-53409-3 Hardback
ISBN 978-1-009-53407-9 Paperback

Cambridge University Press & Assessment has no responsibility for the persistence or accuracy of URLs for external or third-party internet websites referred to in this publication and does not guarantee that any content on such websites is, or will remain, accurate or appropriate.

*To our parents*

# Contents

| | | |
|---|---|---|
| *List of Figures* | | *page* xiii |
| *List of Tables* | | xv |
| *Acknowledgments* | | xvii |
| 1 | Members of Congress Are Politicians, Not Experts | 1 |
| 2 | Committee Hearings and Information Provision in Congress | 12 |
| 3 | Who Testifies in Congress? New Data on Congressional Hearings and Witnesses | 29 |
| 4 | Not All Information Is Equal: How Witnesses Vary in What They Provide to Congress | 53 |
| 5 | When Committees Seek Out Information for Policy Development | 78 |
| 6 | How Control of Government Shapes Information Exchange | 98 |
| 7 | Congressional Capacity and the Search for Specialized Information | 122 |
| 8 | Conclusion: A Partisanly Informed Congress | 140 |
| *Appendix A* | | 153 |
| *References* | | 175 |
| *Index* | | 187 |

# Figures

| | | |
|---|---|---|
| 2.1 | An example of the Truth in Testimony Disclosure Form | page 27 |
| 3.1 | The list of witnesses in hearing transcripts: Example | 32 |
| 3.2 | Number of hearings and witnesses in Congress over time | 38 |
| 3.3 | Number of total words in witness testimonies over time – House | 39 |
| 3.4 | The number of witnesses in House standing committees over time | 39 |
| 3.5 | The number of witnesses in Senate standing committees over time | 40 |
| 3.6 | Number of hearings by type of hearing | 40 |
| 3.7 | Witness affiliations over time | 43 |
| 3.8 | Witness affiliations by House standing committee | 45 |
| 3.9 | Witness affiliations by Senate standing committee | 45 |
| 3.10 | The composition of witness affiliations by majority party | 46 |
| 3.11 | Witness gender over time | 48 |
| 3.12 | Witness gender by committee | 49 |
| 4.1 | Over time changes in individual witnesses' speaking patterns | 61 |
| 4.2 | Changes in witness testimonies by Congress | 61 |
| 4.3 | Proportion of keywords by witness type | 65 |
| 4.4 | Number of keywords by witness type | 67 |
| 4.5 | Proportion of keywords by committees | 67 |
| 4.6 | Proportion of keywords by the gender of witnesses | 69 |
| 4.7 | Proportion of keywords by government type and the majority party | 69 |
| 4.8 | Topics of testimony by witness categories – Total number of statements | 71 |
| 4.9 | Topics of testimony by witness categories – Proportion of statements | 71 |
| 4.10 | An example of research cited in a written statement | 73 |

## List of Figures

| | | |
|---|---|---|
| 5.1 | Frequency of legislative hearings – House, 1961–2016 | 85 |
| 5.2 | Share of referral hearings across a congressional term – House | 85 |
| 5.3 | The effect of referral hearings on witness invitations – House | 87 |
| 5.4 | The effect of referral hearings on witness invitations – Senate | 89 |
| 5.5 | The effect of referral hearings on witness invitations by different periods – House | 91 |
| 5.6 | The effect of referral hearings on witness invitations in policy committees | 93 |
| 5.7 | The effect of referral hearings on witness invitations in constituent committees | 93 |
| 5.8 | Referral hearings and inviting expert witnesses by issue areas | 95 |
| 5.9 | Referral hearings and inviting group witnesses by issue areas | 95 |
| 6.1 | Ratio of bureaucratic witness over time | 109 |
| 6.2 | Ratio of bureaucratic witness across issues | 109 |
| 6.3 | Number of legislative hearings by executive departments | 110 |
| 6.4 | Number of legislative hearings by independent agencies | 110 |
| 6.5 | The effect of divided government on witness invitations – House | 113 |
| 6.6 | The effect of divided government on witness invitations – House | 114 |
| 6.7 | The effect of divided government on witness invitations – Senate | 115 |
| 6.8 | The effect of divided government on witness invitations by different periods – Senate | 115 |
| 6.9 | The effect of divided government on inviting bureaucrats as witnesses by presidential issue priorities – House | 118 |
| 6.10 | The effect of divided government on inviting bureaucrats as witnesses by presidential issue priorities – Senate | 119 |
| 7.1 | OTA Annual Report to the Congress, 1974 | 128 |
| 7.2 | OTA Annual Report to Congress, 1992 | 130 |
| 7.3 | Number of OTA request by House committees, 1990–1995 | 130 |
| 7.4 | OTA elimination on the change in the number of witnesses | 134 |
| 7.5 | OTA elimination on the change in research witness share | 135 |
| 7.6 | Changes in the number of committee staff in the House | 137 |
| A1 | Number of hearings by type of hearing – House | 153 |
| A2 | Number of hearings by type of hearing – Senate | 153 |
| A3 | Number of witnesses by type – House | 154 |
| A4 | Number of witnesses by type – Senate | 155 |
| A5 | Witness gender composition by issue areas – House | 156 |
| A6 | Witness gender composition by issue areas – Senate | 156 |
| A7 | Research witness shares | 173 |

# Tables

| | | |
|---|---|---|
| 3.1 | Types of witness affiliations | page 35 |
| 3.2 | Structure of hearings and witness dataset | 37 |
| 3.3 | Average number of witnesses per hearing by types of hearings | 41 |
| 3.4 | Witness categories by types of hearings | 44 |
| 3.5 | Gender composition by witness affiliation | 50 |
| 4.1 | Examples of witness testimonies containing varying levels of analytical information | 59 |
| 4.2 | Hearing characteristics and witness testimonies | 63 |
| 4.3 | Examples of the most and least analytical testimony | 66 |
| 4.4 | Distribution of reference sources | 74 |
| 4.5 | Top sources for citation | 74 |
| 4.6 | Witness types and citation patterns | 76 |
| 5.1 | Number of legislative hearings and proportions of referral hearings by committee | 92 |
| 5.2 | Number of legislative hearings and proportions of referral hearings by issue | 94 |
| 6.1 | Bureaucratic witnesses under divided vs. unified government | 111 |
| 6.2 | Top issue in the State of the Union address by Congress | 117 |
| 7.1 | Changes in witness invitations before and after the 1995 reform – House | 133 |
| 7.2 | Number of committee staff and witness invitations, 95th–114th Congresses | 136 |
| A1 | The featured words of each topic | 159 |
| A2 | Regression results for divided government and Democratic majority | 162 |
| A3 | Committee intent and witness invitation patterns – House | 163 |
| A4 | Committee intent and witness invitation patterns – Senate | 165 |
| A5 | Mean share of expert and group witnesses by issue | 167 |
| A6 | Summary statistics of the variables | 167 |

| | | |
|---|---|---:|
| A7 | Institutional characteristics and witness invitation patterns – House | 168 |
| A8 | Institutional characteristics and witness invitation patterns – Senate | 170 |
| A9 | Divided government, President's issue priority, and bureaucrats as witnesses – House | 172 |
| A10 | Divided government, President's issue priority, and bureaucrats as witnesses – Senate | 172 |
| A11 | OTA elimination on the number of invited witness | 173 |
| A12 | OTA elimination on the invitation of research witness | 174 |

# Acknowledgments

In the summer of 2019, little did we know that the world would soon face an unprecedented pandemic. It was during this time that the three of us embarked on a project focused on congressional hearings. This book stands as the culmination of our efforts, forged through countless Zoom meetings spanning three different time zones: Pam in San Diego, Ju Yeon in Essex in the UK, and Hye Young in New York City.

The realization of this book wouldn't have been possible without the generosity and insights of our colleagues. We owe our deepest gratitude to Seth Hill, Jaclyn Kaslovsky, Shiro Kuriwaki, Julia Payson, Jon Rogowski, Jim Snyder, and Jan Stuckatz. They were the first to read the work that laid the groundwork for this book and graciously shared their invaluable feedback. Their input was pivotal in shaping the course of this book.

Being first-time authors, we are immensely grateful for the guidance of our mentors throughout this process: Jim Curry, Frances Lee, and Sean Theriault. Renowned scholars in congressional politics and seasoned authors, they not only imparted invaluable knowledge on how to navigate the book publication process but also offered crucial feedback on our manuscript. Their unwavering support and encouragement have been instrumental in cheering us on throughout this journey. Gwyneth McClendon, Julia Payson, Molly Ritchie, and Sharece Thrower shared their own book prospectuses, provided feedback on ours, and introduced us to editors. We thank Brandon Bartels, Sarah Binder, and Forrest Maltzman for feedback at a book roundtable. Frances Lee, Nolan McCarty, and Anthony Taboni's suggestions helped us develop and think through the last step, our title. We are grateful for the support of all these colleagues as they guided us through the book publication process.

We've had the privilege of engaging with various scholarly communities that generously welcomed us to share our work, providing us with invaluable insights. Among these, we extend our deepest gratitude to Craig Volden and Alan Wiseman for their invitations to the Center

## Acknowledgments

for Effective Lawmaking Annual Research Conference. Their support allowed us to exchange ideas and gather invaluable perspectives among scholars and practitioners, enriching our scholarly journey.

We have benefited from excellent research assistance from Matt Asare, Hope Chow, Jack Dwekc, Isabel Feng, Ria Coen Gilbert, Maggie Jia, Annapurna Johnson, Sophia Jordan, Mariah Kallhoff, Victoire Legrand, Jessica Lieban, Cameron Maglio, Kamden Martin, Carlos Paredes, Anna Pelz, and Alan Sun. We are also deeply grateful to two anonymous readers who provided thorough feedback that substantially improved the framing and writing of our book. We thank Robert Dreesen at Cambridge University Press for leading us through the publication process.

The origin of this book project can be traced back years before its first word was officially written. We would like to thank a number of people who have inspired, mentored, and supported us along our academic careers.

My (Pam) time in political science started when Jim Snyder at Harvard introduced me to political science research when I was an undergraduate. Thank you, Jim, for treating me as a serious scholar from the beginning and inspiring me to pursue graduate study with you; your influence throughout my PhD has shaped the course of my academic career. Once I arrived at the University of California San Diego as a new assistant professor, I was welcomed by a department strongly dedicated to making sure junior faculty succeed and benefited from expert mentorship on the book publication process and my academic career in general from Dan Butler, Seth Hill, and Thad Kousser. Thank you to my fellow colleagues Sam Elgin, Sean Ingham, Federica Izzo, Gareth Nellis, and Ben Noble for talking with me about my work and offering help at the drop of a hat. We made a loud and animated junior faculty family that kept our hallways a party and our engagement with each other lively.

My (Pam) academic career and this book was made possible by the unwavering support and love from my husband, Michael, and our dear cat Finn. Michael, you put up with all the hours I spent at the computer, ensured I ate food that wasn't just Chipotle, and always made me laugh no matter what else was going on. I am so lucky that we crossed paths on our mountain bikes and love our little family.

I (Ju Yeon) owe so much love and guidance to my dearest advisor, the late Rebecca Morton, and dissertation committee members, Chris Dawes, Eric Dickson, and Jonathan Woon, who believed in my ability as a scholar and provided unconditional support. My postdoctoral fellowship at Washington University in St. Louis was a breakthrough in my academic career and redefined me as a congressional scholar and data

## Acknowledgments

scientist. I am deeply grateful to my postdoctoral advisor, Jacob Montgomery, for his continued guidance and support. Thank you to Kevin Esterling, Sean Theriault, and Steven Smith for always being welcoming, inspiring, and generous with their time and advice. My gratitude also goes to Craig Volden and Alan Wiseman for inviting me to be part of the Legislative Effectiveness research community, where I met scholars who would become my lifelong academic friends.

My (Ju Yeon) tenure-track career began at the University of Essex. I would like to thank Royce Carroll and Shane Martin for their mentorship during my time at Essex. I have recently moved to the Ohio State University with great excitement. I am extremely grateful to Janet Box-Steffensmeier, Sarah Brooks, Gregory Caldeira, Vladimir Kogan, Marcus Kurtz, William Minozzi, Michael Neblo, and Thomas Nelson for their guidance and support in my various academic pursuits. Thank you to my colleagues, especially Alex Acs, Erin Lin, Molly Ritchie, and Nicole Yadon, for making my new home feel like a home I have known for years. Finally, I give my greatest love and thanks to my husband, Kye Yun Lee, for supporting my academic career in every way possible and always being there for me through thick and thin, and to my little sunshine, Elise Lee, for making my life full of love and joy every day.

I (Hye Young) am immensely grateful to my dissertation committee members Jeffry Frieden, Ken Shepsle, and Jim Snyder at Harvard University, who provided invaluable insights, unwavering support, and scholarly mentorship throughout my academic journey. I am deeply grateful for my colleagues at Vanderbilt University: Larry Bartels, Josh Clinton, Marc Hetherington, Dave Lewis, and Alan Wiseman were exceptionally generous with their time as mentors; Allison Anoll, Brenton Kenkel, Emily Nacol, Cecelia Mo, and Sharece Thrower made my journey as a junior faculty member filled with fun. I also met Mike Sances and Molly Ritchie at Vanderbilt, who became collaborators and friends, and a significant influence on my academic journey.

I (Hye Young) began my time at New York University with Gwyneth McClendon and Julia Payson, which was akin to winning the lottery. Even more colleagues made NYU and the city feel like home: Amy Catalinac, Chris Dawes, Pat Egan, Sandy Gordon, Rakeen Mabud, John Marshall, Carlo Prato, Pablo Querubín, Arturas Rozenas, Cyrus Samii, Shanker Satyanath, Melissa Schwartzberg, Tara Slough, and David Stasavage, all contributed immensely to my professional and personal life in New York. My academic journey and this book would not have been possible without the support and love of my husband, Inkeun Song. I ask myself every day how lucky I am to have him by my side.

*Acknowledgments*

Finally, all three of us would like to express our deepest gratitude to our parents: Chunsheng Eric Ban, Hong Vicky Wan, Ke Lim Park, Myoung Youl Kim, Young Soo Noh, and Jung Mok You. We have carried their unconditional and unfailing love, encouragement, and confidence with us throughout our careers and lives. We dedicate this book to you.

# I

## Members of Congress Are Politicians, Not Experts

I have one goal today, and that is accurate information, accurate information that can help Americans understand what they should do about the coronavirus, and accurate information to help Members of Congress decide what else we ought to be doing about the coronavirus.
– US Senator Lamar Alexander, in the hearing "An Emerging Disease Threat: How the U.S. Is Responding to COVID-19, the Novel Coronavirus," held on March 3, 2020, by the Committee on Health, Education, Labor, and Pensions.

In March 2020, Congress faced the looming threat of the coronavirus spreading to the United States. At that point, members of Congress did not yet foresee the massive impact it would have on public health, the economy, and cultural norms. However, they did realize their need for one thing to sort out what, if anything, they had to do: information. Congress began to collect information on what would soon be named COVID-19 through congressional committee hearings. In the 2019 calendar year, only two hearings mentioned the word "coronavirus." In 2020, this number increased to five hearings in January, thirty-nine hearings in February, and over fifty hearings in the first two weeks of March. By March 2020, Congress was dedicating frequent, full hearings exclusively to the topic of coronavirus response and preparedness.

The Senate Committee on Health, Education, Labor, and Pensions, for example, held a hearing in early March on the emerging threat of COVID-19 and how the United States should prepare to respond. On March 3, 2020, the chairman of the committee at the time, Lamar Alexander, opened the hearing with the above quote, revealing his intention to gather information to help Congress decide how to react to the pandemic.

While at the time, Congress did not believe that the coronavirus would carry a high risk to the United States – during that hearing, Chairman Alexander even stated that he believed "most people in the United States are at low risk" – the committee called a panel of witnesses to inform them about the possible impact coronavirus might have on public health and the global economy. They called four witnesses to testify that day: Dr. Anthony Fauci, Director of the National Institute of Allergy and Infectious Diseases at the National Institutes of Health; Dr. Stephen Hahn, Commissioner of the US Food and Drug Administration; Dr. Robert Kadlec, Assistant Secretary for Preparedness and Response at the Department of Health and Human Services; and Dr. Anne Schuchat, Principal Deputy Director of the Centers for Disease Control and Prevention.

Chairman Alexander emphasized the importance of these four witnesses in providing information at the committee hearing:

The first goal of the hearing is to provide the American people with accurate information. Today's witnesses are respected professionals who have a lot of experience in what we're talking about today and know what they are doing, and I want to take a moment to emphasize their backgrounds ... The reason I go through that is because if we're looking for accurate information, these four ought to be able to provide it. Now, in addition to getting accurate information for the American people, we want it ourselves to know what else we should be doing to limit the damage of the coronavirus to the American people and the American economy.[1]

The chairman specifically highlighted the witnesses' cumulative experience in the country's responses to the Ebola outbreak in Africa, biological threats, other epidemics and flu pandemics, and in healthcare administration and management. Chairman Alexander stressed how these witnesses' firsthand experiences were paramount in providing information to Congress and the American public, which in turn would form the basis for how members of Congress would shape policy.

Indeed, the contrast between the expertise of the four witnesses at this hearing and that of members of Congress cannot be overstated. Members of Congress are politicians – they are not scientists, healthcare professionals, or experts in public health – yet they are responsible for enacting legislation that responds to issues and situations requiring such expertise. They must search for and rely on other individuals to provide information and guidance within highly politicized, complex environments.

Members of Congress are under time constraints and constant pressure to make decisions that have important and potentially far-reaching consequences. Information ranks as one of the members' most important and necessary resources as they fulfill their legislative responsibilities, and various groups and individuals compete to provide information from their own perspectives with the aim of influencing legislators.

The flow of information has a high potential to shape both legislation and new policies. For instance, in the early days of congressional discussions about COVID-19, conflicting opinions abounded on how to prioritize prevention efforts, especially regarding vaccine development, mask mandates, and lockdowns. These opinions were largely divided along party lines, with no shortage of individuals able to provide and amplify their perspectives on the stage of Capitol Hill. *Whom* Congress selected to provide information, and *why* Congress selected those witnesses, would substantially shape the trajectory of policy response.

To that end we ask: From whom do members of Congress seek information, and how does the content of that information vary by the identity of those providing information? How do partisan politics or institutional conditions affect information acquisition? The answers to these questions are paramount to understanding the role of information in legislative institutions and how members enact effective policies.

This book advances our understanding about the roles of information and external witnesses in shaping public policy and political discourse. Understanding how institutional features and partisan-driven incentives influence the quality and diversity of information Congress acquires benefits the American public by revealing potential ways to increase representation and improve lawmaking.

Our key theoretical insight focuses on how partisan incentives determine when committees seek witnesses who can provide analytical input to policy decisions. On the one hand, members of Congress are politicians who respond to political forces. On the other hand, they must make policies and laws that solve real problems. This responsibility is held in tension with the politicized, partisan environment of Congress; members have a serious policymaking role they must perform while pushed by political forces.

Committee hearings and the process of inviting witnesses present a unique setting to examine this tension. While there are various avenues through which committees can collect information, hearings reveal the specific witnesses and information that members of Congress intentionally select to consider and then convey to other members, interest groups, the media, and voters. As committees form policies and legitimize their decisions to other members and external observers, various factors – such as polarization or divided government – can affect whom committees invite to testify.

In other words, witness testimony in hearings is a product of the committee's selective search for information. This is the information that committees have consciously chosen to find and publicly consider to advance their goals. Therefore, we can leverage the material contained in witness invitations and testimonies to examine how partisan incentives affect the information-seeking behavior of Congress and the testimony provided in hearings.

As hearings are public in nature, committees use them and witness invitations to further their political goals such as promoting partisan agendas. Under certain conditions, however, committees are more likely to seek out witnesses who can provide information relevant for policy-making. We present a theoretical framework incorporating how partisan incentives within three categories of institutional conditions – committee intent, interbranch relations, and committees' internal capacities – can affect whom committees choose to provide external information. These conditions grant the incentives and abilities for primary actors in committee proceedings to conduct relatively in-depth searches for information.

We present the most comprehensive analysis, to date, of the information flow between Congress and external groups. Marshaling extensive new data on witnesses and witness testimonies that span 1960 to 2018, we use a new methodological approach to quantify the quality of information that witnesses present. We examine whom Congress invites to provide information and the conditions under which committees turn to certain types of witnesses more often than others.

Our argument yields testable predictions regarding how these conditions affect the information that committees search for and receive. We use our extensive data throughout the book to provide empirical evidence. In doing so, this book answers a central question that bridges research on congressional policymaking, interest group politics, legislative organization, and text-as-data methodology: From whom does Congress seek information, and what drives this information search?

## 1.1 COMMITTEE HEARINGS AND STRATEGIC INFORMATION FLOWS

The congressional committee stage is a critical time during which information is sought and acquired in Congress. Since Woodrow Wilson's declaration in 1884 that "Congressional government is committee government," congressional scholars have placed committee systems at the center of studies of legislative organization. This central importance makes the committee stage a prime market for exchanges of information.

The importance of hearings during the committee stage is noted in both academic literature and contemporary examples. Members of Congress themselves believe that committee hearings provide an efficient way to gather information, publicly establish positions, and exert influence.

Recent examples demonstrate this. In September 2023, the Senate Judiciary Committee held hearings on the best way to govern artificial

## 1.1 Committee Hearings and Strategic Information Flows

intelligence. The hearings were in conjunction with consideration of a bipartisan bill that would deny artificial intelligence companies immunity from user content that violates federal law. At the end of one of these hearings, Senator Richard Blumenthal (D-CT), then Chair of the Subcommittee on Privacy, Technology, and the Law, spoke directly about how information in witness testimonies was useful in developing a framework for the legislation they were considering:

It is so helpful to us. I can go down our framework and tie the proposals to specific comments made by Sam Altman or others who have testified before, and we will enrich and expand our framework with the insights that you have given us. So I want to thank all of our witnesses and again, look forward to continuing our bipartisan approach here.[2]

The next example is from a February 2023 hearing on children's online safety, as Senator Dick Durbin (D-IL) noted:

We'll hear from an outstanding panel of witnesses about the challenges to protecting kids online and the steps we in the Senate and this committee can take to help. I want to thank our witnesses, Kristen Bride and Emma Lembke, who've been personally impacted by this issue. They speak on behalf of many others and they advocate for change to help spare others what they and their families have gone through.[3]

Here, Senator Durban is making clear that the input from the witnesses provides information on why the committee should take action and how they could potentially do so.

As these examples demonstrate, committee hearings are explicitly designed so members can receive external input through witness testimonies. They serve a dual role within the tension between making policy and responding to political forces: They allow committees to search for and receive information necessary for efficient policymaking and, because committee hearings are formal and public, committees are able to control the narrative of this information flow in pursuit of political goals.

While this setting ostensibly allows audiences – such as the media, interest groups, legislators who are not committee members, and other stakeholders – to observe the information flow among external witnesses and committee members, the public nature of a hearing also incentivizes members to use hearings strategically to advance their goals. A committee's choice of witnesses they invite to testify is a prime example of this strategy. In Chapter 2, we detail the witness invitation process and how committees hold hearings; we also outline the theoretical context explaining our focus on witnesses to study the strategic role of information in the legislative process.

## 1.2 HEARING WITNESSES AND TESTIMONIES

To fully understand the informational dynamics in hearings and witness testimonies, it is crucial to identify the types of witnesses who are invited to speak and the types of information they present. In Chapter 3, we provide a detailed explanation of how we constructed our dataset on hearings and witnesses. Our data harness the full names, organizational affiliations, testimony content, and other witness characteristics of 731,810 witnesses who appeared in 74,077 published hearings of the House, Senate, and joint standing committees from 1961 through 2018. This is the most comprehensive collection of data to date concerning those who provide external information to Congress.

This comprehensive dataset allows us to present new descriptive trends showing that certain types of witnesses (e.g., bureaucrats) are more frequently called to testify compared to other types of witnesses (e.g., representatives of nonprofits) and that the composition of witness pools varies by committees or issues. In general, it provides a fuller picture of the groups and individuals who are invited to deliver their views and opinions to members of Congress.

These descriptive patterns show witnesses' various affiliations, which represent meaningful differences in the amounts and types of information that witnesses provide. In Chapter 4, we define and explain the concept of *analytical information* – the amount of falsifiable statements about policies under consideration. We measure the amount of analytical information present in witness testimonies using a new methodological approach that combines (1) dictionary methods using information-seeking statements from a supervised learning method and (2) keywords related to cognitive orientation. We measure and validate the amount of falsifiable statements about the policy under consideration – analytical information – that occur in each witness's testimony.

Through measuring the amount of analytical information present in witness testimonies, we reveal two aspects of witness invitations: They expose *whom* committees select as witnesses, and they have substantial implications for the types of information committees ultimately *receive* from witnesses. This is because, all else equal, the amount of analytical information offered varies by the type of witness. For instance, we find that witnesses who are bureaucrats and those from think tanks and research institutions tend to give testimonies with the highest proportions of analytical information. On the other hand, witnesses who are individual citizens without organizational affiliations and those who represent religious institutions tend to give testimonies with lower proportions of analytical information; instead, they provide more anecdotal or experiential information.

Furthermore, witnesses provide differing amounts of analytical testimony depending on the institutional context. For example, witness testimonies tend to include a greater proportion of analytical information when more members of Congress attend and speak during the hearing. On the other end of the spectrum, witnesses tend to provide less analytical information as the ideological polarization within a committee grows, indicating that greater polarization leads to more partisan hearings at the expense of true analytical fact-finding.

Also, we go beyond our measure of analytical information to examine the amount of information from scientific and academic sources provided to Congress – information that is backed by research evidence. Using examples of climate change hearings held in the House during recent Congresses, we find that the types of witnesses who provide higher levels of analytical information also cite more research evidence in their testimonies. Bureaucrats and individuals associated with think thanks and academic institutions, in particular, use this type of information extensively in their testimonies. Thus, when these witnesses are invited to speak, members of Congress receive large amounts of research-based evidence.

## 1.3 ROLE OF PARTISAN INCENTIVES

The descriptive patterns in Chapters 3 and 4 illustrate how the witnesses who testify in committees can vary and how levels of analytical information differ across witness types. This implies that invitees shape the type of information committee members are offered during hearings. Therefore, we investigate how those who testify in legislative hearings are chosen.

The key to understanding this matter lies in the tension that members of Congress face as lawmakers: They shoulder the serious responsibility of making the nation's policies while facing political forces that incentivize them to pursue political goals with their policymaking. For instance, addressing the COVID-19 pandemic was more complex than simply choosing policies from a menu of options; it involved consideration of how each possible path aligned with various political goals. Imposing lockdowns might prevent spread of the virus but could harm economic growth extensively. Mandating vaccinations for federal workers was likely to reduce hospitalizations due to COVID-19 but could erode support in public health and government officials among those hesitant on vaccination.

Support for any possible path, and consideration of its tradeoffs, can be bolstered or weakened by the information that Congress receives and conveys. And each path is replete with political considerations, the strongest of which lie along *partisan lines*. We argue that partisan-driven incentives can affect the choices of who committees summon to supply external information. As hearings are public, committees use hearings and witness invitations to further their political goals, such as promoting partisan agendas. Under certain conditions, however, committees are more likely to seek witnesses who can provide analytical information.

We begin Chapter 5 by examining the *intent* a committee may have for holding a legislative hearing and how this affects the committee's witness selection. The main distinction of a committee's intent in a hearing is whether there is a bill attached to the hearing (referral hearing) or the hearing is exploratory in nature (nonreferral hearing). In a nonreferral hearing, the chair and committee have not yet advanced a public position with a bill and have the political flexibility and incentive to seek *analytical information* from experts.

In contrast, a referral hearing is anchored to a specific piece of legislation, so committee members are more likely to learn about and disseminate *political information*. Committees can broadcast the views of groups affected by the legislation hoping to garner support for, and gauge the viability of, the bill under consideration. Members elicit information from specific witnesses to assist the majority party delegation with the eventual passage of that bill.

The findings from our extensive dataset point to committees pursuing and obtaining relatively more information from witnesses who provide the most analytical information at the development stages of the policymaking process. This contrasts with the later stages when a specific bill and its corresponding partisan goal are at hand. Furthermore, the varying types of witnesses who speak at referral and nonreferral hearings provide evidence that committee chairs strategically choose the identities of witnesses and the types of information the hearing will generate.

In Chapter 6, we examine a second category of partisan incentives that shapes the information committees seek: the interbranch relationship between Congress and executive agencies. Given the informational advantage that executive agencies possess, we focus on how the political forces surrounding the relationship between the legislative and executive branches manifest in the information-seeking behavior of committees.

We argue that when the preferences between the legislative and executive branches diverge – which is most salient during divided government – committees are less likely to seek information from bureaucrats. By strategically adjusting the frequency of bureaucrats' appearances in legislative hearings under divided government, committees can control input from the executive branch. However, this leaves committees in a dilemma: While limiting input from the executive branch could keep policy outcomes closer to the committee's preferences, the lack of bureaucratic input in policymaking causes an informational void that could lead to inferior policy outcomes for the majority party in Congress.

Using our extensive data on witnesses and a series of regression analyses, we show how committees overcome this problem. Under divided government, committees substitute for bureaucratic input by shifting to two types of witnesses whose testimonies also include a high degree of analytical information: (1) congressional support agencies, such as the Congressional Research Service or Congressional Budget Office, and (2) witnesses from research organizations, such as affiliates of think tanks and academics.

This link between divided government and the invitation rates of bureaucrats sheds light on a new mechanism that explains how divided government affects interbranch relationships through information transmission. A partisan divide between the legislative and executive branches may result in more than the commonly understood barriers to enacting legislation. The divide may also hold implications for the amount of input – information – from the executive branch that Congress incorporates in the formulation of legislation. A partisan divide may, therefore, have significant consequences on the content of bills as well as their implementation by executive agencies.

In Chapter 7, we address how the internal resources of Congress affect the quantity and quality of information that committees receive. Recently, scholars have revealed that the decreasing number of policy and committee staff along with a lack of internal resources has weakened congressional capacity so seriously that Congress is unable to fulfill its institutional duty effectively. One of the most critical factors in this trend is the diminished (or eliminated) role of congressional support agencies, such as the Congressional Budget Office and the Office of Technology Assessment. Scholars have expressed concern that Congress's lack of internal sources of expertise could increase the power of lobbyists and outside groups to influence legislators.

We focus on how the internal capacity of Congress – determined, in part, by the partisan incentives of congressional party leaders – affects how members are informed through the channel of committee witnesses. Our methodological approach takes advantage of a shock to congressional capacity in 1995 when the newly elected House Republican majority downsized the government through their "Contract with America" platform. As part of this downsizing, the Office of Technology

Assessment (OTA) was eliminated. Consequently, committees suffered an immediate reduction in internal information and the absence of a group of OTA staffers who liaised between committees and the scientific community.

Using a difference-in-differences research design, we show that congressional committees that relied most heavily on internally produced information suffered a drastic drop in the number of technical and scientific witnesses they could invite after the OTA's elimination. Our evidence suggests that those committees did not compensate for this loss of information through external witnesses. The partisan-motivated cuts to congressional capacity resulted in a void of technical and scientific witnesses testifying before Congress. These results highlight the importance of strong congressional capacity to bring research-based witnesses to hearings. Without this form of resource and support, the ability and incentive of legislators to identify and process key scientific and technical information decrease significantly.

## 1.4 BROADER IMPORTANCE OF "HEARINGS ON THE HILL"

This book makes three notable contributions. We present the most comprehensive database to date on congressional committee hearings and witnesses who appear before them. Our data greatly expand the time spans of hearings and witnesses covered in previous research while providing novel and valuable data, such as types of witnesses and their individual affiliations. Additionally, our results fill a knowledge gap by empirically demonstrating the effect of partisan considerations on how often, to whom, and why legislators rely on outsiders for information.

More generally, this book advances an understanding of how external groups influence legislators through providing information at congressional hearings, an important venue for congressional deliberation. By revealing which external groups are invited, the conditions driving these invitations, and how the type of information delivered varies by group affiliations, this book highlights one crucial way in which external groups can shape legislative processes.

We conclude the book by discussing the broader implications of Congress's selections of witnesses on the study of legislative politics and policy outcomes for the country more generally. While legislators are tasked with the ever-important job of making and passing policy to address wide-ranging concerns, they are politicians rather than substantive experts. To make well-informed policies, they must rely on the expertise of others.

## 1.4 Broader Importance of "Hearings on the Hill"

Good public policy in a democracy rests on efficient and accurate information flows between legislators and those with firsthand or substantive knowledge. However, this transfer of information occurs within a partisan arena that is increasingly polarized. Partisan-driven incentives can seep into how legislators seek information and to whom they turn. Therefore, how this process unfolds is central to understanding how laws are made and who influences the production of policy.

*Hearings on the Hill* tells the story of how legislators strategically use a central institution of Congress – committees and their hearings – to collect information and advocate for their policy positions. This story is highly relevant to salient issues that the US government and the public are facing today within an atmosphere where the value and use of information and scientific evidence have been questioned. Our findings extend the discussion on the costs and benefits of the quality of the information presented to politicians and prompt further inquiry into the role of research and scientific evidence in shaping public policy in our democracy.

### NOTES

1. From the hearing "An Emerging Disease Threat: How the U.S. is Responding to Covid-19, the Novel Coronavirus," held by the Committee on Health, Education, Labor, and Pensions, US Senate, on March 3, 2020.
2. From the hearing "Oversight of A.I.: Legislating on Artificial Intelligence," held by the Committee on the Judiciary, US Senate, on September 12, 2023.
3. From the hearing "Protecting Our Children Online," held by the Subcommittee on Privacy, Technology and the Law (Committee on the Judiciary), US Senate, on February 14, 2023.

# 2

## *Committee Hearings and Information Provision in Congress*

Thank you again to all the witnesses today for their testimony and for offering their views on the Paycheck Protection Program. By sharing your experiences, we will be able to conduct more effective oversight, and continue to optimize the PPP program. Though I am pleased the program appears to be saving small business jobs, as we intended, your testimonies have confirmed that there are still some issues that need to be addressed.
– Chairwoman Nydia Velazquez in a hearing held on June 17, 2020 by the House Committee on Small Business[1]

We are writing to request information and documents regarding the reported role of ExxonMobil in a long-running, industry-wide campaign to spread disinformation about the role of fossil fuels in causing global warming, and to request your appearance at a Committee hearing on Thursday, October 28, 2021.
– Letter dated September 16, 2021, from the House Committee on Oversight and Reform to ExxonMobil Corporation CEO Darren Woods

Information is one of the most important commodities in congressional politics. That information provides power in Congress may be the least controversial idea among scholars who extensively study the ways in which members of Congress seek, acquire, and control information. The importance of information makes sense considering the context of Congress: Members are time constrained, work in complex environments, make important and consequential decisions, and are constantly pressured to act (Baumgartner and Jones, 2015; Curry, 2015). In this environment, information is one of the most important strategic needs of, and tools for, members of Congress as they consider legislation (Krehbiel, 1991). Members may need information concerning the importance of problems they are asked to address (Baumgartner and Leech, 1998; Kingdon, 1981). They might require information about the likely impact, effectiveness, or unintended consequences a policy proposal may have on their constituents (Krehbiel, 1991; Baumgartner and Jones, 1993) and on their own reelection chances (Hansen, 1991; Arnold, 1990).

However, there are significant variations in legislators' abilities to acquire information. This is due to many factors, including their institutional positions within Congress, their networks of donors and interest groups, and their professional backgrounds before joining Congress. Members' abilities to acquire information are heterogeneous, and this inequality affords party leaders and committee chairs opportunities to use their informational advantages to shape behaviors of rank-and-file members who have limited resources (Curry, 2015). Also, donors reward members with policy expertise through their campaign contributions (Esterling, 2007), and this trend is particularly noticeable at the leadership level: The share of interest group donations through political action committees (PACs) to party leaders in particular has dramatically increased over the last three decades (Ban, Moskowitz, and Snyder, 2021).

Given the power of information in Congress, it is important to understand how, and from what sources, members acquire that information. There are many sources eager to offer information on policies and members' electoral prospects (Gray and Lowery, 2000). Internal organizations of Congress, such as the Congressional Budget Office and Congressional Research Service, serve and assist members and congressional committees in their workflow. Legislators can rely on news media and polling to acquire information. They can reflect on their own interactions with constituents to understand issue priorities and the potential impacts of their actions on their reelection prospects. Existing literature also emphasizes that members of Congress who lack knowledge about a specific issue will rely on the expertise of trusted fellow members (Kingdon, 1989).

Interest groups are another primary source of information for members of Congress. Corporations, nonprofits, and various other groups seek to influence legislators through the provision of information. Thus, members' need for information provides opportunities for external groups to participate and gain influence. Indeed, providing information has long been characterized as a type of lobbying in the formal theory literature (Austen-Smith, 1993; Lohmann, 1995; Schnakenberg, 2017; Awad, 2020; Dellis, 2023). Across all stages of the policymaking process, interest groups are predicted to be most likely to lobby in the form of providing information during the committee stage (Hojnacki and Kimball, 1998). Additionally, extant literature theorizes that interest groups are most likely to provide information-based resources to legislative allies because they will work toward, rather than against, progress on the interest groups' preferences (Hall and Deardorff, 2006; Ellis and Groll, 2020).

The committee stage is a prime market for the acquisition of information because of its importance in the legislative process. Since Woodrow Wilson's famous argument, "Congressional government is committee government" in 1884, congressional scholars have put committee systems at the center of studies of legislative organization. Early work on congressional committees emphasized the distributive rationale behind the organizational structure of committees: The way congressional committees are organized reflects a collective choice made by members when allocating policy benefits. The importance of committees in the politics of information became more salient when this distributive tradition was challenged by informational theories on legislative organization. Unlike the distributive perspective, the informational view explicitly considers the notion of policy expertise and explores how committees' organizational structures help the legislative body acquire information. Further, this theory explores how committees use their informational advantages to persuade the majority in Congress (Gilligan and Krehbiel, 1990; Krehbiel, 1991; Diermeier and Feddersen, 2000).

In particular, the importance of hearings as a tool that committees use to gather and convey information has been noted in the congressional literature (Oleszek, 1989; Huitt, 1954; Truman, 1951; Davidson and Oleszek, 1985). Further, members of Congress themselves believe that committee hearings, specifically, provide an efficient way to gather information, publicly establish their positions, and exert influence (Park, 2017, 2019). However, despite the vast theoretical attention paid to the role of information in legislative organization and interactions between legislators and external groups, there is a lack of systematic empirical work on how committees acquire information and who provides it. Only a handful of recent studies have addressed this question. For example, Kornberg (2023) examines the witnesses invited to various types of hearings and argues that witnesses tend to be selected not on the basis of their expertise but on the basis of their position on the issues under consideration. However, Park (2017, 2019) presents conditions under which witnesses are selected based on their expertise rather than their issue positions by introducing a formal model of the committee's strategic witness selection process and empirically testing its predictions using laboratory experiments.

The relative lack of empirical work on sources of information at the committee stage is particularly surprising given that *witness testimonies during congressional hearings* are designed to provide external input to members. The congressional literature recognizes the importance of hearings during the committee stage as a tool for gathering and conveying information (Oleszek, 1989; Deering and Smith, 1997). Committees hold hearings to help them accomplish their work, and hearings are explicitly designed to feature external witnesses who can provide particular or diverse viewpoints on issues under consideration.

Committees also can collect information through private meetings, phone calls, individual correspondence, or private briefings. However, the process of inviting experts to speak at committee hearings reveals the specific witnesses and information that members of Congress selectively seek to consider and convey to other members, interest groups, the media, and voters during the committee process.

The use of external information – through the selection of witnesses to testify – in a formal, public setting provides members of Congress with information and credibility in legislative decision-making. Formal theorists view information transmission in legislatures as a game of incomplete information where policymakers face uncertainties about the implications and consequences of policy proposals (Austen-Smith and Riker, 1987; Austen-Smith, 1990b; Gilligan and Krehbiel, 1990). Legislators who aspire to transmit reliable information to their fellow members can gain credibility by using external witnesses during hearings. Thus, they must make strategic decisions about whom to invite to testify during the committee stage. Understanding these choices informs a full comprehension of the informational role of committees in the legislative process.

In this chapter, we provide a theoretical context for our focus on witnesses in congressional hearings and the role of the information they provide in the legislative process. First, we review the function of information in congressional committees and how that setting has emerged as a crucial means of information acquisition for legislators. Second, we examine where members of Congress source information and how its importance at the committee stage opens opportunities for groups to provide information. Third, we examine the specific use of hearings and witnesses to facilitate flows of information during the committee stage. In particular, we focus on how the public nature of congressional hearings allows others to observe information flows between witnesses and committee members and affords members of Congress the opportunity to use hearings strategically to achieve their goals. Finally, we provide a primer on the mechanics of committee hearings and the witness invitation process.

## 2.1 SEARCH AND ACQUISITION OF INFORMATION IN CONGRESS

The literature in congressional politics characterizes information in various ways. As Bimber (1991) points out, research on the role of information in congressional politics comprises two strands: Observational studies that mainly focus on how the search for and use of information is related to institutional design and formal models that explain how political actors strategically find information and use it in decision-making.

In his seminal field work on congressional committees, Fenno (1973) illustrates how committees can facilitate information gathering for Congress. His comparative study of six congressional committees in *Congressmen in Committees* focuses on how committee members' goals drive the level of "integration" in a committee (i.e., how the group works collectively both formally and informally). He explains why some committees, such as the Appropriations Committee, come to value expertise and the search for and sharing of information, while other committees, such as the House Education Committee, do not. To Fenno, the answer lies in a system of reciprocity and deference – in Appropriations, full committee members defer to the expertise of subcommittee members, which gives them incentives to specialize in their subject matter. His study reveals how within-committee norms can affect how a committee values information, thus whether the members of a committee will acquire expertise in their subject matter and discount information from outside experts.

Another line of work shows how legislators' choices to search for and reveal information can be affected by rules governing amendments to legislation and the ideological positions between committees and the floor. Gilligan and Krehbiel (1990) show how rules that restrict amendments can incentivize committees to acquire technical information, since the risk of the committee's legislation being modified is lower under closed rules.

Increasing level of polarization may be another factor. Park (2017) shows that as the policy preferences of two competing parties within a committee diverge and the floor median takes a more extreme position, committee members are less motivated to seek information about which policy alternative is optimal because they are already inclined toward their preferred alternative and thus use the hearings for other purposes, such as sending political messages or grandstanding.

In positive theory, formal models, such as those in McCubbins, Noll, and Weingast (1987) and McCubbins and Page (1987), depict information asymmetries between Congress (i.e., committees) and the executive agencies charged with implementing policies. These principal–agent models center on how information acquisition to overcome asymmetries is costly to Congress and how Congress is uncertain about the outcomes of its delegation to agencies. The authors predict that as the cost of Congress acquiring information grows, Congress will impose increasingly more administrative procedures on agencies. This line of research shows how the cost of acquiring information for legislators could affect institutional designs by Congress.

The positive theory literature also has expanded the theoretical framework on the use of information through modeling how a political actor can strategically choose when to reveal private information to others. For instance, models in Austen-Smith and Riker (1987, 1990) and Austen-Smith (1990a) show how a legislator's choice to reveal expert information can increase certainty about a policy's consequences among other legislators. The information asymmetry here is among legislators themselves within Congress. These models highlight the strategic decision of legislators to use information – whether to reveal it to other legislators – and how those decisions are influenced by ideological positions among legislators and the levels of uncertainty about outcomes.

Furthermore, the ideological distance between the committee and the floor also can affect how much information can be transmitted from the committee to the floor (Gilligan and Krehbiel, 1990; Krehbiel, 1991). Formal models have shown that the greater the divergence between committee and floor preferences, the more the floor will discount the information provided by a committee. This is because the floor recognizes that the committee has an incentive to be strategic about the information it reveals.

These models illustrate that the literature in congressional politics identifies the committee as the fundamental entity that acquires and uses information. This is no surprise; scholars emphasize that committees have a strategic policymaking position and view committees as policy experts, gatekeepers, and agenda controllers in their policy areas (Fenno, 1973; Shepsle and Weingast, 1987; Weingast, 1988; Deering and Smith, 1997; Cox and McCubbins, 2005). As such, the committee stage receives specific attention from scholars interested in the relationships between legislators and other political actors and the informational exchanges within those relationships.

## 2.2 SOURCES OF INFORMATION PROVISION TO CONGRESS

Section 2.1 above briefly reviewed how the literature addresses the question of why legislators search for information and under what conditions they reveal more or less information to other political actors. Given that information is such an important commodity in congressional politics, it is important to understand who supplies it.

Formal theories that treat information as a core logic of legislative organizations mostly focus on the information environment rather than types and sources of information. For example, Krehbiel (1991) writes about "key concepts in informational theories," and his main focus is to differentiate incomplete information and asymmetric information. According to Krehbiel (1991), incomplete information is characterized by "assuming that legislators are uncertain about the relationship between policies and outcomes" (p. 68). Asymmetric information "refers to a condition in which some legislators have better knowledge than others about the relationship between policies and outcomes" (p. 68). Most of the formal work examines how information transmission and collective decision-making occurs under either incomplete information or asymmetric information (e.g., Austen-Smith, 1993) and does not seriously consider the information's origins.

Empirical research on information seeking among legislators has focused more explicitly on members' searches for information. Kingdon (1981)'s survey of members and resulting study examines where members are likely to search for information when determining how to vote. Information searches are costly; when members need to find information, they are likely to rely on the most efficient route possible. Kingdon (1981) notes that members frequently take their cues from party leadership or other members. Other scholars document that cue-taking from peer legislators is common (Matthews and Stimson, 1975; Box-Steffensmeier, Ryan, and Sokhey, 2015; Fong, 2020) and that information is distributed formally through instructions from party leaders or "Dear Colleagues" letters (Box-Steffensmeier, Christenson, and Craig, 2019), and informally through conversations or through observing others' voting patterns (Zelizer, 2019).

Other literature focuses on the provision of information by interest groups. Some argue that, while a degree of informational asymmetry among legislators exists, the gap in expertise is much larger between interest groups and legislators (Austen-Smith, 1993). The informational advantage that interest groups possess engendered the theory of lobbying as information transmission: Interest groups are privy to private information about constituent opinions and views on policies, and lobbyists for interest groups can use this private knowledge to convince legislators to take friendly positions (Schnakenberg, 2017; Awad, 2020; Awad and Minaudier, 2024). As Hansen (1991) explains, this transmission of information from interest groups occurs because of legislators' lack of certainty about which positions to adopt on policies. From this perspective, Baumgartner et al. (2002) argue that information in these cases can contribute to issue framing. Further, interest groups and their lobbyists have incentives to be strategic about when and what information to provide.

## 2.2 Sources of Information Provision to Congress

Relatedly, Hall and Deardorff (2006) introduce the idea of lobbying as a way for interest groups and their lobbyists to subsidize (i.e., augment the scarce resources of) legislators who share their preferences. This differs from the previously mentioned forms of lobbying as exchange or persuasion because it does not see lobbyists as changing (or preventing the change of) preferences but instead as a "service bureau" providing resources to legislators who are friendly to an interest group's position. Those resources include the types of information legislators might not be able to access or produce easily. For instance, the in-depth technical policy analysis described in Esterling (2004) and Wright (1996), or specific awareness of the active players in the policy's issue arena such as the issue networks detailed in Carpenter and Lazer (1998). Further, Hall and Deardorff (2006) and Matthews (1973) note that interest groups are not only well positioned to possess these types of information, they also can perform tasks similar to what legislative staff might do, such as synthesizing and summarizing information in reports for legislators or providing information in a form that is useful for speech writing.

Scholars have documented that lobbying to provide information, especially technical policy information, is most likely to happen during the committee stage (Hojnacki and Kimball, 1999). Formal models also highlight that agenda-stage lobbying is generally influential in changing members' beliefs through information provision (Austen-Smith, 1993). Given that a relatively small number of committee members have profound influence on the fate of legislative agendas through gatekeeping and agenda-setting, interest groups have targeted committees to exert their influence (Kollman, 1997). Studies examining the influence of interest groups through campaign contributions also highlight the importance of the committee stage. For example, Hall and Wayman (1990) contend that the committee level, rather than the floor level, should be the focus for scholars studying the influence of money on congressional decision-making. While other studies, such as Grenzke (1989), Wright (1985), or Grier and Munger (1986, 1993) concentrate on whether PAC contributions affect members' voting decisions on the floor, Hall and Wayman (1990) specifically study committee-stage participation in discussions about a subset of legislative bills. They report that interest group money is indeed a driver of legislators' participation at the committee stage. Studies also provide ample evidence that PACs change whom they target based on legislators' committee assignments (e.g., Romer and Snyder, 1994; Powell and Grimmer, 2016; Fouirnaies and Hall, 2018). The motivating reasoning underlying these studies is that the mechanisms for influencing policy decisions are present during deliberations or behind-the-scenes discussions at the committee stage (Hall, 1987; Evans, 1996) – especially prior to committee votes – rather than at the floor stage.

## 2.3 COMMITTEE HEARINGS AS A VENUE FOR INFORMATION PROVISION

Having established that the committee stage is a crucial time for the exchange of information between legislators and external groups, we turn now to describing committee hearings – the institutional setting that is explicitly designed for the flow of information during the committee stage.

Congressional committee hearings are held for one of four purposes: (1) to collect information and opinions on legislation *(legislative)*, (2) to conduct oversight on executive agencies *(oversight)*, (3) to investigate events *(investigative)*, and, in the Senate, (4) to consider presidential nominations as part of the confirmation process *(confirmation)* (Heitshusen, 2017). In legislative hearings, committee members seek and discuss information about the subject matter of proposed legislation or future legislation. While introduction of a bill is not required before holding a legislative hearing, these hearings concentrate on matters specifically related to potential policy.

The other three types of hearings – oversight, investigative, and confirmation – generally involve the executive branch or another body as the subject of the hearing. An oversight hearing is held by a committee as one way of conducting oversight of the executive branch. In oversight hearings, committees pursue a variety of actions relative to an agency, such as reviewing its administration of a program or considering whether a program should be reauthorized. While a legislative hearing is about potential policy ideas or bills, an oversight hearing is about overseeing an executive branch agency's actions.

For instance, an oversight hearing held on October 25, 2017 by the Committee on Veterans' Affairs examined overpayments erroneously made by the Veterans Benefits Administration. The committee heard from witnesses from the US Department of Veterans' Affairs and groups representing veterans. Members of the committee used the hearing to seek information on how overpayments can be prevented and what processes should be established to mitigate the problem. This hearing revealed the committee's oversight of an executive agency and department concerning an existing problem, in contrast to a legislative hearing where the same committee could have focused on policies regarding future benefits for veterans.

## 2.3 Hearings and Information Provision

Investigative hearings are held when committees wish to investigate a governmental official, agency, or incident due to suspected wrongdoing, and they generally involve witnesses giving sworn testimony under oath. Similar to oversight hearings, investigative hearings focus on the actions of another individual or group.

Hearings held by one of the House Select Committees examining the January 6, 2021 attacks on the US Capitol provide an illustrative example of investigative hearings. In June 2022, former Trump White House aide, Cassidy Hutchinson, gave a firsthand account of what she observed leading up to and during the attacks. These types of investigative hearings differ immensely from legislative hearings, as they are centered on the actions of another individual or group rather than an introduced or potential bill.

Confirmation hearings are held when Senate committees consider a president's nomination to an executive or judicial position. They include questioning of the nominee and others who are asked to provide information about the nominee. This examination of a specific nominee distinguishes confirmation hearings from other types of hearings. For example, a hearing to confirm a US Supreme Court Justice is focused on that person's background and qualifications for the post rather than on a current or future legislative issue.

In theory, all committee hearings are important venues for "educative instruments" as committee members collect the information they need from the various witnesses invited to speak (Oleszek, 1989). Therefore, hearings are an integral part of the committee process. Committee chairs have ultimate authority to decide whether to hold hearings and there are various motivations for holding hearings. For instance, a committee chair may hold a hearing to collect information about the details or consequences of proposed bills, or a committee chair may use a hearing to advance or publicize their own opinions or agendas (Park, 2021, 2023). In Chapter 5, we will expand on these possible drivers – what we term *committee intent* – and how they affect witness selection. For now, we focus on the mechanics of hearings and witness invitations.

In any type of committee hearing, members from both the majority and minority parties are given the chance to make statements, ask questions, debate opinions, invite outside witnesses to testify, and question outside witnesses about the topics at hand. In general, hearings provide an opportunity for committee members to engage with external witnesses as members collect information, discuss ideas, and formulate policy. Witnesses who appear in Congress only appear before congressional committees; there are no witnesses who testify on the floor. Therefore, witnesses who appear before congressional committees represent the extent of all external witness testimony in Congress.

Nonetheless, members of Congress can gather information from multiple sources. They can collect information from federal agencies by requesting reports. Lobbyists can provide information to members and their staffers in private meetings. Constituents and other interested parties can write or call members' offices with information. Members can receive information in private Congressional briefings. However, two features stemming from the public nature of hearings make them a fitting venue to study information flows into Congress.

The first feature relates to researchers' data collection and empirical research designs. The public nature of hearings allows us to measure the information flow among legislators and witnesses, which is challenging to observe through private communications. For example, while correspondence between members and bureaucrats can be collected through the Freedom of Information Act (e.g., Lowande, 2018; Lowande, Ritchie, and Lauterbach, 2019; Ritchie, 2018; Ritchie and You, 2019; Ritchie, 2023), it is unlikely to comprise a complete set of the universe of all correspondence. Also, telephone and meeting records, even if obtainable in complete sets, do not record the content discussed or the information conveyed.

Committee hearings, however, are documented word-for-word and made public. These records allow citizens, media, interest groups, and researchers to observe the totality of information provided. We can observe all witnesses who appear before committees along with the statements, questions, and responses exchanged among legislators and witnesses.

The second feature benefits our theoretical argument. The public nature of hearings allows committees to signal their interest in issues and communicate their preferences to other political actors. Holding a hearing instead of requesting a report, for instance, could increase the salience of an issue or force other legislators to pay attention to it. Also, it can be a way to consolidate the agenda-setting power of committees (e.g., Sinclair, 1986) and can allow committees to use their information advantages to shape legislator behavior on the floor (Box-Steffensmeier, Ryan, and Sokhey, 2015; Bianco, 1997; Curry, 2019; Curry and Rosenstiel, 2023).

The signaling function of hearings also applies to actors outside of the legislative body. Existing work suggests that oversight hearings in particular serve to signal committees' willingness to monitor agency actions and overrule them if the actions are too far from the committee's preferred policy (Foreman, 1988). Hearings also can signal a committee's

## 2.3 Hearings and Information Provision

resoluteness to alter the agency's implementation of policies (Cameron and Rosendorff, 1993), making them an effective tool of political control.

The target audience of a hearing can extend beyond other legislators and bureaucrats to include voters and interest groups. Gloseclose and McCarty (2001) publish a model that shows how public bargaining between Congress and the president – and the information generated from that process – can affect voters' approval of the president. Kriner and Schickler (2016) provide empirical evidence that holding investigative hearings on the conduct of the president or executive branch can affect the public's approval of the president and ultimately force the president to change the course of policies initiated by the White House. This suggests that the information generated through hearings could affect voters' perceptions of the executive branch. Park (2023) shows that committee members also send political messages to voters during hearings through "grandstanding," and members who engage in this behavior more than others are rewarded with higher vote shares. Esterling (2007) finds that committee members' engagement in analytical discourse during committee hearings tends to attract more campaign contributions from PACs.

Thus, committee hearings can be strategically important from the chair's perspective. One of main decisions that chairs must make is the composition of the witness pool. The selection of witnesses affects what information is aired publicly in the hearing, thereby revealing the chair's intent for the hearing and the information they hope to convey to the public and other members. It can also signal the likeliness that the hearing will serve as an opportunity for members to grandstand. Various factors, such as the polarization of the relevant issues and the composition of committees, affect whom committee chairs choose to invite as committees form policy and legitimize their decisions to other members and external observers (Hansen, 1991; Krehbiel, 1991; Park, 2017). In other words, witness testimony in committee hearings is a product of members' searching for selective information, and the information aired in hearings is made public to advance the committees' goals.

Committee hearings are an observable source of information flow among legislators and outside interest groups, as well as among legislators and bureaucrats. Studies, such as McGrath (2013), Aberbach (1990), and Dodd and Schott (1979), address the exchange of information among legislators and bureaucrats in oversight hearings, and use the number of days in oversight hearings as a reflection of how Congress reviews, monitors, and supervises executive action. Further, as Aberbach (1990) shows from a survey of congressional staffers, oversight hearings rank very high compared to other techniques of congressional oversight, and they are an important conduit for Congress to collect information from and about executive agencies.

Several existing studies analyze the types of witnesses invited to testify in congressional hearings. Leyden (1995) randomly selects 250 interest groups listed in the *Encyclopedia of Associations* and examines their presence in hearings held in 1985. His approach focuses on which types of interest groups are invited to provide information to legislators during committee hearings. His interviews with committee staffers provide qualitative evidence that the presence of witnesses from interest groups in hearings can be used as a measure of the access an organized interest group has to congressional policymaking. Leyden (1995)'s analysis shows that groups with substantial organizational resources are invited to testify more frequently than those with fewer resources. Gormley (1998) analyzes whether the Republican takeover of Congress after the 1994 midterm election changed the composition of invited witnesses. By analyzing witness lists of six House committees in the years immediately before (1993) and right after (1995) the Republican takeover, he shows that groups that are more sympathetic to the Republican Party – specifically, conservative advocacy groups and business groups – were more likely to be invited as witnesses after the Republican takeover.

Core functions of committees hinge on the selection of witnesses: Gatekeeping, agenda-setting, information collection, and mobilizing support or opposition on a particular legislative issue can be affected by granting access to some and denying it to others (Arnold, 1990; Gormley, 1998). Previous research and case studies show how legislative outcomes and the content of bills can be affected by the information discussed or the conflicts that occur at committee hearings (Baumgartner and Jones, 1993; Brasher, 2006; Burstein, 1999). However, despite some analyses of witness composition in a small selection of hearings during limited time periods, the congressional scholarship has never systematically built a complete, extensive dataset studying the witnesses who testified in committee hearings. To fully understand how information shapes politics at the committee level, it is essential to understand how committees use witnesses to achieve their goals and what types of information witnesses provide to committees.

## 2.4 WITNESS INVITATION PROCESS AND HEARING PROCEDURES

Given their importance to congressional information seekers, we examine who Congress invites to testify at hearings, how committees identify them, and why some witnesses are chosen rather than others.

## 2.4 Witness Invitations and Procedures

Choosing witnesses is often one of the most important tasks in planning a hearing. Among other considerations, committees must decide how many and what type of witnesses to invite. A committee chair assisted by committee staff identifies potential witnesses for a hearing (Heitshusen, 2017; Davis, 2015), and there is no limit to the number of witnesses who may be invited. Witnesses who receive invitations are often eager to testify; if not, committees can exercise their congressional subpoena power to compel a specific person to testify (Davis, 2015). A committee also can schedule multiple days for a hearing, allowing them time to hear from an expanded number of witnesses.

During the consideration of potential witnesses, committee members of the majority party may comment on and provide recommendations to the chair, although chairs decide which witnesses ultimately are invited to testify. The minority party's committee members have been granted protection by chamber rules to call their own witnesses on at least one day of each hearing. Formally, the inclusion of the minority's witnesses can be accomplished by a majority of minority committee members submitting a request to the chair. Typically, however, these rules are not officially invoked and the minority party works informally with the majority party to ensure that witnesses representing the minority's views are invited (Heitshusen, 2017; Davis, 2015). There are specific rules and norms in some committees regarding witness selection. For example, in the Senate Finance Committee, the committee rules allow every committee member to choose their own witnesses to testify.

Committees select witnesses in various ways. They can simply invite their allied groups (Kollman, 1997); interest groups are eager to testify in hearings since they garner unique access to members of Congress (Leyden, 1995). Committee staffers can contact allied groups with expertise on a hearing issue and ask them to suggest potential witnesses (Parrott, 2019). To find witnesses from academia or research-oriented institutions, committee staffers search for publications about the hearing topic, identify the authors, and invite them to testify.

For their study of citizen witnesses, Van Der Slik and Stenger (1977) surveyed witnesses who were invited to testify in congressional committees and subcommittees in 1974. Some citizens initiated a request to testify, but most were contacted by the member of Congress or the member's staff from the district where they lived. Sometimes, celebrities or best-selling authors are invited to trigger heightened social awareness around an issue. For example, after his book, *Unsafe at Any Speed*, became a national bestseller and alarmed the public regarding unsafe practices in the automobile industry, young lawyer and consumer activist Ralph Nader testified on traffic safety before the Senate Committee on

Government Operations in 1966.[2] Nader's appearance played a significant role in the passage of the Traffic Safety Act of 1966 (Oleszek, 1989). Ben Affleck, a famous film actor and director, testified at a 2014 Senate Foreign Relations Committee hearing in his capacity as founder of the Eastern Congo Initiative. He discussed the mass killings plaguing the Democratic Republic of the Congo, and his appearance as a witness generated unusually high media attention to the hearings and the issues discussed.

Generally, once potential witnesses are identified, committee staff interview them and confirm their willingness to testify in hearings. Then, in both the House and the Senate, the committee chair sends a formal letter of invitation to the selected witnesses. Committees may also request that witnesses submit biographical information and a printed version of their written testimony. However, committee rules vary on whether a witness is required to submit written testimony in advance of hearings. For example, the House Committee on Appropriations does not require witnesses to submit written testimonies at federal budget hearings (CRS, 2006). In addition to submitting a resume, nongovernment witnesses must complete the "Truth in Testimony Disclosure Form" and disclose the name of organizations that they represent, as well as any federal government grant or contract received in the previous two fiscal years (House Rule XI, clause 2(g)(4)). Figure 2.1 shows a sample Disclosure Form. Daniel Hinkle, State Affairs Counsel at the American Association of Justice, testified before the subcommittee on Consumer Protection and Commerce of the Committee on Energy and Commerce on "Autonomous Vehicles: Promises and Challenges of Evolving Automotive Technologies" on February 11, 2020. Because Mr. Hinkle was a "nongovernment" witness, he was required to submit this Disclosure Form along with his ten-page written statement in advance of his subcommittee appearance.

After extensive preparation, committee chairs will begin a hearing with an opening statement that introduces the hearing's purpose. The ranking member will follow with their opening statement and other committee members also may make opening statements, typically subject to a five-minute limit, though there is variation. After opening statements, the chair introduces each witness and the witnesses give their oral testimony in an order pre-arranged by the committee. Although some committees give the chair the authority to decide how long a witness may speak, oral testimony is usually brief and limited to a five-minute rule. After witnesses present their testimonies, members may question the witnesses; members generally have five minutes to engage with each witness until every member has had the opportunity to question each witness (CRS, 2006). After

**Truth in Testimony Disclosure Form**

In accordance with Rule XI, clause 2(g)(5)*, of the *Rules of the House of Representatives*, witnesses are asked to disclose the following information. Please complete this form electronically by filling in the provided blanks.

**Committee:** Energy and Commerce

**Subcommittee:** Consumer Protection and Commerce

**Hearing Date:** February 11, 2020

**Hearing Title** :

Autonomous Vehicles: Promises and Challenges of Evolving Automotive Technologies

**Witness Name:** Daniel Hinkle

**Position/Title:** Senior State Affairs Counsel

**Witness Type:** ○ Governmental ○ Non-governmental

**Are you representing yourself or an organization?** ○ Self ○ Organization

**If you are representing an organization, please list what entity or entities you are representing:**

American Association for Justice

**If you are a non-governmental witness, please list any federal grants or contracts (including subgrants or subcontracts) related to the hearing's subject matter that you or the organization(s) you represent at this hearing received in the current calendar year and previous two calendar years. Include the source and amount of each grant or contract.** *If necessary, attach additional sheet(s) to provide more information.*

None.

**If you are a non-governmental witness, please list any contracts or payments originating with a foreign government and related to the hearing's subject matter that you or the organization(s) you represent at this hearing received in the current year and previous two calendar years. Include the amount and country of origin of each contract or payment.** *If necessary, attach additional sheet(s) to provide more information.*

None.

Figure 2.1 An example of the Truth in Testimony Disclosure Form

the question-and-answer period ends for the last witness, the committee chair closes the hearing.

## 2.5 SUMMARY

Members of Congress need to acquire and convey information to wield influence in Congress. The committee stage is when the search for and use of information is most salient. Various groups and individuals recognize legislators' demand for information, and thus compete for access by providing a variety of information to members. One avenue through which this information can be publicly transmitted is congressional hearings, which are designed to invite external input in a public, formalized setting. Although there has been much focus on the role of information in the legislative process, relatively less is known about the witnesses invited to speak before Congress and the types of information they provide.

Committee chairs and committee members recognize how hearings and the information conveyed there can influence the public, other members, bureaucrats, interest groups, and the media. Therefore, chairs have incentives to strategically hold hearings to advance their goals. Selecting witnesses is an important step in this strategic decision, since the set of witnesses and the information the witnesses provide can shape the framing, credibility, and arguments surrounding the issue under consideration. As such, the selection of witnesses is one of the most orchestrated and strategic aspects underlying a hearing.

Given that the composition of the witness pool can be a signal to other political actors, understanding what influences the invitation patterns of different types of witnesses is especially important. In Chapters 5–7, we develop our argument about how partisan incentives underlying a committee's intent for a hearing, the relationship between Congress and the executive branch, and the internal capacity of Congress all affect who is invited to be a witness. We use a novel, comprehensive dataset of witnesses and testimonies to test and evaluate our theories.

We proceed by first painting a descriptive picture about witness invitation patterns in Congress and describe the original dataset we will use. In Chapter 3, we describe the comprehensive, machine-readable dataset we constructed on congressional witnesses and their testimonies for the 1960–2018 time period.

## NOTES

1. From the hearing "Paycheck Protection Program: Loan Forgiveness and Other Challenges," held by the Committee on Small Business, US House, on June 17, 2020.
2. This committee no longer exists, and its area of oversight is now under the Senate Homeland Security and Governmental Affairs Committee.

# 3

## Who Testifies in Congress? New Data on Congressional Hearings and Witnesses

Right now, we have our most diverse Congress in history – and as Chairs of the Tri-Caucus, it is our responsibility to ensure that this House is doing everything possible to represent the full diversity of the American people. That is why we are calling on our own Committees, our own colleagues, to join us by inviting witnesses that reflect all the communities we represent: urban and rural, from every socioeconomic class, of every racial background, and evenly include experts of every gender.
– Congressional Tri-Caucus (Asian Pacific American, Black, and Hispanic) Chairs in a Letter to House Committee Chairs and Ranking Members on December 12, 2019.

Chapter 2 described how congressional hearings are venues for members to acquire and publicly communicate information – information that can shape the framing, credibility, and arguments surrounding the issue under consideration. To fully understand informational dynamics in Congress, we examine the types of witnesses invited to provide this information and the types of information they ultimately present to committee members.

This focus is not merely academic. As the chapter-opening quote illustrates, the issue of who exactly is invited to testify has been very important to legislators in Congress. On December 12, 2019, the chairs of the Congressional Tri-Caucus – which includes members of the Congressional Asian Pacific American Caucus, the Congressional Black Caucus, and the Congressional Hispanic Caucus – announced a new initiative to increase the diversity of witnesses and outside experts testifying before House committees. In their letters, the Tri-Caucus chairs lamented that "People of color and women are experts in their fields, but are not always called as witnesses before Congress." Speaker Nancy Pelosi (D-CA12) responded in a Press Release on December 12, 2019 that Congress needs to listen to "the full range of voices and values in our community, so that the People's House continues to be a reflection of the American people whom it is our great honor to serve."

The Tri-Caucus's concerns about diversity and representation are grounded in the fundamental concern that who testifies before Congress affects the *information* that members hear, convey, and use. This concern extends beyond the race and gender of witnesses, as other characteristics and variables may influence the types of information they present to Congress. Scholars recognize this and have studied the types of interest groups appearing in hearings and how the information they present shapes legislative outcomes.

For one, Leyden (1995) randomly selected 250 interest groups from *The Encyclopedia of Associations* and examined the number of times each group in the sample testified at hearings held in 1985. He shows that groups with more resources – measured as the number of lobbyists and research staff they hired – are more likely to appear in hearings. Another researcher analyzed the presence of labor unions in hearings across thirteen years, finding that organizational resources – such as the number of lobbyists and the density of union membership in sectors – are associated with a greater presence of labor unions at the Capitol (Albert, 2013). By analyzing committee hearings during 1974, Van Der Slik and Stenger (1977) show that those from the middle and upper middle classes with higher levels of education comprised the dominant type of witnesses in hearings, even among citizen witnesses.

Other studies track the appearance of witnesses over time and offer longitudinal comparisons. Talbert, Jones, and Baumgartner (1995) collected an impressive amount of information on nearly 10,000 witnesses who appeared in hearings on pesticide and tobacco issues from 1945 to 1986. With this data, they reveal that nonlegislative hearings exhibited more stacking of witnesses – inviting witnesses with a similar perspective – which helped committees assert their jurisdiction over particular issues. Flemming, MacLeod, and Talbert (1998) traced the groups that appeared at Senate hearings on federal judicial appointments from 1945 to 1992 and show that the number of witnesses from state and local organizations declined over time, while national groups have dominated confirmation hearings since 1980. Cameron et al. (2020) show that the number of groups involved in the Supreme Court nomination process increased over time with the groups focusing on identity issues, such as the National Association for the Advancement of Colored People, becoming the most active participants. Finally, Gormley (1998) compared interest groups that testified in congressional hearings immediately before and after the Republican takeover of Congress in 1995, finding that groups more sympathetic to the new Republican majority – business groups, conservative advocacy groups, and individuals in the legislative branch – were more frequently invited to testify in hearings after the Republican takeover of the House.

Although this existing research contributes to our understanding of witness attendance in congressional hearings, all the studies are limited in at least one significant way: They focus on a particular type of hearing (e.g., the nomination process or issue-specific hearings), or they examine only a particular type of interest group (e.g., business groups or labor unions), or they cover only a specific, narrow time period (e.g., before and after the Republican takeover of the House in 1995). To fully understand the factors determining witness appearances and how political motivations affect witness invitation patterns, it is crucial to construct a comprehensive dataset that allows comparison of witness appearances across all types of hearings, groups, and time periods. We provide exactly that.

In this chapter, we explain in detail how we constructed the most comprehensive data on hearings and witnesses to date. We will use this dataset in Chapters 5–7 to provide empirical evidence for our theory of how political motivations drive information seeking in Congress. To illustrate the descriptive power of this dataset, however, we first focus on two characteristics of witnesses – affiliation and gender – which we use as proxies for (1) the types of information that committee members seek in hearings and (2) the diversity of witnesses they hear from. We present detailed descriptive patterns of how these two characteristics vary across time, issue, and committee, imparting a more complete picture of those who are invited to present their views and opinions to members of Congress.

## 3.1 DATA CONSTRUCTION PROCESS

We constructed a new dataset on congressional committee hearings and witnesses from 1961 to 2018 to examine who committees invite to testify. There are two main sources of data on congressional committee hearings: ProQuest Congressional, which manages the data previously provided by the Congressional Information Service; and the Government Publishing Office (GPO).[1] ProQuest provides hearing data going back to 1824, while the GPO's coverage of House and Senate committees does not become frequent until 1997. Even after 1997, the GPO's coverage is not comprehensive. Additionally, while both ProQuest and the GPO provide witness lists for each hearing, ProQuest presents witness affiliation information in a more organized fashion. For these reasons, we use data from ProQuest Congressional to construct our dataset.

| WITNESSES | |
|---|---:|
| Kay Brown, Director, Education, Workforce, and Income Security, U.S. Government Accountability Office | 8 |
| Prepared statement | 11 |
| Answers to submitted questions | 92 |
| Joseph S. Campbell, Deputy Assistant Director, Criminal Investigation Division, Federal Bureau of Investigation | 28 |
| Prepared statement | 30 |
| Charles Harwood, Acting Director, Bureau of Consumer Protection, Federal Trade Commission | 37 |
| Prepared statement | 39 |
| Answers to submitted questions | 97 |
| Gail Hillebrand, Associate Director, Consumer Education and Engagement, Consumer Financial Protection Bureau | 52 |
| Prepared statement | 54 |
| Answers to submitted questions | 108 |
| William H. Sorrell, Attorney General, State of Vermont | 58 |
| Prepared statement | 60 |

Figure 3.1 The list of witnesses in hearing transcripts: Example
Notes: This is the list of witnesses presented in the official hearing transcript produced by the House Committee on Energy and Commerce. The hearing was held on May 16, 2013, under the title, "Fraud on the Elderly: A Growing Concern for a Growing Population."

Figure 3.1 shows an example of ProQuest witness lists as they appear in the official hearing transcripts. Some committees independently document witness information for a subset of their hearings. Therefore, we compared the ProQuest information with that provided by the committees to confirm that ProQuest witness lists reflected the same information.[2] There were some instances where the ProQuest lists omitted some witnesses from a hearing, but we did not find any pattern in this occasional missing data – it was random and the percentage of missing data is trivial in the context of the total number of hearings and witnesses.[3] Therefore, we treat the missing data as random noise.

For the 1961–2018 period, our dataset includes the full names and organizational affiliations of 731,810 witnesses who appeared at 74,077 published hearings of the House, Senate, and Joint standing committees. These published hearings do not include hearings that were not initially made available for public record, such as hearings containing sensitive information for national security or private personal information, or hearings held in executive session of the Senate when it considers treaties or items introduced by the President. ProQuest Congressional continues to release portions of unpublished hearings each year, but for the period covered by our data (1961 to 2018), there may be some unpublished hearings that are not included in our data.[4] For each hearing, we recorded the following information in our dataset: hearing title, date, name of the (sub)committee holding the hearing, and any bill numbers considered in the hearing.

Compared to data on congressional hearings previously used by scholars, our dataset is the most comprehensive in terms of both the years covered and the breadth of information. For example, the existing data on congressional hearings in the Policy Agendas Project (PAP) provides no information on witnesses. Some of the previous research analyzing witnesses employs only a small sample of hearings over a short period of time (e.g., Leyden, 1995; Flemming, MacLeod, and Talbert, 1998; Delevoye, 2020). Thus, the congressional scholarship to date has not systematically constructed or used a complete dataset of witnesses who testified in committee hearings over an extended period of time across different types of hearings. Therefore, our novel, comprehensive dataset on hearings and witnesses is a valuable resource for examining how hearings were organized, which groups and individuals gained access to members of Congress through hearings, and what types of information and opinions witnesses conveyed to committee members.

We further process our data by constructing important variables that capture witnesses' characteristics. Our key interest is the witnesses' affiliations, which are used to characterize groups in the political process and provide a fair approximation for the types of external groups invited to congressional hearings. For example, Burstein and Hirsh (2007) categorize a witness's organizational affiliation into five groups: private interest organization, state or local government, federal executive branch, US Congress, and individuals testifying on their own behalf or as experts. Gormley (1998) divides witnesses into twelve categories from congressional officials to nonprofit organizations. Overall, witness affiliations are frequently used in existing studies, which reflects that they are a distinctive characteristic of witnesses.

Other witness characteristics, such as ideology, are also potentially interesting features to explore; however, these characteristics are untenable due to either imprecise measurement or systematic unavailability. For instance, the ideology of outside groups has received considerable theoretical attention in the literature on legislative organization and lobbying (e.g., Kollman, 1997). However, although witness ideologies could be extracted from campaign contributions (Bonica, 2016), not all witnesses or their organizational affiliations make political contributions, which would be necessary for an ideological assessment. This limitation would lead to significant missing data problems.

Therefore, we focus on the one clear, salient, and readily available characteristic that committees use: a witness's organizational affiliation. The interest group literature commonly cites witnesses' affiliations and the types of their affiliations (e.g., corporations, membership organizations, labor organizations) to characterize groups that are present and active in the political process (e.g., Yackee and Yackee, 2006; Schlozman et al., 2015). From the committee's perspective, affiliation types can be good proxies for the overall composition and diversity of the invited witnesses, even though resources and opinions may vary within affiliation types. Thus, for the purpose of this study, we focus on the affiliations of witnesses.

We assigned an affiliation to each witness through the following process. First, we parsed the information about each witness – which consists of a string of characters – using regular expressions to generate three witness-level variables: a witness's affiliation, last name, and first name. This was particularly challenging due to the irregular format of the raw data, which varies significantly across years and committees. Below are some examples of such irregularities:

- DEMPSEY, Martin E., Gen. – Chairman, JCS, VA.
- COATS, Daniel; nominee to be Director, Office of the Director of National Intelligence
- BERGMANN, Scott, Senior Vice President, Regulatory Affairs, CITA – The Wireless Association
- MYLES, Curtis Las Vegas Monorail Co.

These examples illustrate that the name and affiliation of each witness are not always separated by a special character. Even when the words are consistently separated by commas – as in the first and third examples – the location of the institution that a witness represents can be in the last string or in the second- or third-to-last string, depending on whether the state and city names are included. We identified most of these irregularities through an automated parsing process and then performed extensive manual cleaning to accurately extract witness affiliations.

We then classified all affiliations into eighteen types for analysis: agriculture; corporations; trade associations; federal executive branch bureaucrats; congressional personnel, including members, staff, and legislative support agencies; state and local government personnel; (K-12) educational institutions; think tank and university researchers; membership organizations; nonprofit organizations; labor unions; government judicial bodies; lawyers and lobbyists; health-related organizations; Native American groups; religious organizations; individual citizens with no organizational affiliation; and international organizations or foreign nationals. Table 3.1 lists the names of the eighteen types, the percentage of each type in our dataset, an example of a witness affiliation (or title) in each type, and a broader parent category. We devised nine parent categories for the eighteen affiliations to allow clearer graphical presentations of our data in Table 3.1.

This classification was done carefully: (a) we first created a list of affiliations of potential witnesses based on existing data from five sources (explained in more detail below); then (b) we assigned one of our predetermined categories to each organization or job category; and finally

## 3.1 Data Construction Process

Table 3.1 *Types of witness affiliations*

| Type | Composition (%) | Example | Parent category |
|---|---|---|---|
| Agriculture | 1.64 | American Farm Bureau | Business |
| Corporation | 8.85 | Ford Motor Co. | Business |
| Trade association | 6.48 | Chamber of Commerce | Business |
| Bureaucrat | 24.96 | Department of Defense | Bureaucrat |
| Congressional | 9.81 | Congressional Budget Office | Congressional |
| State and local government | 10.56 | Mayor | Local government |
| (K-12) educational | 1.06 | Superintendent | Local government |
| Think tank and university | 8.45 | MIT | Research |
| Membership association | 9.45 | Veterans of Foreign Wars | Membership assoc. |
| Nonprofit | 7.52 | Environmental Defense Fund | Nonprofit |
| Labor Union | 2.29 | AFL-CIO | Labor |
| Judicial | 0.94 | District Court | Other |
| Lawyers and lobbyists | 1.33 | American Bar Association | Other |
| Healthcare | 1.66 | American Hospital Association | Other |
| Native American | 1.24 | National Congress of American Indians | Other |
| Religious | 0.60 | US Catholic Conference | Other |
| Citizen | 2.77 | Resident | Other |
| International | 0.39 | World Bank | Other |
| Total number of witnesses | 731,810 | | |

*Notes:* This table shows the distribution of witness affiliation types, an example organization in each category, and the parent category of the affiliation type for the period 1961–2018.

(c) we merged the list with our new witness dataset by matching affiliations from both datasets. This process involved both automated matching and extensive manual cleaning. The result is a dataset that, for the first time, systematically catalogs the organizational affiliations of every witness who has testified before Congress from 1961 to 2018.

Our list of organizations, groups, and federal bureaucratic agencies came from five sources. First, we extracted the names of clients and lobbying firms from the Lobbying Disclosure Act data available at LobbyView.org (Kim, 2018). Second, we obtained a list of organizations or employers of political donors from the Database on Ideology, Money in Politics, and Elections by (Bonica, 2016). Third, we collected a list of departments and agencies of the federal bureaucracy from the Office of Public Management. Fourth, we used the Washington Representatives Directory, which includes organizations that are active in Washington, DC politics (Schlozman et al., 2015). Finally, we collected a list of foreign governments and international organizations from the Correlates of War Project.

Together, these five datasets identified 1,063,223 unique names of groups with which witnesses could potentially be affiliated. There are 23,519 out of 731,810 witnesses (3.1 percent) with missing affiliation information; in these cases, the only information available is the name of the witness without further information about their organizational affiliation. There was no systematic pattern to this missing affiliation by year or committee.

Moreover, potential witnesses vary along another dimension that is important for descriptive representation and may influence legislative outcomes: gender. Congressional scholars have documented gender gaps in many activities that can influence legislators' policy choices, such as staffing decisions, campaign contributions, and who becomes a lobbyist (LaPira, Marchetti, and Thomas, 2020; Ritchie and You, 2021). Similarly, as the Tri-Caucus Chairs' statement on witness diversity suggests, there may be a gender gap in the witnesses who appear and testify at committee hearings, which may directly affect the types of information delivered to committee members. To extract the gender of witnesses, we use an R package called gender that predicts the gender of each witness based on the first name. Finally, in a separate dataset, we parse witness testimonies by statements to measure the analytical information present in the testimony, which we will explain in detail in Chapter 4.

After constructing the witness-level variables, we extracted hearing- and committee-level variables for each hearing. For the hearing-level variables, we collected information on the title, date, committee and subcommittee, whether the hearing considered a specific bill, the summary of the hearing topic, and the issue areas of the hearing from the PAP database on congressional hearings. We also classified hearings into three types: legislative, oversight or investigative, and nomination hearings. We identify nomination hearings as those that considered a nomination. For oversight or investigative hearings, we follow McGrath (2013) and classify

## 3.2 Trends in the Number of Hearings and Witnesses

Table 3.2 *Structure of hearings and witness dataset*

| (A) Hearing level | (B) Witness level | (C) Committee level |
|---|---|---|
| Title | First name | Number of committee members |
| Date | Last name | Gender composition of committees |
| Committee | Affiliation | Party affiliation |
| Subcommittee | Gender | DW-NOMINATE scores |
| Hearing type | Text of testimony | |
| Bill reference | | |
| Summary | | |
| Issue code | | |

non-nomination hearings as oversight or investigative if the PAP's description of the hearing includes one or more of the following words: "oversight," "review," "report," "budget request," "control," "impact," "information," "investigation," "request," "explanation," "president," "administration," "contract," "consultation," and/or "examination." This is the same set of words used to filter these types of hearings by McGrath (2013). We classify hearings that are neither oversight (or investigative) nor nomination hearings as legislative hearings.

Next, we constructed committee-level variables based on the committee and subcommittee names associated with the hearings. Committee characteristics include the total number of committee (subcommittee) members, the gender composition of committee (subcommittee) members, and the party affiliation and DW-NOMINATE scores of committee (subcommittee) members. Data on committee membership are from Stewart and Woon (2017). In the absence of a readily available subcommittee-level dataset, we manually collected and recorded the subcommittee membership of all standing committees for the 101st–105th Congresses from the Congressional Directories published by the GPO.[5]

Table 3.2 summarizes the dataset we constructed at the hearing, witness, and committee levels during 1961–2018 – the most comprehensive picture of congressional hearings and witnesses to date.

### 3.2 TRENDS IN THE NUMBER OF HEARINGS AND WITNESSES

Figure 3.2 illustrates the total number of witnesses who appeared in each two-year Congress in each chamber from 1961 to 2018. Several major patterns emerge. First, the number of witnesses peaked in the 1970s, when there were 28,703 external witnesses in the 95th House (1977–1979) and 17,055 in the 93rd Senate (1973–1975). This is consistent with the increase in the number of subcommittees after passage of the

## Who Testifies in Congress?

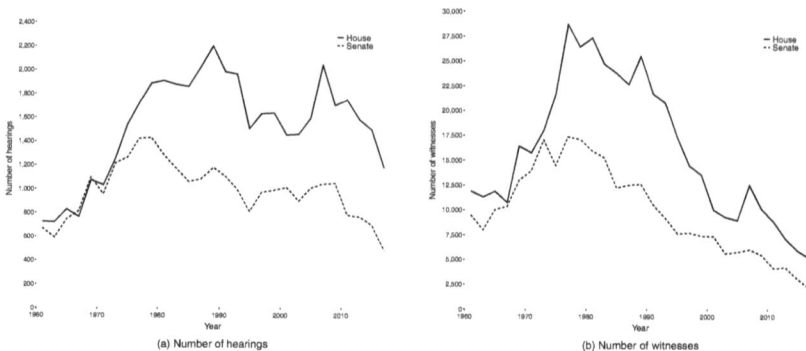

Figure 3.2 Number of hearings and witnesses in Congress over time
Notes: Panel (a) shows the total number of hearings held by congressional committees in each two-year Congress in each chamber. Panel (b) shows the total number of witnesses who have appeared in committee hearings in each two-year Congress in each chamber.

1973 Subcommittee Bill of Rights, since a greater number of subcommittees likely increased the number of hearings held and thus the number of witnesses. These maxima have declined over time to the minima seen in recent years; the number of witnesses in Congress has declined since the 1980s, with roughly one-fifth as many witnesses testifying in Congress today than at the peak in the late 1970s.[6] One possible contributor to this trend is a reform in 1995 that drastically cut the number of subcommittees, causing the opposite effect as the 1970s reforms (Deering and Smith, 1997). Other contributors to the decline in numbers of hearings and witnesses could include the rise of partisan polarization that shifted power and resources from committee chairs to party leaders, increased lobbying by interest groups, and increased time demands for fundraising (Quirk, 2005; Quirk, Bendix, and Bachtiger, 2018; Lee, 2015).

At first glance, the numbers of witnesses follow similar trends in the House and the Senate: when the number of witnesses rises (falls) in one chamber, it also rises (falls) in the other. However, there are two differences between the chambers. First, the number of witnesses and the level of hearing activity in the House has been greater than the number of witnesses and the level of hearing activity in the Senate. Second, the Senate has had a clear downward trajectory in the level of hearing activity since the 1970s, while the House has had bigger swings in the level of hearing activity across time.

Because these patterns are at the aggregate level, they might not tell the full story about the amount of information that Congress gathers from hearings over time. Therefore, we also count the total number of words contained in testimonies before Congress using the available transcripts of House committee hearings during the 105th through the 114th

## 3.2 Trends in the Number of Hearings and Witnesses

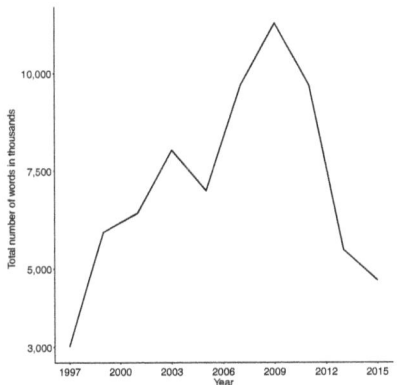

Figure 3.3 Number of total words in witness testimonies over time – House
Notes: This graph shows the total number of words in testimony for each Congress from 1997 to 2016.

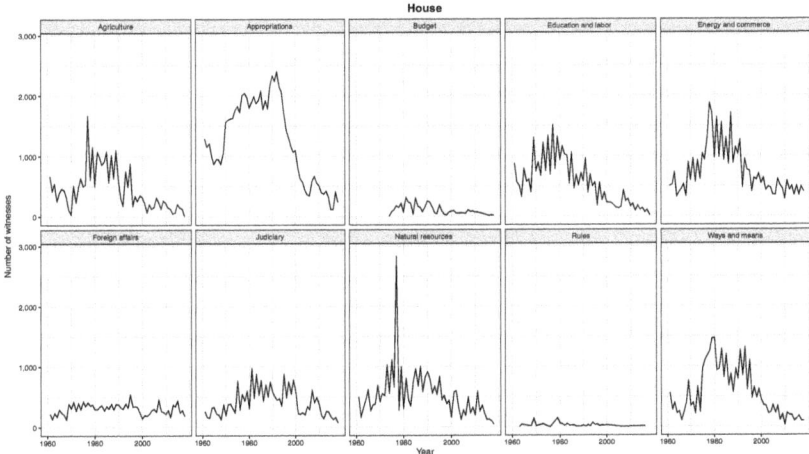

Figure 3.4 The number of witnesses in House standing committees over time
Notes: The panels in this figure show the total number of witnesses in each Congress for a selected set of House standing committees for the period 1961–2018.

Congresses. While we have detailed records of hearings and witnesses from 1961 to 2018, our data on the word-for-word transcripts only spans House hearings from 1997 through 2016. Figure 3.3 shows the trend over time in the number of words in witness testimonies for that time period. The trend is broadly similar to the pattern seen in the number of hearings.

There are also interesting patterns across committees. Figure 3.4 breaks down the number of witnesses who testified in the House by committee over time. It is immediately clear that there are some House committees – Appropriations, Energy and Commerce, and Ways and Means – that have historically invited more witnesses than other committees. Those that focus on procedural or internal matters, such as Budget and Rules, have historically called the fewest number of witnesses.

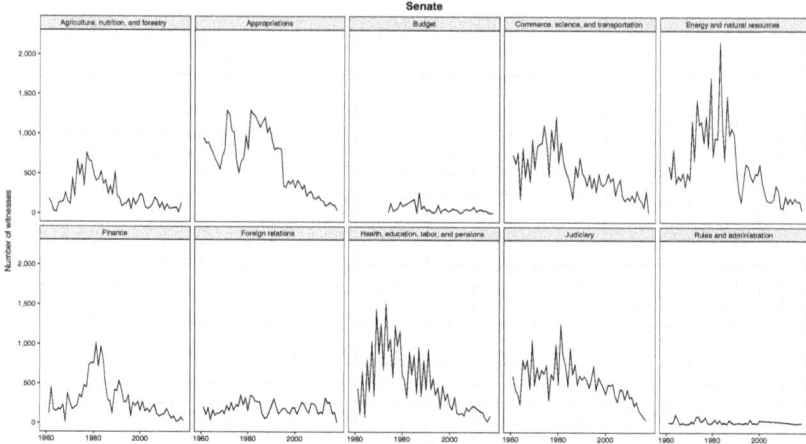

Figure 3.5 The number of witnesses in Senate standing committees over time
Notes: The panels in this figure show the total number of witnesses in each Congress for a selected set of Senate standing committees for the period 1961–2018.

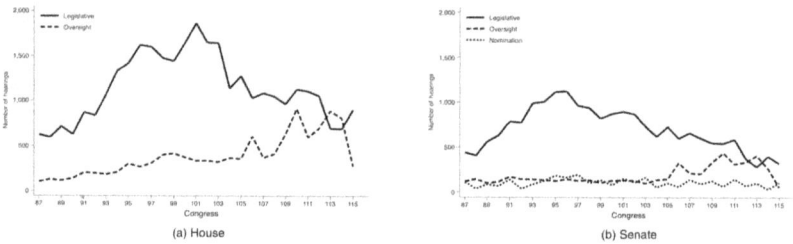

Figure 3.6 Number of hearings by type of hearing
Notes: Panel (a) shows the number of legislative and oversight hearings in the House for the period 1961–2018. Panel (b) shows the number of legislative, oversight, and nomination hearings in the Senate for the period 1961–2018.

Among the Senate committees, Figure 3.5 shows that committees that hosted the highest number of witnesses are Energy and Natural Resources; Health, Education, Labor and Pensions; and Appropriations. Similar to their House counterparts, the Budget and Rules and Administration Committees show the lowest numbers of witnesses.

We also examine the number of hearings and the average number of witnesses per hearing by the three hearing types: legislative, oversight, and nomination. Because the primary purpose of each type of hearing varies, we look for different patterns in the number of hearings and witnesses per hearing over time.

Figure 3.6 shows the total number of hearings by Congress in the House (Panel (a)) and Senate (Panel (b)). The number of legislative hearings increased until the late 1980s, followed by a sharp decline from 1990 to the mid-2000s. By contrast, the number of oversight hearings

## 3.2 Trends in the Number of Hearings and Witnesses

Table 3.3 *Average number of witnesses per hearing by types of hearings*

| | House | | Senate | | |
|---|---|---|---|---|---|
| Decade | Legislative | Oversight | Legislative | Oversight | Nomination |
| 1960s | 14.9 | 16.1 | 14.7 | 11.9 | 4.3 |
| 1970s | 14.7 | 16.5 | 13.4 | 14.0 | 5.2 |
| 1980s | 12.2 | 15.1 | 12.9 | 11.0 | 6.3 |
| 1990s | 9.3 | 14.3 | 9.1 | 10.5 | 7.3 |
| 2000s | 6.2 | 6.7 | 6.0 | 6.4 | 6.4 |
| 2010s | 4.7 | 4.5 | 4.5 | 5.1 | 6.3 |
| Total hearings | 32,153 | 11,227 | 20,156 | 5,329 | 3,123 |

*Notes:* This table shows the average number (mean value) of witnesses invited to hearings by decade for different types of hearings in the House and Senate.

increased steadily until the mid-1990s and increased sharply since then. In the 112th Congress (2011–2012), the number of oversight hearings exceeds the number of legislative hearings in the House for the first time in our dataset.

The Senate shows a similar trend to that in the House: Legislative hearings increased until the 1980s but have declined since then. However, the number of oversight hearings has increased significantly since the mid-1990s, so the number of legislative and oversight hearings has been similar in the most recent years. The number of nomination hearings has been consistent over time, with little fluctuation. However, as the number of legislative hearings has declined significantly, nomination hearings have increased as a percentage of total hearings.

Table 3.3 shows the number of witnesses per hearing by type of hearing in each decade. The average number of witnesses per legislative hearing in the 1960s was 14.9 in the House, but that number dropped to 4.7 in the 2010s. House oversight hearings consistently featured about 15 witnesses per hearing through the 1990s, but this number plummeted in the 2000s and 2010s. Although the number of House oversight hearings increased over time, the average number of witnesses called to testify at oversight hearings declined. This may be related to the 1995 Republican takeover and its reform agenda, which drastically reduced the number of congressional staff and the budgets of legislative support agencies (Kosar, 2020). In the Senate, patterns for legislative and oversight hearings were similar to those in the House. One interesting difference is the average number of witnesses appearing at nomination hearings. In the 1960s, that average number was 4.3, and it increased to 7.0 in the 2010s. Combined with the patterns shown in Figure 3.6, the number of nomination hearings and the average number of witnesses invited to speak have not changed significantly, which contrasts starkly with legislative and oversight hearings.

In Figures A1 and A2, we plot the average number of witnesses per hearing in the House and Senate over time – this figure confirms the patterns in Table 3.3. Figure A1 shows the changes in the average number of witnesses per hearing in the House. The average number of witnesses in oversight hearings is more volatile until the early 1990s and has declined since then. For legislative hearings, there has been a steady decline in the average number of witnesses since the mid-1990s. Figure A2 shows the changes in the average number of witnesses by type of hearing in the Senate. Oversight hearings show the most variation over time; the number of witnesses per legislative hearing has declined since the 98th Congress (1983–1984); and the number of witnesses in nomination hearings increased over time until the 1990s. Since the 109th Congress (2005–2006), the average number of witnesses per nomination hearing has been slightly higher than the average number of witnesses in other types of hearings.

### 3.3 COMPOSITION OF WITNESS AFFILIATIONS

We now turn to the characteristics of witnesses testifying before congressional committees with a primary focus on their affiliations. As explained earlier, external groups' affiliations are often used to examine the degree of representation of interest groups in the political process (e.g., Schlozman, Verba, and Brady, 2012; Yackee and Yackee, 2006). By using witnesses' affiliations in our analyses, we can identify which types of groups are more present in congressional hearings, and thus examine which types of groups are able to provide information to legislators through this channel.

The composition of witness affiliations over time is shown in Figure 3.7 using the nine parent categories described earlier in this chapter (see Table 3.1 for a match between types and categories).[7] Overall, bureaucrats represent the plurality of witnesses at each point in time and their presence has increased since the mid-1990s (104th Congress). Witnesses representing business interests – including corporations, trade associations, and agriculture – rank second in the number of appearances, and their presence increased during the 1980s.

The appearances of congressional personnel – along with those from membership associations, state and local governments, and labor unions – have declined over time. In particular, the number of witnesses representing membership organizations and subnational governments has

## 3.3 Composition of Witness Affiliations

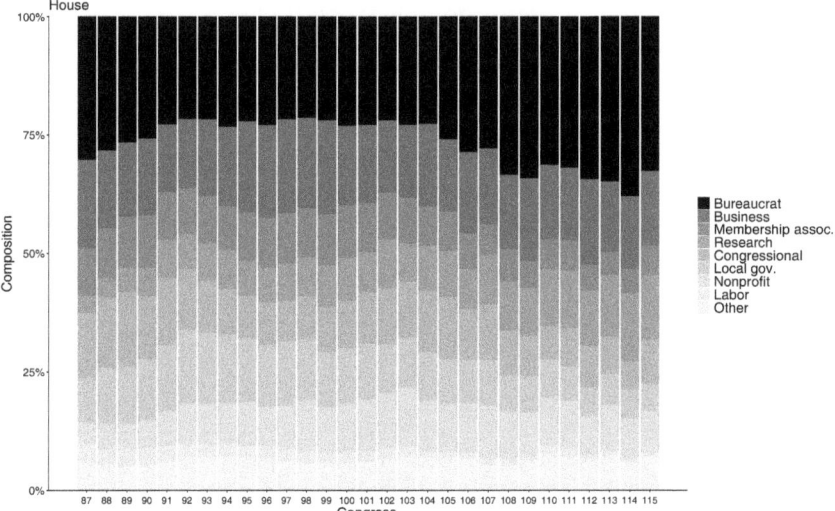

Figure 3.7 Witness affiliations over time
Notes: This figure shows the composition of witness affiliations by Congress over time.

declined sharply. For example, representatives of the Sierra Club, one of the largest environmental membership organizations in the US, were invited to congressional hearings 111 times in 1973. In 2010, there was only one instance of a Sierra Club representative appearing as a witness in a hearing.

Appearances of other types of witnesses have increased over time. For example, the percentage of witnesses from think tanks and research institutions has gradually increased to be the third highest in the most recent years. This may reflect that the number of think tanks in the US has increased dramatically over time (McGann, 2020). Also, the complexity of the issues Congress addresses has increased, compelling members to rely more on expert witnesses (LaPira, Drutman, and Kosar, 2020). Representatives of nonprofits also appeared more frequently over time. The most common types of nonprofits in our dataset are concerned with the environment, such as the Wilderness Society and the Natural Resources Defense Council. This may be related to the rapid growth of environmental and conservation nonprofits in the US, as well as increased interest in and concern for environmental protection (Taylor, 2016).

We observe differences in the composition of witnesses across the different types of hearings. Table 3.4 presents the percentages of witnesses from the nine categories defined in Table 3.1 by type of hearings. Overall, oversight hearings included more witnesses from the bureaucracy than legislative hearings. Given that oversight hearings involve the review,

Table 3.4 *Witness categories by types of hearings*

| Witness category (%) | House | | Senate | | |
|---|---|---|---|---|---|
| | Legislative | Oversight | Legislative | Oversight | Nomination |
| Business | 15.0 | 12.5 | 16.4 | 13.3 | 1.7 |
| Bureaucrat | 34.9 | 49.6 | 32.7 | 47.6 | 55.3 |
| Congressional | 7.7 | 5.1 | 7.0 | 5.1 | 30.6 |
| Local government | 8.4 | 6.1 | 9.8 | 7.0 | 1.7 |
| Research | 9.5 | 8.8 | 9.1 | 8.7 | 0.7 |
| Membership association | 7.8 | 5.0 | 7.8 | 5.0 | 1.5 |
| Nonprofit | 6.8 | 5.3 | 7.0 | 5.6 | 2.1 |
| Labor | 2.2 | 1.3 | 1.9 | 1.3 | 0.4 |
| Other | 7.7 | 6.3 | 8.3 | 6.4 | 6.0 |
| Total | 100 | 100 | 100 | 100 | 100 |

*Notes:* The *Business* category includes agriculture, corporations, and trade associations. *Local government* includes state and local government and K-12 educational institutions. *Other* category includes judicial, lawyers and lobbyists, healthcare, citizen, Native American, religious, and international.

monitoring, and supervision of the implementation of government programs by the executive branch, it is intuitive that bureaucrats account for nearly half of all witnesses appearing in oversight hearings. Interestingly, nonbureaucratic witnesses – such as business- and research-based witnesses – frequently appeared in oversight hearings. In stark contrast to legislative and oversight hearings, individuals from government organizations (e.g., bureaucrats and congressional staff) accounted for 85 percent of the witnesses at nomination hearings in the Senate. This is largely because nominees for positions in the federal executive branch are coded as bureaucrats, and members of the Senate and House of Representatives appear as witnesses in nomination hearings.

Interesting variations also emerge when examining the descriptive patterns by committee. For example, Figures 3.8 and 3.9 show the average witness affiliation by committee in the House and Senate, respectively. It is immediately apparent that the type of witnesses invited by committees varies widely.

Bureaucrats strongly dominate the type of witnesses in the Committees on Armed Services, Foreign Affairs, Veterans' Affairs, and Government Operations, perhaps reflecting the strong administrative focus of these committees. On the other hand, business witnesses are relatively

## 3.3 Composition of Witness Affiliations

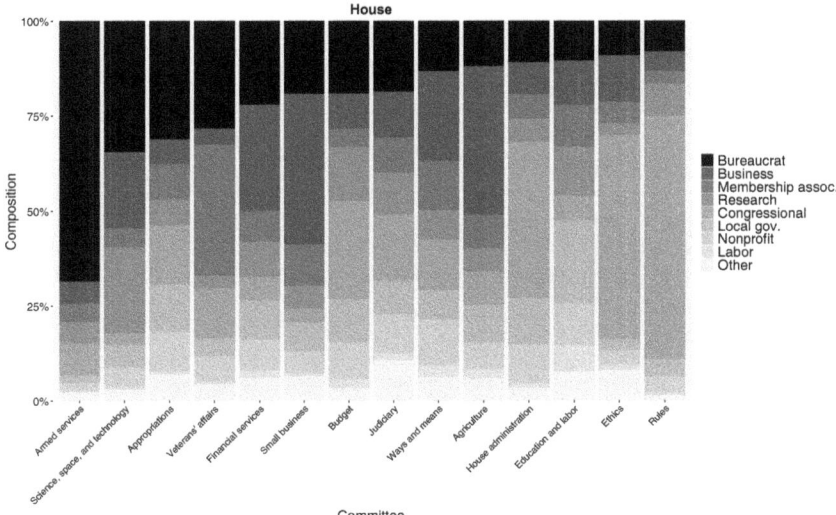

Figure 3.8 Witness affiliations by House standing committee
Notes: This figure shows the aggregate witness composition by House standing committees for the period 1961–2018. The committee order is sorted by the proportion of bureaucratic witnesses (high to low).

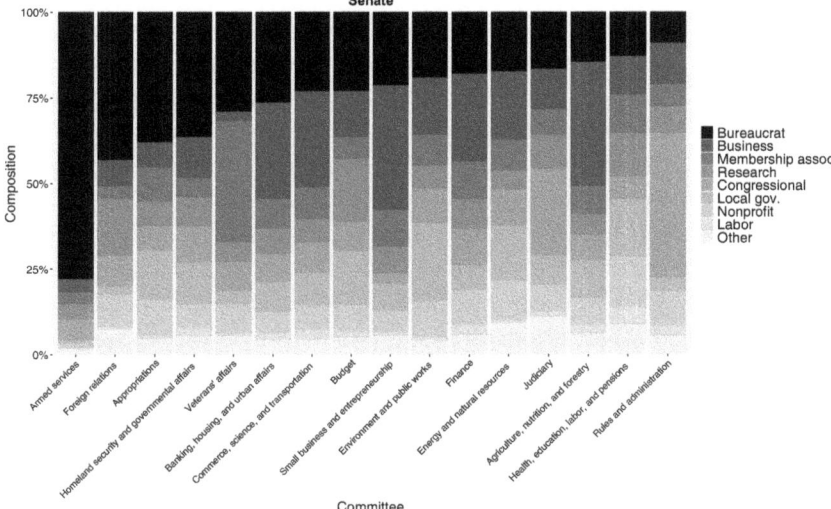

Figure 3.9 Witness affiliations by Senate standing committee
Notes: This figure shows the aggregate witness composition by Senate standing committees for the period 1961–2018. The committee order is sorted by the proportion of bureaucratic witnesses (high to low).

more prevalent in the Agriculture, Banking, Energy and Commerce, and Small Business Committees, reflecting the need for information from outside sources in these industries. When we examine the composition of witnesses by major issue area, hearings dealing with issues such as

45

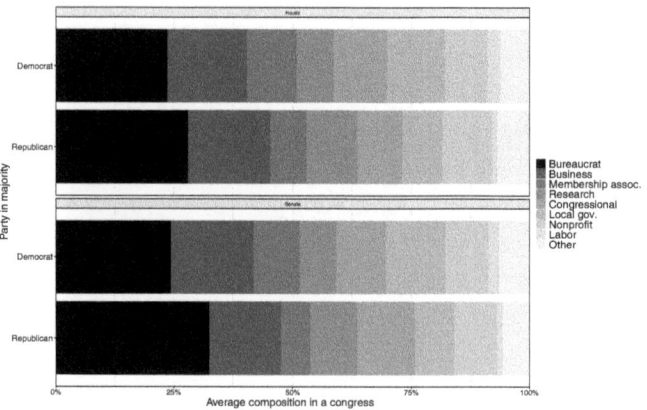

Figure 3.10 The composition of witness affiliations by majority party
Notes: The top panel shows the composition of witnesses by majority party in the House. The bottom panel shows the composition of witnesses by majority party in the Senate.

defense, international affairs, government operations, immigration, and technology hosted more witnesses from the bureaucracy. Hearings on issues such as agriculture, domestic commerce, energy, foreign trade, and macroeconomics had more witnesses from the business sector.

Next, we examine whether the frequency of witness affiliations varies by the majority party in each chamber. Figure 3.10 shows the composition of witness affiliation categories by the majority party in the House and Senate. There is no significant difference in the composition of witness affiliations by majority party status in either chamber. The Republican majority tended to invite more bureaucrats and research-oriented witnesses (think tank and university personnel) than the Democrats when there was a Democratic Party majority. The Democratic majority tended to invite more witnesses from membership associations, state and local government, and labor unions than the Republicans do when there was a Republican majority. One caveat: Given that each party had majority party status in different Congresses and they may have held hearings on different issues, the differences in witness affiliations may simply reflect the time trend, their issue priorities, or both. To fully understand why Democrats and Republicans invite different types of witnesses for a similar type of hearing, we need to control for time, committee, and issue. We present a more comprehensive analysis of this in Chapter 6.

## 3.4 COMPOSITION OF WITNESSES BY GENDER

We close this chapter by examining an issue in the literature on congressional policymaking: how women's voices and presence affect policymaking. This topic is not the focus of our book, but we use this context to

## 3.4 Composition of Witnesses by Gender

demonstrate how the descriptive power of our dataset can inform other important research areas.

Existing literature documents a significant gender gap in activities – such as campaign contributions, staffing decisions, and the gender composition of lobbyists – which could influence legislators' policy choices (Malbin, 1980; Romzek and Utter, 1997; Grumbach, Sahn, and Staszak, 2022; Ritchie and You, 2021; LaPira, Marchetti, and Thomas, 2020; Krook and O'Brien, 2012). Legislators' interactions with individuals and groups shape their perspectives and policy choices (Hertel-Fernandez, Mildenberger, and Stokes, 2019), and scholars raise concerns that women's policy inputs do not match men's influence even on issues that predominantly affect women (Mendelberg, Karpowitz, and Goedert, 2014). Congressional hearings are no exception.

On February 16, 2012, Planned Parenthood posted a commentary on Facebook concerning a House Oversight hearing hosted by Chairman Darrell Issa (R-CA) about contraceptive coverage. Planned Parenthood noted that Congress invited an all-male panel to testify on President Obama's proposal requiring health insurance companies to cover contraception (Flock, 2012). The exclusively male panel of witnesses testifying on an issue intrinsically linked to women's health generated widespread controversy. Two female Democratic members walked out of the House oversight hearing and Representative Carolyn Maloney of New York declared:

What I want to know is, where are the women? I look at this panel and I don't see one single individual representing the tens of millions of women across the country who want and need insurance coverage for basic preventive health care services, including family planning.

This example clearly illustrates that women's presence at a hearing about contraceptive coverage would have increased the visibility of the opinions of the population most directly affected by the policy in question. The lack of female witnesses at congressional hearings in general – in which information is formally and publicly gathered and conveyed – could limit women's visibility and influence in policymaking thereby affecting the quality and impact of legislative outcomes. For instance, research from Clayton, O'Brien, and Piscopo (2019) indicates that women's equal presence in policymaking bodies adds more legitimacy to decision-making processes and increases institutional trust.

As the committee phase is a central decision-making stage in congressional politics, other existing work uncovers gender underrepresentation by examining witnesses who testified before a specific subset of Senate committees (Agriculture; Commerce, Science & Transportation; Foreign

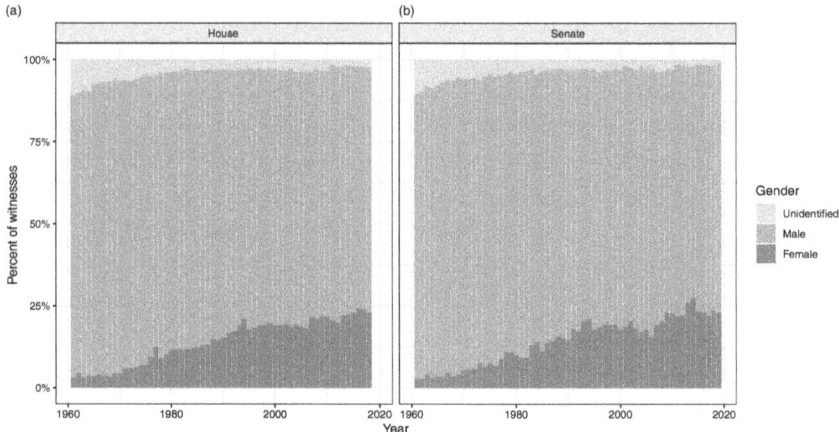

Figure 3.11 Witness gender over time
Notes: These two figures show the gender composition of witnesses in the House (a) and the Senate (b) over time.

Relations; and Health, Education, Labor and Pensions) from 2003 to 2015 and finds that women comprised a minority (23.7 percent) of the witnesses (Pressman, 2020). This study, however, is limited to these specific Senate committees during a limited time period.

Our witness dataset, on the other hand, provides a comprehensive understanding of the gender composition of witnesses in congressional hearings over time and across committees. For example, Figure 3.11 shows how the gender composition of witnesses has changed over time in the House (Panel (a)) and Senate (Panel (b)). In both chambers, the percentage of female witnesses has been low throughout the period and has never approached parity with male witnesses. The percentage of female witnesses ranged from a minimum of about 8 percent in the House and 4 percent in the Senate during the late 1960s, and gradually increased to a maximum of about 24 percent in the House and 26 percent in the Senate near the end of the time period. This trend is relatively similar across committees over time. Furthermore, there is no difference in the gender composition of witnesses in legislative and oversight hearings: men comprised an average of 87 percent of witnesses in the House and 88 percent in the Senate in both types of hearings.

Figure 3.12 shows the gender composition by committee in a stacked bar chart. For each standing committee, we aggregate the ratio of female and male witnesses across years. In the House, the Committee on Education and Labor had the highest percentage of female witnesses from 1961 to 2018, while the Committee on Foreign Affairs ranked near the bottom in terms of the ratio of women testifying before Congress. In the Senate, the Health, Education, Labor, and Pensions (HELP) Committee hosted

## 3.5 Summary

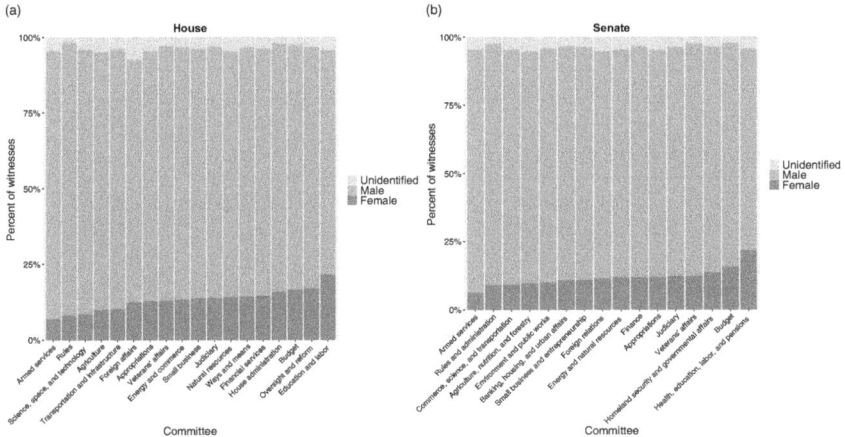

Figure 3.12 Witness gender by committee
Notes: These two figures show the gender composition of witnesses in House standing committees (a) and Senate standing committees (b).

more women as witnesses, while the Armed Services Committee had very few women as witnesses. Figures A5 and A6 show the gender composition of witnesses by hearing topic and illustrate a similar relationship to the gender composition by committee. Women were more likely to be invited to testify at hearings dealing with education and social welfare issues. This is consistent with the trends we see in Figure 3.12, as these are the issues under the jurisdiction of the House Education and Labor Committee and the Senate HELP Committee – the two committees with the highest (though still low) percentages of female witnesses.

Table 3.5 shows the gender breakdown by witness affiliations. Although women are significantly underrepresented in all types of witness affiliations, there are variations. There are more female witnesses from nonprofit organizations and the "Other" category – which includes witness types such as "citizen" and "healthcare." By contrast, groups of witnesses from business organizations, bureaucrats, congressional personnel, and labor unions are more male dominated.

### 3.5 SUMMARY

In this chapter, we provide patterns and trends that describe the witnesses who provide information through testimony at congressional committee hearings. To do so, we use our new, comprehensive dataset on congressional witnesses for the period 1961 to 2018. These data offer detailed descriptive statistics on the number of hearings, number of witnesses, types of witness affiliations, and witness genders across time, committees, and issues.

Table 3.5 *Gender composition by witness affiliation*

|  | House | | Senate | |
| --- | --- | --- | --- | --- |
| Witness categories | No. witness | Female witness (%) | No. witness | Female witness (%) |
| Business | 75,600 | 7.8 | 47,068 | 6.3 |
| Bureaucrat | 110,597 | 11.0 | 70,513 | 10.5 |
| Congressional | 46,473 | 8.6 | 24,983 | 7.2 |
| Local government | 51,056 | 14.9 | 33,314 | 13.0 |
| Research | 37,747 | 12.6 | 22,195 | 11.2 |
| Membership assoc. | 43,571 | 14.3 | 25,262 | 13.2 |
| Nonprofit | 34,166 | 25.1 | 20,524 | 23.1 |
| Labor | 10,739 | 10.4 | 5,850 | 8.1 |
| Other | 52,515 | 20.3 | 35,818 | 19.6 |
| Total | 462,464 | 13.2 | 285,527 | 12.1 |

*Notes:* The *Business* category includes agriculture, corporations, and trade associations. *Local government* includes state and local government and K-12 educational. *Other* includes judicial, lawyers and lobbyists, healthcare, citizen, Native American, religious, and international.

These pattern reveals both the stable and dynamic natures of the diversity of witnesses who have testified in congressional hearings. On the one hand, bureaucrats and business interests have consistently ranked first and second in terms of the frequency of witness appearances over the decades. The composition of witness affiliations by committee and issue has changed little over time. Committees that heavily invited bureaucrats, such as the Armed Services Committee in the 1960s, have continued to invite bureaucrats at substantially high levels; hearings on agricultural issues in the 1960s hosted disproportionate numbers of witnesses from business interests and continued this practice into the 2010s. And perhaps one of the most consistent trends is that the presence of female witnesses has never approached parity with the presence of male witnesses over the past sixty years.

On the other hand, there is evidence of changes in the composition of witnesses. Although the average number of witnesses in hearings has declined since the 1990s, the proportion of research-based witnesses has increased. This increase has come at the expense of witnesses from membership organizations, state and local governments, and congressional personnel – all of whom appeared less often over time. And while female witnesses never comprised even half of the witness pool, there has been an upward trend in their numbers since the 1960s. Female witnesses made

## 3.5 Summary

up less than 10 percent of all witnesses in the 1960s; that percentage gradually increased until the end of our data's time span in 2018 when nearly one-quarter of all witnesses in congressional hearings were female.

However, despite the increasing gender diversity of witnesses, critics note that a significant lack of racial and class diversity remains. This is particularly evident in hearings on certain issues, such as technology – an increasingly important policy area that includes broadband access, antitrust concerns, and artificial intelligence. Chin et al. (2021) observe that racial minority witnesses were conspicuously absent from hearings on technology policies in the 116th Congress, even though these issues could disproportionately and negatively affect racial minorities and low-income households.

In recent years, the issue of witness diversity has begun to attract the attention of members of Congress. In 2021, the House Office of Diversity and Inclusion began tracking – albeit in broad and aggregate terms – witnesses' geographic, racial, and sexual orientation characteristics. It will be interesting to follow this effort and observe trends in witness diversity and the extent to which formal institutional initiatives within Congress – such as the House Office of Diversity and Inclusion and the Senate Democratic Diversity Initiative – might change the composition of witnesses testifying before Congress.

Ultimately, the public, the media, and scholars care about the types of witnesses who testify in Congress because the information they provide receives both a formal platform and a spotlight during an important stage of policymaking: the committee stage. However, the descriptive landscape of witness composition we paint in this chapter is only the tip of the proverbial iceberg. In Chapter 4, we explore the *types of information* that witnesses provide and whether those with different affiliations provide different types of information. In Chapters 5–7, we explain *why* committees turn to the types of witnesses shown in the patterns explained in this chapter.

### NOTES

1. While individual committees provide real-time information on current hearing schedules and may have records of past committee hearings available on their committee-specific websites, this information is not systematically provided on each committee's website systematically for every hearing going back in time. The two sources discussed earlier – ProQuest and the GPO – are the two primary sources that provide and maintain data on committee hearings.
2. While the witness information provided by the committees may be the most accurate documentation of the witnesses who appeared at a hearing, this information is not provided by every committee or for every hearing, so it cannot be used as a comprehensive data source.

3. The percentage of missing data was even higher in the GPO data.
4. For more details about the unpublished hearings excluded from the ProQuest's Congressional Hearings data, see the following document: https://comparativeagendas.s3.amazonaws.com/codebookfiles/Hearings_Codebook_19.1.pdf
5. These directories were digitized by the HathiTrust Digital Library Project using Google Books.
6. While the trend in the number of witnesses is declining sharply over time, the points seen in the last two years of the chart (2017 and 2018) do not include all the hearings held, as hearing data are not yet fully available for the most recent Congresses. For example, classified hearings held in recent Congresses may not yet have been declassified (compared to classified hearings that have been declassified over time).
7. Figures A3 and A4 present trends in the number of witnesses by eighteen specific types over time for the House and the Senate, respectively.

# 4

## Not All Information Is Equal

### How Witnesses Vary in What They Provide to Congress

Over two weeks in January 2021, the price of GameStop stock rose 1500 percent, a surge that Elon Musk commemorated with a tweet proclaiming "Gamestonk." This reflected the actions of Reddit users in the WallStreetBets subreddit, who initiated a short squeeze in response to an investment newsletter predicting GameStop's price would fall. Several large hedge funds were in a short position – poised to make money if the stock price fell, but to lose money if it rose. The sudden, sharp increase in GameStop's stock price and the resulting market volatility – driven by the actions of amateur individual investors – caused these hedge funds to lose billions of dollars.

Many of these WallStreetBets investors in GameStop were what the industry calls "retail traders" – individuals who invest in a single stock rather than hedge funds or other mutual funds – who used brokerage firms and trading platforms such as Robinhood and TD Ameritrade. The resulting financial event, in which WallStreetBets retail investors profited by driving up GameStop stock prices and hedge funds lost by being on the wrong side of the bet, led Robinhood to temporarily halt purchases of GameStop on its trading platform on January 28, a move Robinhood said was necessary to preserve its own collateral and liquidity.

Robinhood lifted the temporary ban the next day but continued to impose severe restrictions on GameStop trading, claiming that the restrictions were necessary for it to meet the collateral required to execute trades. Retail investors – the self-proclaimed Davids facing the Goliaths of hedge funds and large investment firms – were infuriated by Robinhood's restrictions that prevented them from continuing the short squeeze and were suspicious of Robinhood's ties to hedge funds that were losing money.

In the aftermath, it became clear that Robinhood was facing a $3 billion margin call from the Depository Trust & Clearing Corporation. This meant that – in order to cover the transactions that Robinhood's users were initiating on GameStop – Robinhood would have to come up with $3 billion to cover the trades, a requirement that led Robinhood to halt trading instead. Robinhood's users, however, did not see this as a valid justification; they considered it Robinhood's responsibility to its users to cover their trades. Dozens of lawsuits were filed against Robinhood, Robinhood was thrust into the media spotlight, and calls for regulatory action and oversight rang out.

Various government agencies were concerned about the Robinhood and GameStop trading activity, from the perspective of protecting retail investors (the concern of the US Securities and Exchange Commission), the potential systemic risks that had been exposed (the concern of Treasury Secretary Janet Yellen), and possible market manipulation related to the short squeeze (the concern of the Senate Banking Committee). In response, the US House Financial Services Committee, led by Chairwoman Maxine Waters (D-CA), held three days of hearings aimed at uncovering the facts of what happened and gathering information to develop legislative responses.

On its first day of hearings, the committee heard from Keith Gill, a retail investor from WallStreetBets who had invested in GameStop. In his testimony, Gill provided the following information:

I'm just an individual whose investment in GameStop and posts on social media were based upon my own research and analysis ... Social media platforms, like Reddit, YouTube, and Twitter are leveling the playing field. The idea that I used social media to promote GameStop stock to unwitting investors and influence the market is preposterous. My posts did not cause the movement of billions of dollars into GameStop shares ... I consider myself and my family fortunate with our investment. When the stock price broke $20 in December, I knew my investment was a success. I was so happy to visit my family in Brockton for the holidays. The money would go such a long way for us ... I am grateful to be in a position to give back to and support my family. As for what happened in January, others will have to explain it. It's alarming how little we know about the inner workings of the market.

His testimony and answers to the questions posed by the Committee highlighted his personal perspective on the events and their impact on his own life. Another witness, Vicki L. Bogan, an associate professor at Cornell University, was invited to inform committee members about the design of investment applications such as Robinhood, reflecting the Committee's concern that Robinhood's design may have led retail investors to take unnecessary, uninformed risks. She was asked about this in questions from members of the committee:

**Representative Cindy Axne:** Dr. Bogan, you have done some tremendous research in behavioral finance. Just a quick question to start, can app design influence what decisions people using that app make?
**Professor Vicki Bogan:** Thank you for the question. Absolutely. App design and the way the platform is designed and the user interface can influence the type of decisions that a retail investor makes, almost on an unconscious level. And I want

## Witness Testimonies and Analytical Information

to make a clear point, there is a difference between retail investor access, which is great and provided by appropriations; retail investor environment, which kind of is ease of use; and retail investor manipulation, in that there are certain behavioral science techniques that are used to trigger investors to behave in a particular way that may not be in their best interest.

**Representative Cindy Axne:** And that is why Robinhood has behavioral researchers, correct?

**Professor Vicki Bogan:** I can't speak to why they have behavioral researchers, but I can say that some of the features of their platform have been shown in research to elicit particular behaviors, such as more trading. For example, they have a list of kind of the most popularly traded stocks. That brings attention to particular types of stocks, and we know from the research that just having attention to particular stocks increases trading in those stocks, whether or not it is in the best interest of the investor to do so.

**Representative Cindy Axne:** So, as you mentioned, it increases trading, and do you think that encourages savings and investment or do you think that just encourages greater tendency toward more trades?

**Professor Vicki Bogan:** Yes, there is a difference between investment and trading. Just trading multiple times a day for trading's sake, the research is very clear that is never in the best interest of a household. Buy and hold is the conventional wisdom. And so, buying is fine, but this multiple trading and turning portfolios has never been shown to be beneficial to a retail investor.

In this exchange, the committee member asked the witness to publicly provide information about how the design of an app by a company such as Robinhood can lead a user to engage in increased trading. In her responses, Professor Bogan refers to academic research and makes several falsifiable statements on the subject.

While both Keith Gill's and Vicki Bogan's testimonies provided information to the committee, the *type* of information differed. The form of Keith Gill's information was an anecdote that established his personal experience. The form of Vicki Bogan's information was an analysis of the issue at hand from a falsifiable standpoint.

The difference was, in fact, intentional. When calling the hearing, Chairwoman Waters emphasized her expectation of the different types of information that different types of witnesses would provide. She made this clear in her statement summarizing the testimony given on both hearing days:

In our first hearing on those events, we received testimony from the CEOs of trading app, Robinhood; Wall Street firms, Citadel and Melvin Capital; and social media company, Reddit; as well as Keith Gill, a trader involved in WallStreetBets on subreddit. We heard directly from those involved in the short squeeze and volatility and we got the facts.

In our second hearing, we received testimony from a number of capital markets experts and investor advocates to hear their views and begin to assess possible legislative and regulatory steps that may be necessary. We examined conflicts of interest in the market. We scrutinized payment for order flow, potential systemic risks to our financial system, the gamification of trading, the clearance and settlement process for trades, and the evolution of trading with the rising use of social media and new technologies.

Clearly, Keith Gill's testimony informed committee members about what happened, while Vicki Bogan's testimony was part of the information-gathering process to begin "possible legislative and regulatory steps." Both types of information are useful, but the latter is singled out as necessary input for considering possible legislative action.

How can we think about the content of the testimony and how it relates to the invited witnesses? The descriptive patterns Chapter 3 showed the varied composition of witnesses in terms of their affiliations. When committees select witnesses, their affiliations may be the clearest, most relevant characteristics present, but do affiliations capture meaningful differences in the amount and type of information witnesses provide? In this chapter, we illustrate several ways to explore how the content of witnesses' testimony may vary by their affiliations.

As shown in the GameStop example earlier, the content of testimony can vary considerably. The existing empirical literature has focused on one way to measure information: the amount of falsifiable statements about the policy under consideration. Esterling (2004, 2007) refers to this type of information as *analytical* discourse; other scholars name it "policy-analytic knowledge" or "technical information" (Bradley, 1980). This contrasts with nonanalytical information, such as what is conveyed in anecdotes or personal material and is categorized as "ordinary knowledge," "experiential discourse," or "political messages" (Esterling, 2007; Park, 2021). Analytical information is by no means unbiased or nonpartisan – technical information can still be gathered in a biased way or presented in a partisan fashion – it is simply a type of information that is characterized by its falsifiable nature.

Of course, nonanalytical information is also politically useful, especially for politicians to understand and connect with constituents (Esterling, 2007). However, analytical information is a necessary input for technical policy development and the type of information on which positive theories have focused on for the most part (Krehbiel, 1991). Furthermore, the decline in the analytical capacity of Congress emphasizes the importance of understanding the quantity and quality of analytical information that external witnesses provide (Burgat and Hunt, 2020).

We examine the amount of analytical information present in witness testimonies and show that witnesses of different types offer different amounts of analytical information. This chapter describes how witness

## 4.1 Analytical Information in Witness Testimonies

affiliations can capture meaningful differences in the information that witnesses ultimately provide.

### 4.1 ANALYTICAL INFORMATION IN WITNESS TESTIMONIES

#### 4.1.1 Data and Measurements

To examine the content of testimony, we collected transcripts of House hearings in the 105th through 114th Congresses (1997–2016) from the Government Publishing Office (GPO). We analyzed each witness statement or speaking instance – their speeches, questions, answers, and other statements.

To determine which types of witnesses provide more analytical information in hearings, we quantify three aspects of their testimonies: the number of words each witness spoke in a hearing; the number of keywords conveying analytical information that each witness used in a hearing; and the proportion of these keywords out of all the words each witness spoke in a hearing. First, the number of words is the most comprehensive measure, as it can contain both analytical and nonanalytical information. Second, the number of keywords measures the absolute amount of analytical information provided by a witness in a hearing. Third, the proportion of keywords addresses how efficiently a witness conveys analytical information in her testimony. We use the proportion of keywords as our main dependent variable for the following reason. The absolute number of keywords that witnesses speak is important, but it is likely the result of various external factors – such as the length of a hearing or the frequency of questions – that are strategic decisions made by committee members rather than by the witnesses themselves. However, the proportion of keywords characterizes the testimony style of individual witnesses, which is intrinsic to each witness. The unit of analysis is the individual witness in each hearing.

We identify the set of keywords that may convey analytical information using several sources: information-seeking statements from Park (2021), words related to cognitive orientation from the Harvard IV-4 dictionary, and any additional word stems that are similar to those in the first two groups.

First, we refer to the grandstanding score introduced in Park (2021), which measures the intensity of political messages conveyed in each statement made by committee members during congressional hearings using the same hearing transcript data analyzed in this study. As a byproduct of the score, members' statements with low scores are largely either procedural statements or information-seeking statements. We use the frequent words in these statements while screening out words relevant to procedural statements.[1]

Second, we additionally collected words that are related to cognitive orientation from the Harvard IV-4 dictionary. Specifically, we selected thirty-two words in the following subcategories: "know" (e.g., analyt, calcul, and correl), "causal" (e.g., caus, consequ, and odd), "compare" (e.g., less, higher, and better), and "quan" (e.g., approx, averg, and disproportion) and stemmed these words for the analysis.

Third, to supplement the list, we identify twenty-eight additional word stems that are relevant to analytical information but are not included in the list of words described above (e.g., diagnosi, survey, examin, investig, and measure) or are words with meanings similar to words in that list but are not included in the list (e.g., "percentag" is similar to "percent"; "contrast" is similar to "differ"; and "result" is similar to "consequ"). In total, we use 134 keyword stems for this study. The full list of keywords can be found in the Appendix Section A.2.1.

## 4.2 VALIDATION OF THE MEASUREMENT OF ANALYTICAL INFORMATION

To validate our measure of the analytical information conveyed in witness testimony, we constructed a human-coded validation measure for the 100 sample paragraphs of witness testimony through the following procedure. First, we randomly selected 1,000 witness statements and kept only those statements with more than 80 words. Then, if a statement contained multiple paragraphs, we separated the statement into paragraphs. Among the paragraphs or single-paragraph statements, we kept only those with more than 50 words and less than 150 words. Second, we measured the proportion of keywords for each paragraph.[2] Third, we conducted random block sampling to construct a set of 100 sample paragraphs to be human-coded. We selected twenty paragraphs from each of the following five blocks: 0–0.05, 0.05–0.1, 0.1–0.15, 0.15–0.2, and 0.2 or higher. The thresholds were chosen to divide the range of keyword proportions into five equidistant smaller ranges. Fourth, each of the 100 sample paragraphs was randomly paired with another paragraph to create 1,000 pairs. Fifth, each of the two trained research assistants compared 500 pairs and selected the one that seemed more analytical. That is, a paragraph is analytical if it contains a verifiable, fact-based, objective, or positive statement as opposed to a statement that is nonverifiable, experiential, opinion-based, subjective, or normative. After collecting the coders' choices, we fit a Bradley–Terry model to measure the latent trait in the sample paragraphs and constructed a continuous measure following the procedures introduced in Carlson and Montgomery (2017).

## 4.2 Validation of Analytical Information

We then computed the correlation coefficient between our measure, the proportion of keywords, and the human-coded score resulting from the Bradley–Terry model. We find that the correlation coefficient is 0.6, which indicates that these two measurements tend to go in the same direction. This procedure provides a statistical validation of our measure.

We further substantively validate our measurement strategy by examining witness testimonies containing different levels of analytical information. Table 4.1 shows three examples from the 100 sample paragraphs

Table 4.1 *Examples of witness testimonies containing varying levels of analytical information*

| Information on speaker and hearing | Statement | Prop. of keywords |
|---|---|---|
| Craig Rosenthal at Pension Rights Center before the House Committee on Ways and Means in a hearing titled Defined Benefit Pension Plan Funding Levels and Investment Advice Rules (October 1, 2009) | "The IRS relief allowed companies to look back to interest rates that were in effect in October 2008, which are substantially higher and, therefore, derived lower liabilities than interest rates in effect at the beginning of 2009. So that lookback, while very helpful for plans, did reduce plan liabilities by approximately 10 to 20 percent, based on our study." | 0.254 |
| Michael Farley at American Red Cross before the House Committee on Energy and Commerce in a hearing titled Charitable Contributions on September 11 (November 6, 2001) | "If the donor restricts their contribution for a particular purpose, then we honor that designation, but when we initiate a fund-raising initiative and make a case as to what the funds are being used – what the need is, the funds that we received, we presume that because the donor has responded to that without condition, it would be used for that purpose." | 0.1 |
| Gary Brock at Baylor Healthcare System before the House Committee on Ways and Means in a hearing titled Physician-Owned Specialty Hospitals (March 8, 2005) | "Well, definitely they would because they are going to have more involvement, more operating knowledge about that facility. All of these facilities that we operate in partnership with our physicians, they also retain active staff privileges on our other hospitals. So, they are extensions of their practice. They are extensions of our hospitals." | 0 |

of testimony. We chose these three paragraphs based on the following criteria: the paragraph with the largest proportion of keywords; the paragraph in which the keywords make up 10 percent of the total number of words (proportion = 0.1), which is about the midpoint of the range of keyword proportions in this sample dataset; and the paragraph with no keywords. The first example statement is about pension plans; it contains analytical information about the effects of a policy obtained from the witness's study. This is the statement with the highest percentage of keywords among the 100 sample paragraphs. In the second example, a representative of the American Red Cross explains how they use charitable donations. Similarly, the third example statement explains how the witness's facilities operate and their relationship with physicians. The second and third statements may be useful field information, but they are not typical examples of analytical, research-driven information as defined in this study. Consistent with this observation, the proportion of keywords for these statements is 0.1 and 0, respectively. In summary, the comparison of these three example paragraphs suggests that statements with a higher proportion of keywords are indeed more likely to provide information that is considered analytical as defined in this study.

## 4.3 DESCRIPTIVE STATISTICS

Before examining the differences among witness types, we first examine the time trend from 1997 to 2016 in the number of words and analytical keywords witnesses spoke during committee hearings and how their speaking patterns have changed by looking at the proportion of keywords included in their testimony. These descriptive statistics are presented in two ways. First, we compute the average of each measure across Congresses using the witness-hearing-level measures we constructed. The first two panels of Figure 4.1 show that witnesses tended to speak more words and analytical keywords over time. The average proportion of keywords contained in each witness's testimony in each hearing (the third panel of Figure 4.1) slowly increased until 2012 but decreased in the last two Congresses analyzed. Thus, it appears that the amount of information – both analytical and nonanalytical – provided by each witness has generally increased, while their testimony has not necessarily become more analytical.

However, this analysis provides limited information about how much information congressional committees gained from public hearings. As shown in Figure 3.2, the number of witnesses invited by House committees declined dramatically over this twenty-year period, but the number of hearings did not decline as dramatically. These statistics together suggest

## 4.3 Descriptive Statistics

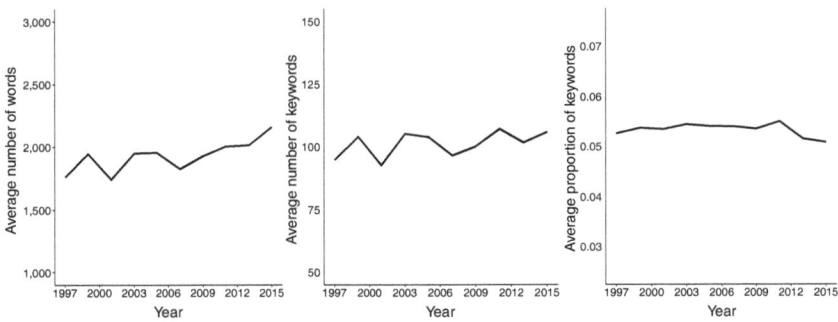

Figure 4.1 Over time changes in individual witnesses' speaking patterns
Notes: Panels (a) and (b) show the number of words or keywords that a witness spoke on average in a hearing across time (across Congresses). Panel (c) computes the average proportion of keywords contained in witness testimonies in each Congress using the witness-hearing-level data.

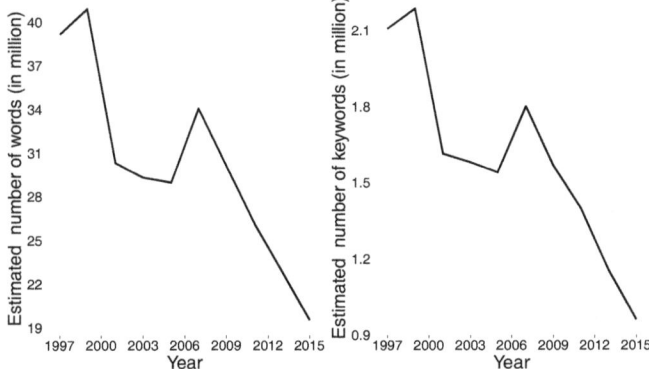

Figure 4.2 Changes in witness testimonies by Congress
Notes: The average number of words spoken by witnesses in each hearing multiplied by the total number of witnesses invited to House committee hearings in each Congress is plotted on the left; the same for the average number of keywords is plotted on the right. Entries are in millions of words.

that each witness may have received more opportunities to speak at each hearing, which might have rendered the average amount of information that an individual witness provided to increase over time. However, from these statistics, it is unclear whether the absolute amount of information that committees collected may have decreased or not.

To further address this issue, we multiplied the average number of words and of keywords, respectively, by the number of witnesses invited to House committee hearings in each Congress to estimate the total number of words and keywords contained in all testimony in each Congress. We plot them in Figure 4.2. As expected, both the number of words and the number of keywords decreased over time. Because both measures show a similar trajectory, these estimates are largely driven by the decline in witness invitations, and that decline is not offset by the increased amount of information provided by individual witnesses. This finding implies that the role of congressional committees in gathering all types of policy-relevant information – including analytical information – through public hearings has declined significantly over time.

## 4.4 REGRESSION ANALYSIS AND RESULTS

Using the three measures of witness testimony as dependent variables, we conduct a regression analysis to examine which types of witnesses tend to provide more analytical testimony. Thus, the main explanatory variable of interest is the type of witness affiliation, which we include in the model as fixed effects for witness affiliation types. In these regression models, we include the following control variables. At the hearing level, we include the number of committee members who spoke, the number of witnesses present at a hearing, the number of times a witness was asked to speak at a hearing, the gender of a witness, an indicator for whether a bill was considered (referral hearings), and an indicator for subcommittee hearings. At the committee level, we include the absolute difference in the DW-NOMINATE score between the Democrats and Republicans on the committee, the absolute difference in DW-NOMINATE scores between the committee chair and the floor median, and the absolute difference in the DW-NOMINATE score between the committee median and floor median, the proportion of female committee members, and the average legislative effectiveness score of committee members who spoke in a hearing (Volden and Wiseman, 2014). We also include Congress fixed effects, committee fixed effects, and hearing issue fixed effects (from the Policy Agendas Project).

The regression equation is shown below:

$$\text{Proportion of keywords}_{fhict} = \alpha_0 + \beta * \text{Hearing Characteristics}_h$$
$$+ \gamma * \text{Committee Characteristics}_{ct}$$
$$+ \alpha_f + \alpha_i + \alpha_c + \alpha_t + \varepsilon_{fhict},$$

where the subscripts indicate witness affiliations $f$, hearings $h$, issue $i$, committee $c$, and Congress $t$.

The results of this regression are shown in Table 4.2. Columns (1) and (2) analyze the number of words and keywords that witnesses spoke in a hearing, which captures the amount of information they provided. The regression result shows that each witness spoke less when there were more witnesses; when the witness was female; when a bill was being considered; when a hearing was held by a subcommittee rather than a full committee (only on the number of words), as subcommittee hearings tend to be shorter; when committee members were more polarized by

## 4.4 Regression Analysis and Results

Table 4.2 *Hearing characteristics and witness testimonies*

|  | Dependent variable | | |
|---|---|---|---|
|  | Words (1) | Keywords (2) | Keywords/words (3) |
| Number of members | 5.742*** | 0.167*** | 0.0001*** |
|  | (1.057) | (0.063) | (0.00002) |
| Number of witnesses | −29.202*** | −1.672*** | −0.00000 |
|  | (0.994) | (0.059) | (0.00002) |
| Female witness | −125.913*** | −5.284*** | 0.001*** |
|  | (10.637) | (0.634) | (0.0002) |
| Number of statements | 67.234*** | 3.442*** | −0.0001*** |
|  | (0.337) | (0.020) | (0.00001) |
| Bill | −90.832*** | −3.257*** | 0.0004 |
|  | (10.820) | (0.645) | (0.0002) |
| Subcommittee hearing | −48.798*** | −0.193 | 0.002*** |
|  | (13.753) | (0.820) | (0.0003) |
| |Comm. Dem-Comm. Rep| | −722.651*** | −41.097*** | −0.004*** |
|  | (117.565) | (7.007) | (0.001) |
| |Floor Median-Comm. Chair| | −227.853*** | −10.716*** | −0.002*** |
|  | (52.177) | (3.110) | (0.001) |
| |Floor Median-Comm. Median| | −576.510*** | −12.352* | 0.003* |
|  | (107.804) | (6.425) | (0.002) |
| Prop. of female members | 519.939*** | 34.338*** | −0.001 |
|  | (141.032) | (8.405) | (0.002) |
| Avg. LES of committee | 6.986 | 0.326 | −0.0002** |
|  | (4.423) | (0.264) | (0.0001) |
| Constant | 2,244.428*** | 115.950*** | 0.049*** |
|  | (111.070) | (6.620) | (0.001) |
| Witness type FE | Yes | Yes | Yes |
| Issue FE | Yes | Yes | Yes |
| Committee FE | Yes | Yes | Yes |
| Congress FE | Yes | Yes | Yes |
| Observations | 32,512 | 32,512 | 32,512 |
| $R^2$ | 0.658 | 0.609 | 0.108 |
| Adjusted $R^2$ | 0.657 | 0.608 | 0.106 |

Notes: *$p < 0.1$; **$p < 0.05$; ***$p < 0.01$.

party line; when a committee chair took a more ideologically extreme position; and when committee members on average took more ideologically extreme positions. The finding that female witnesses spoke fewer words could be because they were asked questions less often, they voluntarily gave shorter answers, or they were interrupted by committee members more often. The finding that members allowed witnesses less time to speak in referral hearings and in ideologically biased or polarized committee environments may be because in these cases committee members are likely to have established policy positions rather than exploratory interests, and they only need witnesses to provide short answers to specific questions. On the other hand, witnesses spoke more as the number of committee members increased (because members could ask witnesses more questions), and when there are a larger number of female committee members.

Column (3) analyzes when witnesses provided analytical information more efficiently. It is noteworthy that witnesses conveyed analytical information more compactly in hearings where more members attended and spoke – potentially busier or more important hearings – and in subcommittee hearings, which tend to be shorter and may place more time constraints on hearing participants. Female witnesses provided more analytical information. In addition, ideological polarization within a committee tended to hinder witnesses' effective delivery of analytical information, but the ideological extremism of the committee chair and the committee as a whole had mixed effects. Interestingly, the average legislative effectiveness score of committee members did not promote the collection of information from witnesses overall; it negatively affects the collection in the third model, although the magnitude is very small.

Since we are primarily interested in how witness affiliations correlate with the amount of analytical information presented in witness testimony, we now turn to an analysis of the coefficients on witness affiliation types. Figure 4.3 shows the coefficients on the witness type fixed effects from an ordinary least squares regression predicting the proportion of keywords used by a witness in a hearing. Here, witnesses representing nonprofit organizations are set as the reference group.

The figure shows that bureaucrats and witnesses from think tanks and research institutions gave testimony with the highest proportion of analytical information. On the other hand, individual citizens with no organizational affiliation and those representing religious institutions provided the lowest proportion of analytical information, which seems naturally consistent and gives confidence that our measurement is substantively valid.

There is a clear gap between the types of witnesses who provide the most and least analytical testimony. Based on Figure 4.3, the difference between the coefficients for bureaucrats and citizens is 0.016. Given that the witnesses in this analysis tended to speak an average of 1,923 words in a hearing, bureaucrats were likely to use an average of 31 more analytical keywords in a hearing than ordinary citizens. To further examine

## 4.4 Regression Analysis and Results

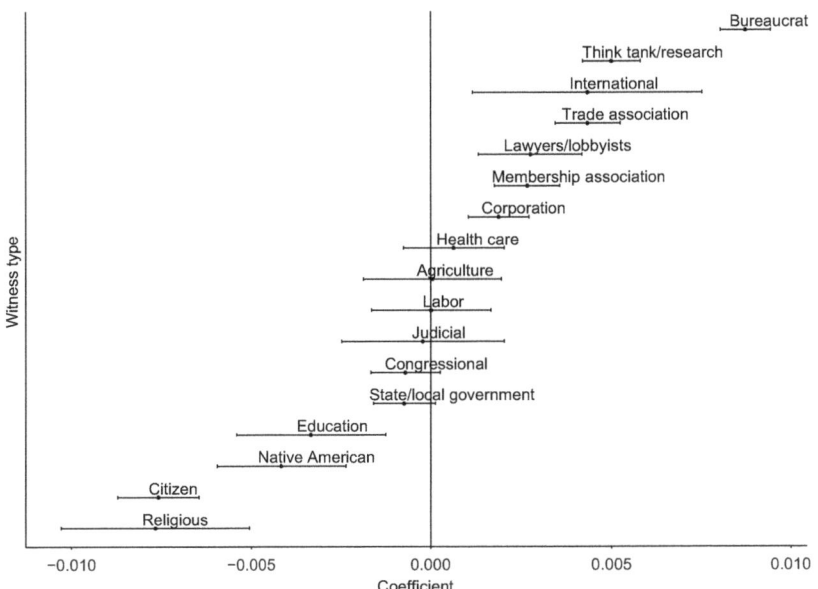

Figure 4.3 Proportion of keywords by witness type
Notes: This figure shows the coefficients on the witness type fixed effects when the outcome is the proportion of keywords in witness testimonies. The vertical line indicates the 95% confidence interval. The reference group is witnesses from nonprofit organizations.

whether this difference is substantively noticeable, in Table 4.3 we provide two sample statements selected from those containing at least fifty words.[3] The first statement has the largest proportion of keywords among those made by bureaucrats; the second is the statement with the smallest proportion of keywords among those made by citizen witnesses. In the first statement, a bureaucrat informs committee members about different discount rates applied at different stages of policymaking and during the implementation process. In the second statement, the parent of a drug overdose victim explains his experience with his son anecdotally. The contrast between these two statements illustrates how our measure successfully captures the difference in the levels of analytical information. We provide additional representative sample statements to confirm this finding in Appendix Section A.2.2.

Alternatively, when the number of keywords spoken is used as the dependent variable, the top two and bottom two groups remain the same. The coefficient plot from this model is shown in Figure 4.4, and there are notable changes in the three groups. Judicial witnesses and state and local government witnesses moved up in the rankings – from 11th to 3rd and from 13th to 7th, respectively – suggesting that they used more analytical words. But at the same time, they used more words, which

Table 4.3 *Examples of the most and least analytical testimony*

| | With the largest proportion of keywords | With the smallest proportion of keywords |
|---|---|---|
| Statement | "When projects are authorized, when there is a Chief's Report and the Congress authorizes a project, the economic analysis that is done on that calculates a benefit to cost ratio. And that benefit to cost ratio is based on a 3.125 discount rate. When the Office of Management and Budget evaluates projects for funding, including in the President's budget, that benefit to cost ratio is evaluated at a 7-percent discount rate. So the budgeting discount rate is different from the authorization discount rate that's used." | "When Michael came home that night and I confronted him and was talking to him, he had eye contact like we do now. But when he was sitting on the sofa and nobody was confronting him, he was comatose. He was in the ozone. He was sitting with his mouth hanging open, staring at the floor. I knew that there was something wrong with him that night. I could tell that he had taken something." |
| Speaker | Jo-Ellen Darcy, Assistant Secretary, Civil Works, Department of Army | Brad Alumbaugh, parent of drug overdose victim |
| Type | Bureaucrat | Citizen |
| Proportion | 0.247 | 0 |

decreased the proportion of keywords. Thus, they may provide more analytical information in absolute terms than when they are measured on the proportion of keywords. In contrast, agricultural witnesses dropped from 9th to 15th, indicating that they spoke fewer analytical words than other types of witnesses, but they also spoke much fewer words overall.

## 4.5 VARIATION ACROSS OTHER CONDITIONS

In addition to our primary focus – examining variations in information provision across witness affiliations – we examine such variations across important institutional factors and witness gender. First, we show variation in the proportion of keywords in witness testimony across committees. For this analysis, we fit a new regression model because committees and major issue areas are likely to overlap significantly. All parts of the model remain the same as the third model in Table 4.2, except it omits issue fixed effects.

Figure 4.5 shows the coefficients on the committee fixed effects from the regression result. We find that testimony was most analytical in

## 4.5 Variation across Other Conditions

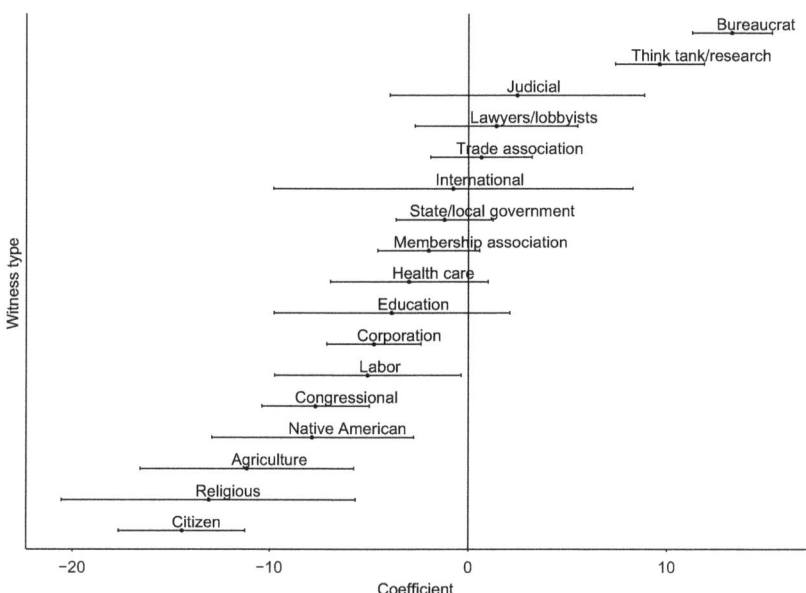

Figure 4.4 Number of keywords by witness type
Notes: The figure shows the coefficients on the witness type fixed effects when the outcome is the number of keywords in witness testimonies. The vertical line indicates the 95% confidence interval. The reference group is witnesses from nonprofit organizations.

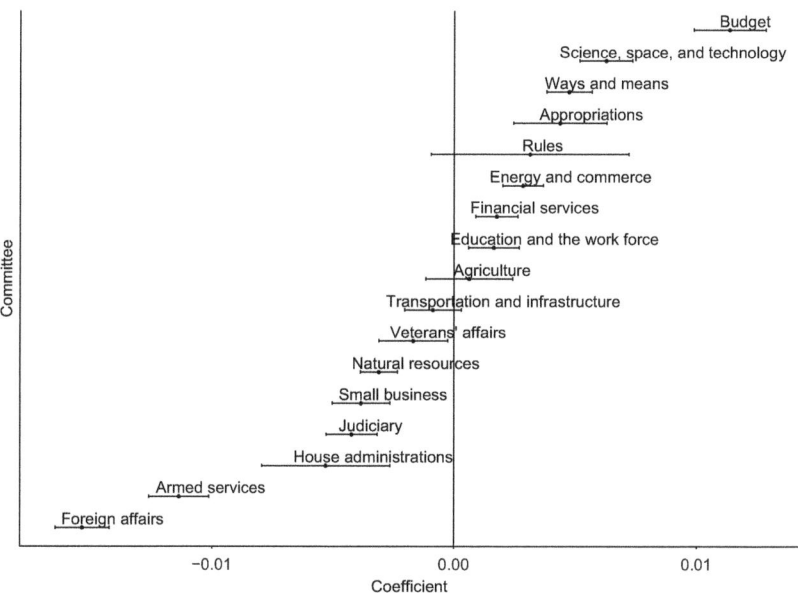

Figure 4.5 Proportion of keywords by committees
Notes: The figure shows the coefficients on the committee fixed effects when the outcome is the proportion of keywords in witness testimonies. The vertical line indicates the 95% confidence interval. The reference group is the Oversight and Reform Committee.

hearings held before the Appropriations and Science, Space, and Technology Committees; it was least analytical in hearings held before the Armed Services and Foreign Affairs Committees. This is consistent with the existing findings in Park (2021): Members of the latter two committees – which deal with foreign affairs and security issues where the president has predominant policymaking power – have less incentive to gather policy-relevant information because they have relatively less power to make policy changes in their jurisdictions compared to other committees. As a result, members of these committees tend to focus on making relatively more political statements than on questioning witnesses to gather information for legislative language. By contrast, it is intuitive to expect that members of the Science, Space, and Technology Committee would be most dependent on analytical research given the committee's jurisdiction. The Appropriations Committee sets spending and revenue levels for the federal government given the outstanding deficit and national debt. Therefore, the committee's hearings focus on analytical fiscal conditions, which increases the use of analytical terms by witnesses.

Second, while our study focuses on the primary characteristics of witnesses' affiliations, gender may be another important aspect that affects the quantity and quality of information Congress receives. Congressional scholars document gender differences in many activities, such as staffing decisions, campaign contributions, and who becomes a lobbyist, which can influence legislators' policy choices (Ritchie and You, 2021; LaPira, Marchetti, and Thomas, 2020). Similarly, we see a gender gap in the witnesses who appear and testify at committee hearings. Our gender effect results presented in Table 4.2 suggest that female witnesses spoke fewer words and keywords than male witnesses. However, the proportion of keywords was higher for female witnesses, suggesting that they were more precise and efficient in providing analytical information, even though the total amount of information they conveyed may be less than that of male witnesses. These effects are visualized in Figure 4.6.

Gender dynamics also are present among committee members. Patterns from our data show that the gender composition of committee members has significant effects on the characteristics of witness testimony. The results in the first and second models in Table 4.2 illustrate that as the proportion of female committee members increased, (a) witnesses spoke more, and (b) witness testimony contained more analytical information.

Finally, we examine whether the information-gathering efforts of House committees are hindered under divided government and whether there is any partisan effect depending on which party controls the majority of seats in the House. We conduct another set of regressions by

## 4.5 Variation across Other Conditions

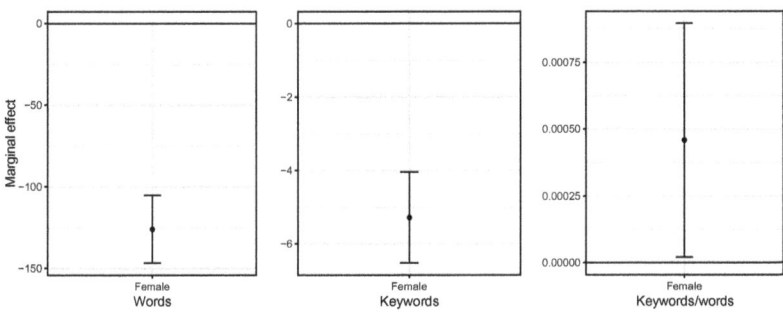

Figure 4.6 Proportion of keywords by the gender of witnesses
Notes: The reference group is male witnesses. The plots show the marginal effect of the female witness variable on the total number of words, the total number of analytical keywords, and the proportion of analytical keywords of the total number of words.

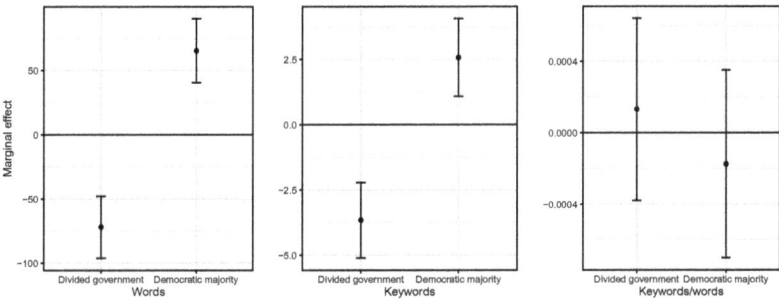

Figure 4.7 Proportion of keywords by government type and the majority party
Notes: The reference group for the *Divided Government* variable is Unified Government. The reference group for the *Democratic Majority* variable is Republican Majority. The plots show the marginal effect of each variable on the total number of words, the total number of analytical keywords, and the proportion of analytical keywords of the total number of words.

adding binary indicators for divided government and Democratic majority control of the House. However, because these characteristics vary by Congress, we use president fixed effects instead of Congress fixed effects to control for any time trend.[4] Figure 4.7 shows the regression coefficients for these indicators on each of the three dependent variables. Consistent with general expectations, witnesses tend to provide fewer words and keywords under divided government than under unified government. However, the proportion of keywords is not affected by the type of government. Regarding the partisan difference, committee members were more successful in eliciting information from witnesses when the Democratic Party controlled the chamber. The number of words and the number of keywords contained in the testimonies increased under the Democratic majority, but the proportion of keywords was not affected.

The evidence discussed in this section shows that the amount of analytical information in witness testimonies varies by the type of witness affiliation. Furthermore, the amount of analytical information can also vary by the gender of the witnesses and by institutional conditions such as ideologically polarized environments, the gender composition of committee members, divided versus unified government, and partisan control of the chamber.

Namely, witness affiliations matter. They capture differences in the amount of information provided by witnesses by a meaningful metric: analytical information. We demonstrate this further by turning next to analyzing the content of hearings.

## 4.6 CONTENT ANALYSIS IN WITNESS TESTIMONIES

In this section, we analyze whether and how different types of witnesses provide testimony by focusing on the types of content they deliver in hearings on the same broader issue. For this analysis, we focus on hearings held on the issue of "health," which is a major topic category in the US Policy Agendas Project. We chose this issue because these hearings invited the most diverse set of witnesses in our witness dataset compared to hearings on other major issues.

Using the statements that witnesses made in House committee hearings on health-related issues from the 105th to 114th Congresses and the stm R package, we fit a structural topic model with twenty topics (within the "health" issue) to explore latent topics in witness testimonies.[5] Table A1 shows the twenty words with the highest probability of appearing in each topic. We then grouped the twenty topics into six meaningful topic categories – (a) [medical] practice, (b) insurance, (c) government (e.g., policy implementation and monitoring), (d) legislation, (e) research, and (f) junk topics (e.g., common nouns, verbs, adjectives, and adverbs) – to simplify the analysis, which compares topic focus across nine witness categories. We use only the first five topic categories for analysis.[6]

Figure 4.8 shows the number of statements made by witnesses in each witness category on each of the five topic categories. In health-related hearings, witnesses from bureaucratic agencies and research institutions were invited and testified at the highest rate, suggesting that these hearings were largely focused on gathering analytical information.

To compare the topic focus of each group of witnesses, Figure 4.9 shows the proportion of testimony from the same group of witnesses in each topic category. Witnesses from government agencies provided testimony primarily on topics related to government (e.g., implementing and monitoring the progress of policy programs) and medical practice. Witnesses from research institutions provided the largest proportion of research-based testimony. This analysis illustrates the differences in the

## 4.7 Use of Evidence in Witness Testimonies

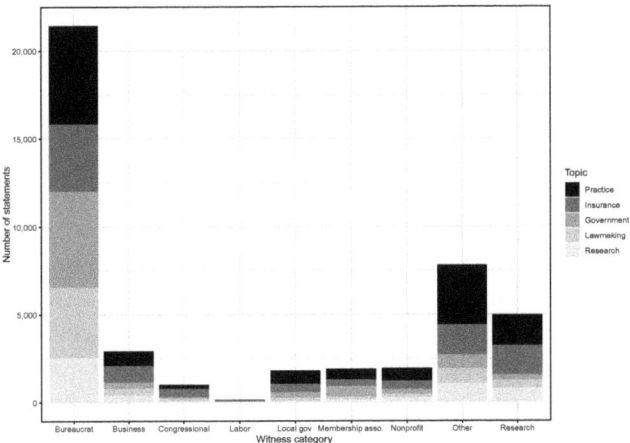

Figure 4.8 Topics of testimony by witness categories – Total number of statements
Notes: This graph shows the number of statements made by witnesses in each category on each topic.

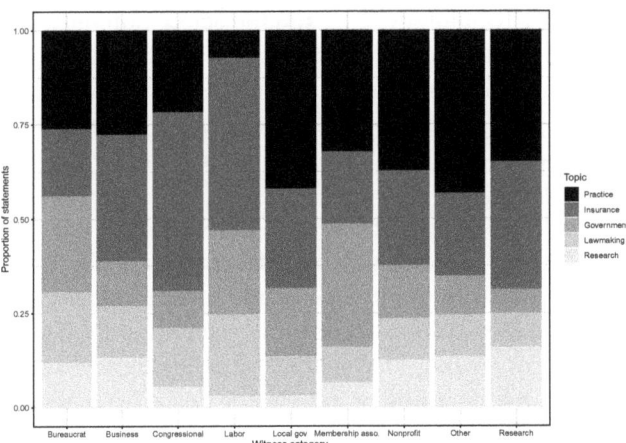

Figure 4.9 Topics of testimony by witness categories – Proportion of statements
Notes: This graph shows the proportion of topics on which witnesses in each category testified.

content of testimony that different types of witnesses provided to congressional committees, even when they were invited to discuss much the same issue.

### 4.7 USE OF EVIDENCE IN WITNESS TESTIMONIES: CLIMATE CHANGE HEARINGS

Up to this point, we have examined how different witness types present different degrees of analytical information. This is useful, especially for achieving empirical breadth across a variety of topics over an extended period of time. But the quantity of analytical information aggregated at the witness type level does not fully reveal the types of information, evidence, and research findings that witnesses present to members of Congress. In this section, we go beyond a measure of analytical information and examine specific sources of evidence that witnesses cite in their congressional testimony in the context of climate change: an issue ripe for scientific information and academic research.

For this focus, we concentrate on climate change hearings held in the House of Representatives during the 110th through 115th Congresses (2007 through 2019). Using hearing title and summary information, we identify hearings that contain keywords such as "climate change," "global warming," and "greenhouse gas" to identify hearings on climate change. We focus on the three House committees that held the most hearings on topics related to climate change (the numbers in parentheses indicate the number of hearings on climate change for the 110th–115th Congresses): Committee on Energy and Commerce (36), Committee on Science, Space, and Technology (41), and the Select Committee on Global Warming established in the 109th and 110th Congresses (37). In total, there were 114 hearings on climate change in these House committees. Eighty hearings (70.2 percent) were held under the Democratic majority and thirty-four hearings (29.8 percent) were held under the Republican majority in the House.

To understand the sources of research and studies cited by witnesses, we used PDF files of the hearing transcripts and manually extracted the citations and references that witnesses made to scientific works or other organizations. The transcripts include both oral testimony and statements written prior to the hearing and submitted as attachments to the transcript. We search for citations or references made by a witness at any point in the transcript and create indicator variables that capture whether the reference was made during a speech or in the written testimony.

Although the number of hearings is modest (i.e., 114 hearings held by the 3 committees), extracting citations and references was time consuming. Because the format of the materials varied by committee and witness, we could not apply an automated code for machine reading. Therefore, we extracted citations and references manually from all the hearing transcripts. Figure 4.10 shows how research is cited in a prepared statement submitted by a witness: Michael Mann, Distinguished Professor of Atmospheric Science at Pennsylvania State University. He was invited to testify at a hearing entitled "Climate Change: Assumptions, Policy Implications, and the Scientific Method," held by the House Committee on Science, Space, and Technology during the 115th Congress. Prior to his appearance at the hearing, Dr. Mann submitted a seventeen-page

### References

1. M.E. Mann, B.A. Steinman, and S.K. Miller, "On forced temperature changes, internal variability, and the AMO", *Geophysical Research Letters*, vol. 41, pp. 3211-3219, 2014. http://dx.doi.org/10.1002/2014GL059233
2. K. Tung, and J. Zhou, "Using data to attribute episodes of warming and cooling in instrumental records", *Proceedings of the National Academy of Sciences*, vol. 110, pp. 2058-2063, 2013. http://dx.doi.org/10.1073/pnas.1212471110
3. G.A. Schmidt, D.T. Shindell, and K. Tsigaridis, "Reconciling warming trends", *Nature Geoscience*, vol. 7, pp. 158-160, 2014. http://dx.doi.org/10.1038/ngeo2105
4. M. Huber, and R. Knutti, "Natural variability, radiative forcing and climate response in the recent hiatus reconciled", *Nature Geoscience*, vol. 7, pp. 651-656, 2014. http://dx.doi.org/10.1038/ngeo2228

Figure 4.10 An example of research cited in a written statement
Notes: This figure shows the references used in the written statement submitted by a witness Michael Mann of Penn State University for the hearing entitled "Climate Change: Assumptions, Policy Implications, and the Scientific Method" in the House Committee on Science, Space, and Technology in 2017.

statement outlining his views on global warming, climate change, and greenhouse gas regulation. In it, he cites several studies, research findings, and journals, such as the *Geophysical Research Letters* and *Nature Geoscience*. His citations were mostly in footnotes or references, as shown in Figure 4.10.

In total, we identified 3,137 instances of citations and references made by witnesses in the 114 climate change hearings. During the witnesses' oral testimony, 388 references (12.3 percent) were cited; therefore, most research citations appeared in the witnesses' written testimony. We recorded each citation and reference in full as it appeared in the transcript and then categorized the reference source into five different types: academic, think tank, government report, international, and other.

Table 4.4 shows the distribution of reference sources. The most common are academic papers, accounting for 36.5 percent of all citations. There are over 300 unique journals and academic publications (e.g., a book published by a university press) cited by witnesses in climate change hearings. Research published in academic journals, such as *Nature, Science* and *The Journal of Climate Change*, is highly cited by witnesses in congressional hearings. Table 4.5 shows the top five journals that witnesses cited; the numbers in parentheses indicate the total number of citations. All of the top five sources are peer-reviewed journals with impact scores (as of 2021) ranging from 4.2 (*Journal of Geophysical Research*) to 69.6 (*Nature*).[7] Although there are concerns about deliberate efforts by industry to produce research denying human causes of climate change or global warming (e.g., Oreskes and Conway, 2011), the research evidence presented to congressional committees from academic sources appears to come from sources with scientific authority.

Government publications are the second most common type of source that witnesses cited. Publications produced by federal and state

Table 4.4 *Distribution of reference sources*

| Type | Frequency | Share (%) | Example |
|---|---|---|---|
| Academic | 1,147 | 36.56 | Michaels, P. J. and P. C. Knappenberger, 1996, "Human Effect on Global Climate?" *Nature*, 384: 522–523 |
| Government | 781 | 24.90 | "EPA Study of the Effects of Global Warming" |
| International | 328 | 10.46 | "Intergovernmental Panel on Climate Change Report" |
| Think tank | 291 | 9.28 | Mintzer, I., 1987, "A Matter of Degrees: The Potential for Controlling the Greenhouse Effect," Report No. 4, *World Resources Institute* |
| Other | 590 | 18.81 | "As China Roars, Pollution Reaches Deadly Extremes," December 26, 2007, *The New York Times* |
| Total | 3,137 | 100 | |

*Notes:* This table shows the distribution of reference source types in oral and written testimony of witnesses in climate change hearings.

Table 4.5 *Top sources for citation*

| Rank | Academic | Government |
|---|---|---|
| 1 | *Nature* (101) | Department of Energy (230) |
| 2 | *Science* (74) | Environmental Protection Agency (112) |
| 3 | *Journal of Climate* (48) | National Research Council (77) |
| 4 | *Journal of Geophysical Research* (40) | Department of Commerce (50) |
| 5 | *Geophysical Research Letter* (35) | NASA (42) |

*Notes:* Numbers in parentheses indicate the number of total citations by witnesses from each source.

government agencies accounted for 24.9 percent of all citations in witnesses' written and oral testimony. Table 4.5 shows the top five government agencies in order of numbers of citations. Reports from the Department of Energy, the Environmental Protection Agency (EPA), the National Research Council, the Department of Commerce (particularly the National Oceanic and Atmospheric Administration), and the National Aeronautics and Space Administration (NASA) are highly cited.

## 4.7 Use of Evidence in Witness Testimonies

Federal agencies have produced a significant amount of publications. For example, a search result on the GPO website using the keywords "Department of Energy" returns 26,402 publication results.[8] Feldman (1989) studies bureaucrats in the US Department of Energy and finds that analysts' information is often not used in policymaking. But analysts produce it "because it is the only way they can hope to influence policymaking" and because bureaucrats "value the work" for intrinsic, professional, and social reasons. Carpenter (2001) argues that bureaucratic information and the ability to act on it form a pillar of bureaucratic autonomy. Our analysis suggests that congressional hearings could be a valuable venue for bureaucrats to cite federal agency publications in their testimonies.

The *International* category includes research or other types of publications from international organizations or foreign governments. Given our focus on climate change hearings, reports from the International Panel on Climate Change (IPCC), an international body established in 1988 by the World Meteorological Organization (WMO) and the United Nations Environment Programme (UNEP) to assess the science of climate change, were heavily cited. Out of 326 citations from international sources, publications produced by the IPCC were cited 162 times (49.3 percent). The next most cited publications were from the International Energy Agency, an international organization that coordinates various global energy systems.

Table 4.6 shows the result of a cross-tabulation between types of witnesses in climate change hearings and the sources of citations from each type of witness. For each witness, we present the proportion of citation sources. For example, 40.7 percent of the citations submitted or mentioned by bureaucrats appearing in climate change hearings were from academic sources and 34.2 percent of the sources were from government publications. Academic and government sources are widely cited by all types of witnesses. Witnesses representing business interests tended to cite more sources from reports published by trade associations, which are included in the "Other" category of source types. Witnesses from nonprofit organizations, many of which are environmental groups, showed a higher proportion of citations from international sources, especially ICPP reports.

Overall, this analysis suggests that academic research and technical government publications are important sources of information that witnesses relay. It also confirms our analysis on the analytical information: bureaucrats and individuals associated with think tanks and academic institutions provide more research-based evidence to members of Congress.

Table 4.6 *Witness types and citation patterns*

| Witness type | Citation source | | | | | |
|---|---|---|---|---|---|---|
| | Academic | Government | International | Think tank | Other | Total |
| Bureaucrat | 40.7 | 34.2 | 12.1 | 3.0 | 10.0 | 100 |
| Business | 18.1 | 27.6 | 9.3 | 10.5 | 34.6 | 100 |
| Nonprofit | 19.8 | 20.8 | 16.4 | 16.0 | 27.0 | 100 |
| Think tank and university | 47.7 | 18.9 | 9.0 | 10.5 | 13.9 | 100 |
| Other | 20.1 | 35.5 | 10.7 | 7.0 | 26.7 | 100 |

*Notes:* This table shows the distribution of citation sources for each witness type in climate change hearings. Each row sums to 100 (%). The *Business* category includes corporations and trade associations. The *Other* category includes all other types of witnesses: Agriculture, Citizen, Congressional, Healthcare, International, Labor, Membership association, Native American, and State and local government.

## 4.8 SUMMARY

The patterns described in this chapter demonstrate that not all testimony provides the same type of information and committees may receive different amounts of analytical information depending on the types of witnesses they invite. Specifically, bureaucrats and witnesses from research-oriented institutions provide the most analytical testimony; female witnesses provided analytical information more efficiently than male witnesses; and committees collected more information – especially analytical information – under unified government than under divided government and when the Democratic Party held the majority instead of the Republican Party. In addition, our analysis of health policy hearings confirmed that committees invite different types of witnesses to inquire about different aspects of policy. Finally, by manually extracting research citations from witnesses' oral and written testimony in climate change hearings, we illustrate which types of research are presented by which types of witnesses.

Importantly, the descriptive examples in this chapter show that witness affiliations capture meaningful differences in the information provided by witnesses. This foundation allows a greater scope of analysis using witness affiliations, as the availability of transcripts of committee hearings (1997–2016) is dwarfed by the data availability of witnesses (1961–2018).

Taken together, the findings and patterns illustrated in this chapter motivate our argument that the composition of witnesses has important implications for committees, as witness invitations not only indicate from whom committees choose to hear but also signify the different types of information committees may ultimately receive.

## 4.8 Summary

### NOTES

1. From the list of 200 most frequent word stems in the statements in the lower quartile of the score, we selected 74 word stems that were deemed relevant to bills (e.g., bill, law, and legisl), sources of information (e.g., inform, letter, record, and report), research (e.g., author, data, estim, and studi), statistics (e.g., percent, rank, and rate), logical relationship (e.g., relat, associ, and differ), cost – benefit calculation (e.g., benefit, budget, cost, and dollar), policy consequences (e.g., change, effect, impact, and increase), and deliberation (e.g., discuss, possibl, and review). Then, we added one more word stem and two special characters: "statist," "%," and "$." These word categories can be considered as constituting a typical policymaking process that includes collecting information and data; analyzing them; assessing costs, benefits, and possible consequences of policy alternatives; and, finally, deliberating and deciding among the alternative choices.
2. Note that although the actual measure we use for the analysis is constructed at the witness-hearing-level – determined by calculating the total number of keywords a witness spoke in a hearing divided by the total number of words they spoke in that hearing – for purposes of presentation, we calculate the proportion of keywords for each sample paragraph.
3. In the regression analysis, the proportion of keywords was measured for each witness in each hearing. However, it is difficult to compare such long texts that summarize all speaking instances in a hearing. To make it easier to compare the sample testimonies, we again measure the proportion of keywords for each instance of speech that the witnesses made.
4. The regression results are reported in Table A2.
5. We fit unsupervised topic models without specifying covariates. We fit models with ten, twenty, and thirty topics. Ultimately, we chose the twenty-topic model because (1) the topic clusters resulting from the ten-topic model seemed to require more detailed topic classifications, while (2) the topic clusters from the thirty-topic model seemed to be saturated with several overlapping topics. Thus, we proceeded with the twenty-topic model.
6. The twenty topics are grouped into six categories as follows: (a) "Practice" includes medical practice, medical treatment, virus, medication, disease, youth health, and drug; (b) "Insurance" includes health insurance, Medicare & Medicaid; (c) "Government" includes inspection, crisis management, and veterans' health; (d) "Lawmaking" includes lawmaking and hearing procedures; (e) "Research" includes analysis, medical research, and stem cell research & women's health. The three junk topics tend to contain common words (e.g., peopl, can, get, know, and realli). We labeled each of the twenty topics based on the twenty words with the highest probability of appearing, as well as the twenty words that appeared most frequently and were the most exclusive in each topic.
7. Impact score is a measure of the importance of a scientific journal. It measures the annual average number of citations to recently published articles from that journal.
8. https://catalog.gpo.gov/F?func=find-b&find_code=WRD&local_base=GPO01 PUB&request=Department+of+Energy (accessed July 29, 2022).

# 5

# When Committees Seek Out Information for Policy Development

The descriptive patterns in the Chapters 3 and 4 provide a picture of how the witnesses who testify before committees can vary and how different types of witnesses provide different levels of analytical information. This implies that whom the committee invites to testify affects the types of information they receive during hearings. Because we are interested in whom Congress invites to provide information to produce policy, we focus on legislative hearings. We examine how members of Congress decide who will testify in legislative hearings and the conditions leading committees to invite the types of witnesses who provide higher levels of analytical information for policy development.

Members of Congress are politicians. They are naturally driven by political considerations in the numerous decisions they make in their jobs. Choosing witnesses to speak in public committee hearings is no exception. Strong political considerations emerge between parties, and majority and minority committee members may follow diverging goals set by their leadership. Simultaneously, however, members are lawmakers tasked with the serious responsibility of making the nation's policies. They must hold this lawmaking duty in tension with the political forces they face, especially along partisan lines.

In the following chapters, we present a theoretical framework incorporating how three categories of explanatory factors – committee intent, interbranch relations, and committees' internal capacity – affect how committees choose witnesses. The dominant actor in committee proceedings – chairs and majority members – seek witnesses to impart analytical information under three conditions that are driven by partisan considerations. In this chapter, we begin by examining the intent for a legislative hearing and how it affects a committee's selection of witnesses.

## 5.1 COMMITTEE INTENT IN LEGISLATIVE HEARINGS

On March 26, 2019, the House Committee on Education and Labor held a subcommittee hearing entitled, "Protecting Workers' Right to

## 5.1 Committee Intent in Legislative Hearings

Organize: The Need for Labor Law Reform." In Subcommittee Chairwoman Federica S. Wilson's opening statement, she said the hearing was called "to examine the threats to workers' rights and explore proposals that will improve the quality of life for millions of workers and their families." This hearing did not have a referred bill attached to it; the intent of the hearing was to discuss "the strengths and weaknesses in the current state of labor law and identify proposals that hold employers that violate the law accountable, protect collective action, and modernize labor laws for a changing economy." The subcommittee called four witnesses, ranging from a professor of sociology to an automotive glass worker. They gave prepared testimony and answered questions from members on a variety of topics concerning the labor movement and labor unions. The sociology professor from Washington University in St. Louis, Jake Rosenfeld, addressed issues such as historical trends, the state of the current labor movement, and the level of public support for labor unions; the automotive glass worker, Cynthia Harper, provided first-hand accounts of working conditions, attempts to unionize at her company, and the aftermath of that failed unionization attempt.

Overall, the hearing focused on gathering and disseminating information from these witnesses on existing problems in labor law reform, the facts and opinions surrounding unions, and possible policy solutions. The hearing was open-ended and concluded with a call for congressional action, reflected in the chairwoman's closing statement: "As our witnesses have made clear, Congress must act now to stop violations of workers' rights and reverse decades of wage stagnation and income inequality. I thank my colleagues for an informative hearing. I thank the witnesses for coming."

Compare this hearing to one held by the same committee and subcommittee on May 8, 2019, entitled, "The Protecting the Right to Organize Act: Deterring Unfair Labor Practices." Unlike the hearing described earlier, a specific bill was attached to this hearing: H.R. 2474, the Protecting the Right to Organize (PRO) Act. Subcommittee Chairwoman Wilson opened the hearing by stating: "Today we are holding the first legislative hearing on H.R. 2474 ... this hearing will focus specifically on the provisions of the bill that prevent employers from violating workers' rights through coercion, retaliation, and delay." While these two hearings focused on the same topic of labor law reform, the May hearing concentrated on the items in H.R. 2474, which had been referred to the committee.

This hearing also featured four different witnesses: the president of the AFL-CIO, a worker who suffered retaliation when he tried to unionize, a partner at a labor law firm, and the executive director of a think tank.

The vast majority of members' questions at this hearing were about provisions in H.R. 2474. For example, Ranking Member Virginia Foxx asked, "In the event of a collective bargaining impasse, H.R. 2474 requires employers and unions to enter arbitration, allowing the unelected bureaucrats to write a binding union contract. The bill states that the contract 'shall be based on the wages and benefits other employers in the same business provide their employees.' Does that mean that under this standard a mom and pop retail small business would have to accept the same union contract terms as a mega corporation like Walmart or Amazon? What effect would this mandate have on small businesses and their employees?"

Members from both parties asked for the witnesses' opinions on specific provisions of the bill and the consequences and effects they anticipated from the bill. Members of the minority party highlighted the potential drawbacks or unintended consequences of the proposed legislation, particularly for small businesses. Members of the majority party highlighted the benefits and need for the proposed legislation, particularly noting how it would offer more protections for workers during union organizing efforts than existing law. Chairwoman Wilson concluded the hearing by urging Congress to pass H.R. 2474, stating that "as our witnesses have made clear, Congress must enact the PRO Act to deter violations of workers' rights and reverse decades of wage stagnation and income inequality."

While both the March and May hearings in the Education and Labor Committee were held on the same legislative issue of labor law reform, they differed in one crucial characteristic: whether they had a specific bill attached to the hearing that defined the position the committee was considering. The March hearing had no bill attached to it – therefore, no public position yet established in its proceedings – and focused on exploring a range of opinions and expert testimony on labor law reform. The May hearing was held on a specific bill, H.R. 2474, that had been referred to the committee. By choosing to take up the bill for discussion during the May hearing, the committee publicly communicated that the position in H.R. 2474 was one it was specifically considering. Accordingly, the May hearing concentrated on the provisions of the bill, why this particular bill was needed, and its advantages and disadvantages.

Even so, both hearings were still legislative hearings. As Chapter 2 introduced, committees use hearings for a variety of reasons, one of which is to gather and communicate information and opinions on legislation. These *legislative hearings* are not held for oversight of executive agencies, investigations, nominations, or resolutions; they are hearings that focus on legislative issues. Committee members may use legislative hearings for a variety of purposes: to gather and provide information, to persuade other members and constituents, to defuse conflict, or to signal potential problems with legislation. As such, witness invitation patterns may vary based on the committee's intent – more specifically, the chair's intent – for holding the legislative hearing.

Committees use witnesses and their testimonies to build their case in a hearing, whether it is to advance (or defeat) a referred bill or a legislative issue in general. More specifically, usually the committee chair shapes a hearing, rather than the committee as a whole.

Scholars and observers of Congress agree that hearings are controlled by the committee chair who typically exercises tight control over the schedule of testimony. Committee chairs view hearings as tools to promote their own agendas and can use hearings both offensively (e.g., to promote or advocate for an issue or to assert jurisdiction) and defensively (e.g., to remove an issue from public debate or promote the view that it belongs to a rival committee). Talbert, Jones, and Baumgartner (1995) specifically note that some hearings are "booster" hearings – they focus on promoting a particular issue and building support for a solution. Other hearings are "critical" hearings – they attack existing policies or the lack of existing policies.

Furthermore, the fact that hearings are controlled by the committee chair makes hearings more useful to the majority party than to the minority party. This is because they are designed to benefit the majority and are held when it benefits the majority. Talbert, Jones, and Baumgartner (1995) interviewed staffers who emphasized that hearings are usually stacked with witnesses to support the goals of the majority party. They noted that the minority party could, by procedure, have its own witnesses added to the hearing, but it usually requires "considerable" resources and effort to do so.

A long line of scholarship also shows how committees can use their informational advantages to shape legislative behavior on the floor through the provision of information. Rank-and-file members depend on cues and information from committee leaders and committee staff when they cast votes on the floor (Curry, 2019). These cues are the strongest between committee members and noncommittee members in their networks, when the floor votes on legislation in a committee's jurisdiction (Fong, 2020).

Other research offers evidence supporting the idea that the broader context of a hearing may affect both the types of witnesses the committee seeks and the types of information the committee obtains. When the intention behind the hearing is gaining information about a new issue or why a problem exists, scholars reveal that the chair is more likely to invite witnesses with diverse points of view (Leyden, 1995; DeGregorio, 1994; Huitt, 1954). Earlier evidence also shows how committees may plan to invite different types of witnesses for different types of hearings. Talbert, Jones, and Baumgartner (1995) examined hearings on four topics (pesticides, smoking, drug abuse, and civilian nuclear power) from 1945 to 1986 and found that nonlegislative hearings hosted a higher proportion of witnesses from industries in the committee's "home venue" (e.g., witnesses in the agricultural industry testifying before the Agriculture Committee) than hearings that considered a referred bill.

A chair can hold a hearing without including a bill that was referred to the committee – a nonreferral hearing – or a hearing with a bill attached to it – a referral hearing. The committee chair, as gatekeeper, faces several options when considering whether to attach a bill to a hearing. The purpose of a nonreferral hearing can be broad and likely reflects the chair's intent to learn about the issue area or potential legislation. Without a referred bill under consideration, committee members do not have a specific piece of legislation on which they can focus their questions and comments. Rather, the nonreferral hearing is, mechanically, broader in scope and open to a larger context for discussion.

While these types of hearings do not directly consider a bill moving through the legislative process, they are still valuable to committees. For example, Talbert, Jones, and Baumgartner (1995) find that nonreferral hearings can be particularly effective in helping committees define an issue, frame a debate, or assert jurisdiction.[1] In fact, the earlier nonreferral hearing may lay the groundwork for understanding why the committee later takes direct action on related legislation. In a nonreferral hearing, the committee itself has not yet defined or advanced a public position on a bill and thus has the flexibility and incentive to seek *analytical information* from experts. Given this situation, the chair and committee members may seek expert information about the details of what is needed to create policy from a narrower set of witnesses who can provide expertise on the issue.

By contrast, a referral hearing is tied to a specific piece of legislation and its purpose is to consider the specifics of the referred bill in order to decide further committee action (or lack thereof) and garner support for their decision. Naturally, the topics of discussion are more limited in this type of hearing compared to nonreferral hearings. While no formal rules require that the discussion or question-and-answer periods concentrate on the bill at hand, a referral hearing is more likely to focus on the policy consequences of the bill, the implementation of the bill, or what could be amended in the bill than a nonreferral hearing held on the same subject.

## 5.1 Committee Intent in Legislative Hearings

Thus, it is more likely that committee members in a referral hearing intend to learn *political information*, a type of information that allows the committee to gauge the specific views of certain groups and showcase the viability of the bill under consideration. Members may wish to learn and disseminate information about the positions and arguments for or against the specific bill before them from various stakeholders, especially constituents and specific interest groups.

As the majority party in the committee hopes to garner support for a bill, they are likely to seek out group witnesses to disseminate political information in a way to *advocate* for the bill. For example, the Subcommittee on Commerce, Manufacturing, and Trade (of the Committee on Energy and Commerce) held a hearing on April 18, 2013, on the Global Investment in American Jobs Act of 2013. This bill would direct the Secretary of Commerce to recommend ways that Congress could increase the nation's ability to attract foreign direct investment. The subcommittee chair, Republican Lee Terry, clearly advocated for the bill's passage, declaring in his opening statement that the panel of experts invited as witnesses would label the bill "a no-brainer" for attracting foreign investment in the United States. In the first question of the hearing, the chair asked Nancy L. McLernon, president and CEO of the Organization for International Investment, what "low-hanging fruit" that was blocking foreign investment could be removed. McLernon, representing an association obviously in favor of foreign investment, replied "I think what is really important about this bill is that it seeks to uncover those very things ... and what I think that this legislation and what this study can do is it puts investment policy front-brain." Indeed, McLernon's opening statement forcefully illustrates her support for legislation that recruits more investment from global companies:

The Global Investment in American Jobs Act seeks to do just that. The legislation recognizes that the U.S. cannot compete for 21st century investment with a 20th century policy mindset. It aims to equip policymakers with a forward-thinking strategic approach to capture new investment in this increasingly competitive, yet opportunity-rich, global environment. The interagency review and recommendations would provide Congress a roadmap for further action to attract global manufacturers, service providers, and innovators to our shores. If enacted, the legislation will send a powerful message at home and abroad that the US is working to improve its investment climate for [foreign direct investment] in a thoughtful and bipartisan manner.[2]

In this first question-and-answer and opening statement of the hearing, the committee's chosen witness is plainly advocating for the bill and its passage. By summoning this witness from an association in support of foreign investment and placing her testimony first, the committee chair is intentionally seeking out information to advocate for the bill.

Furthermore, existing research suggests that diverse lobbying coalitions are useful to committees' assessments of the viability of legislation by offering political information from various groups (Phinney, 2017; Lorenz, 2020). Similarly, committee members may wish to seek information from a wide range of witnesses – such as groups likely to be affected by the legislation – to learn and broadcast political information in their effort to garner support. Thus, we expect referral hearings to include a more diverse set of witnesses, particularly those who can inform politicians about the political ramifications or offer arguments in support of the bill under consideration in the hearing.

Generally, committee chairs may seek out different types of witnesses based on their intent for the hearing; they may change the scope of information they seek and those they invite to testify. This leads to our hypothesis on committee intent:

*Committee Intent Hypothesis: Committee members will invite a narrower range of witnesses and relatively more witnesses who can provide analytical information in non-referral hearings than in referral hearings. Committee members will invite a more diverse set of witnesses and relatively more witnesses from groups that are likely to be affected by legislation in referral hearings than in non-referral hearings.*

## 5.2 HOW WITNESS COMPOSITION VARIES IN REFERRAL VERSUS NONREFERRAL HEARINGS

Our main analysis focuses on legislative hearings in the House of Representatives from 1961 to 2016. In total, there were 32,134 legislative hearings in the House; 31.7 percent (10,176) of them had a bill (or bills) attached, and 68.3 percent (21,958) were held without a bill attached. Figure 5.1 shows the frequency of legislative hearings in the House during a congressional term, which consists of two sessions. Figure 5.1 aggregates the total number of legislative hearings per day during each congressional term from the 87th Congress through the 114th Congress. Hearing activity closely follows the congressional calendar: A new Congress begins in January and the number of legislative hearings gradually increases until the end of March; Congress adjourns until the second week of April and the number of hearings increases again. Congress is usually not in session in August, so there are few hearings, and they increase again in the fall. As the second session begins, members are busy campaigning as November approaches, so there is a dramatic decrease in the number of legislative hearings in late September and October, which was not seen in the first session.

## 5.2 Witnesses in Referral and Nonreferral Hearings

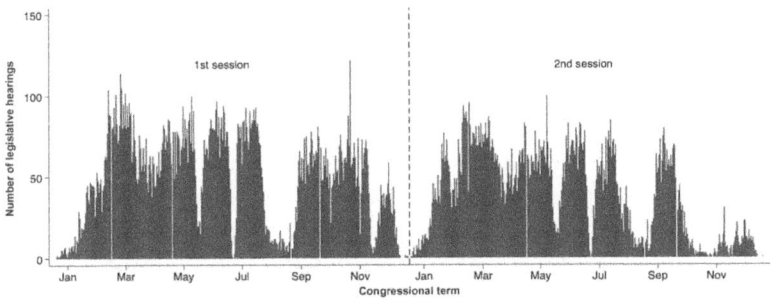

Figure 5.1 Frequency of legislative hearings – House, 1961–2016
Notes: This figure shows the total number of legislative hearings at the daily level over a Congress (two years) in the House of Representative.

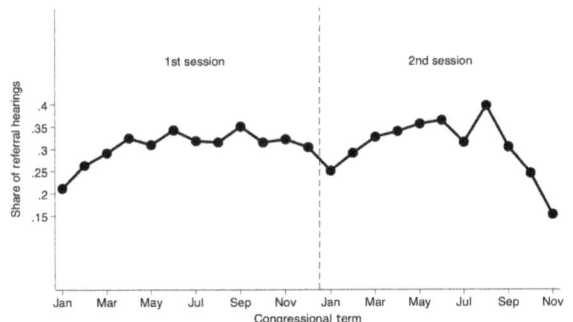

Figure 5.2 Share of referral hearings across a congressional term – House
Notes: This figure shows the share of referral hearings among legislative hearings over a congressional term.

As noted earlier, a nonreferral hearing on a legislative issue may precede a referral hearing. The former may lay the groundwork for the development of a bill; once a bill is developed, a committee chair may hold a referral hearing. In this case, the difference in the numbers of referral and nonreferral hearings may simply be caused by the timing of a hearing. If so, we should expect a disproportionate share of nonreferral hearings in the early days of a congressional term and more referral hearings as the term progresses.

Figure 5.2 shows the proportion of referral hearings during a congressional term (twenty-four months). For each month, we aggregate the total number of legislative hearings and calculate the proportion of referral hearings. The proportion of referral hearings increases until April and then remains stable until the end of the first session. As the Congress's second session begins, the proportion of referral hearings decreases, but after the first month of the second session, the pattern stabilizes as it does in the first session, until the campaign season for the general election begins in September. As a Congress nears its end, toward the end of its second session, the proportion of referral hearings plunges, as nonreferral hearings dominate legislative hearings in the House.

Figure 5.2 shows that there is no monotonic relationship in referral hearings. Rather than seeing fewer referral hearings at the beginning of a congressional term and increasing over time, which would have been the case if Congress starts with nonreferral hearings and advances to referral hearings as the term proceeds, we instead observe the above patterns where the share of referral hearings varies *within* a Congress. Committee chairs, thus, are not simply waiting to hold more referral hearings as the term progresses but are deciding to hold more referral hearings at various points within a term.

We use the following regression and ordinary least squares estimation to examine whether the presence of a bill attached to a hearing affects the types of witnesses invited to testify (*Committee Intent Hypothesis*):

$$Y_{hict} = \beta \text{Hearing Characteristics}_{hict} + \gamma \text{Committee Characteristics}_{ct} + \alpha_i + \alpha_c + \alpha_t + \varepsilon_{hict}, \tag{5.1}$$

where subscripts indicate hearing $h$, committee $c$, issue $i$, and Congress $t$.[3] The outcome variable $Y_{hict}$ measures (1) the quantity of witnesses and (2) the diversity of witness types present at a given hearing, along with the percentage of witnesses of each affiliation type present at the hearing. *Hearing Characteristics* includes the main hearing-level variable of interest that proxies for the committee's intent for the hearing: whether a bill was attached to the hearing. In addition to this key explanatory variable, we include control variables, such as *Subcommittee* (which equals 1 if the hearing was held at the subcommittee level and 0 otherwise). We include committee, issue, and Congress fixed effects. While we use a committee-level fixed effect, we also include committee-level control variables in *Committee Characteristics*$_{ct}$, such as the total number of committee members and the absolute difference in DW-NOMINATE scores between the committee chair and the floor median, as they may be of interest in the estimated results.[4] Standard errors are clustered at the committee level.

Figure 5.3 presents the coefficient plots for the selected outcome variables of interest when a hearing considers a specific bill in the House, a referral hearing.[5] The outcome variable "No. Witness" is the number of witnesses invited to testify at the hearing. In referral hearings, committees tend to invite more witnesses. The outcome variable "Diversity" represents the diversity of witness types and is based on the Herfindahl index of the witness types present in a given hearing. For the eighteen

## 5.2 Witnesses in Referral and Nonreferral Hearings

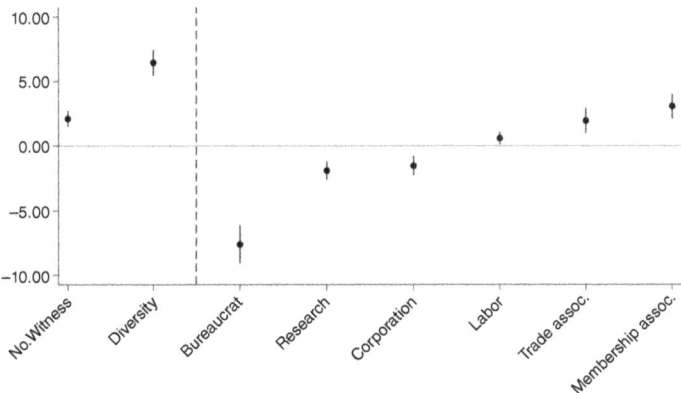

Figure 5.3 The effect of referral hearings on witness invitations – House
Notes: Each plot indicates the regression coefficient for each outcome measure (x-axis). The y-axis shows the regression coefficients: "No.Witness" is the number of witnesses, "Diversity" is one minus the Herfindahl index, and the others are the percentage shares of witnesses. The groups not shown in the plot have coefficients that are not statistically significant. The plots are presented with 95% confidence intervals.

possible witness types, we calculate each type's share of the total number of witnesses in a given hearing. For ease of interpretation, we take one minus this Herfindahl index to create our outcome variable, such that a higher value indicates more diversity of witness types in a hearing and a lower value indicates less diversity. The results in Figure 5.3 show that referral hearings had more invited witnesses and greater witness diversity than nonreferral hearings.

The types of witnesses called more often in nonreferral hearings than in referral hearings are those with a negative significant coefficient in Figure 5.3. First, the share of one type of witness – bureaucrats – is of interest because of their particular knowledge of policy production and needs (Bendor, Taylor, and Gaalen, 1987; Gailmard and Patty, 2012a; Patty and Turner, 2021) and the higher level of analytical information (as we illustrate in Section 4.4) they bring to committees. Note that in Chapter 6, we examine how partisan control of government affects the presence of bureaucrats in committee hearings. Here, we show that the relative frequency of the presence of bureaucrats is related to the committee's intent for its hearings. The results show that committees tend to seek out bureaucrats – their analytical and expert information about policy production and needs – more often when they were not considering a specific bill than when they were considering an already developed one.

Second, the results also show that committees invited relatively more witnesses from think tanks or universities ("Research") to nonreferral hearings than to referral hearings. Think tanks and universities are also of interest because of the potential information they can bring to committees and because they are relatively credible sources of information. While they certainly be politically motivated or biased, speakers and studies from think tanks and universities carry relatively more scientific weight compared to other types of witnesses (such as those from corporations or trade associations) because of their connections to academic research. The result in Figure 5.3 shows that nonreferral hearings hosted a higher proportion of witnesses from think tanks or universities than referral hearings when a bill has already been drafted. This result suggests that committees seek out and receive relatively more information from think tanks and universities in the developmental stages of the policymaking process than in later stages when a specific bill is at hand. The same is true for corporate witnesses: Committees also tend to seek information from corporations more often in hearings without bills than in hearings with attached bills.

However, the opposite is true for witnesses from labor unions, trade associations, and membership associations. Witnesses from these mass-based groups were more likely to be invited and testify at referral hearings than at nonreferral hearings (positive coefficients in Figure 5.3). This suggests that once committees are further along in the policymaking process and are considering a specific bill, they are more interested in learning political information from witnesses who represent those who will be affected by the legislation or who represent a diverse group of individuals and organizations. This allows committees to gather information about the electoral consequences of a particular bill and helps them predict the viability of bills in the legislative process. Additionally, mass-based groups, such as the National Organization for Women (NOW), are well connected with other interest groups (Box-Steffensmeier, Christenson, and Craig, 2019). Therefore, inviting representatives of these types of groups when a committee is considering a particular bill helps the committee gather information about the views of allied groups.

Figure 5.4 shows the results for Senate hearings.[6] As in the House, referral hearings hosted more witnesses and had greater witness diversity than nonreferral hearings. Similar to patterns in the House, bureaucrats and witnesses from think tanks or universities were invited to referral hearings less often than nonreferral hearings; witnesses from labor unions, trade associations, and membership organizations were invited more often to referral hearings than to nonreferral hearings. These patterns are the same as those seen in the House; the only differences are slight in magnitude. Overall, the effect of having a bill attached to a hearing is similar in both chambers.

## 5.3 Variation across Time, Committees, and Issues

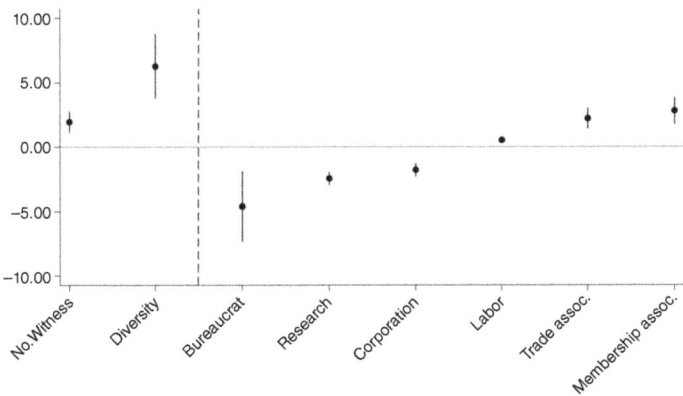

Figure 5.4 The effect of referral hearings on witness invitations – Senate
Notes: Each plot indicates the regression coefficient for each outcome measure (x-axis). The y-axis shows the regression coefficients: "No.Witness" is the number of witnesses, "Diversity" is one minus the Herfindahl index, and the others are the percentage shares of witnesses. The groups not shown in the plot have coefficients that are not statistically significant. The plots are presented with 95% confidence intervals.

Thus, evidence from both chambers support our hypothesis. Committees seek different types of witnesses based on the purpose of the hearing, which is primarily determined by the committee chair's decision to hold a hearing with or without a bill. When a committee seeks testimony to learn about an issue or potential legislation in a nonreferral hearing, our results show that they invited a narrower set of witnesses and relatively more witnesses who can provide analytical information. When a committee seeks testimony to convey a particular view or message about a bill, our results show that they invited a more diverse set of witnesses and relatively more witnesses from groups likely to be affected by the legislation.

### 5.3 VARIATION ACROSS TIME, COMMITTEES, AND ISSUES

In this section, we provide a broader picture by examining heterogeneous effects of committee intent. We examine the effect of referral hearings on witness invitation rates across time periods, committee types, and issue areas. For the analysis, we focus on legislative hearings held in the House of Representatives.

Our data covers periods of dramatic partisan changes in the House and Senate, allowing us to explore whether over-time changes to the political environment altered patterns depicting who informed Congress at committee hearings. We approach this descriptively by examining how the effects identified in Section 5.2 varied over time periods of substantial institutional change in Congress.

Two major, notable reform efforts occurred during our study period. The first is a reform of House committees in the 1970s: The Legislative Reorganization Act of 1970 increased the number of permanent staff on standing committees and the analytical capacity of committees. Congressional research organizations, such as the Government Accountability Office (GAO) received greater resources and responsibilities (Oleszek, 2021). Congress also overhauled the seniority system regulating committees: Senate Democrats adopted rules in 1973 that gave more independent power to subcommittees. This "subcommittee bill of rights" led to a dramatic increase in the number of committee hearings and legislative activities.

The second critical event occurred in 1995. After winning the 1994 midterm elections, a newly empowered House Republican majority implemented substantial institutional changes in the chamber. Among various changes, the ones relevant to our research include a reduction in the number of committee staff, the elimination of the Office of Technology Assessment (a congressional support agency within Congress), and more leadership control granted to subcommittee and committee chairs. Altogether, the reforms implemented in the Republican takeover empowered the party's leadership (Oleszek, 2021).

Therefore, we divide our overall time span into three periods: 1961–1973, 1974–1994, and 1995–2016. We examine how the effect of committee intent varied by running the same regression as in Eq. (5.1) for the three periods.

Figure 5.5 shows the coefficient on the variable *Referral Hearing* for various outcomes considered in Section 5.2. Compared to the results presented in Figure 5.3, which covers the entire period, we see largely similar patterns across the different time periods.

However, some interesting variances appear. During the early period (1961–1973), referral hearings hosted more diverse witnesses, fewer expert witnesses, and more group witnesses. But those patterns are less clear than compared to patterns in the middle period (1974–1994, the era of committee-centered governance), when we see our theoretical expectations borne out most plainly. The final period (1995–2016) shows a similar pattern to the previous period, though the coefficients are less precisely estimated.

To analyze the heterogeneous effect of committee type and issue area, we sort witnesses and committees into broader categories.[7] We divide witnesses into two broad groups: those from the bureaucracy, research organizations, and corporations are classified as *expert witnesses* and those from labor unions, trade associations, and membership associations are classified as *group witnesses*. We attend to these witnesses in

## 5.3 Variation across Time, Committees, and Issues

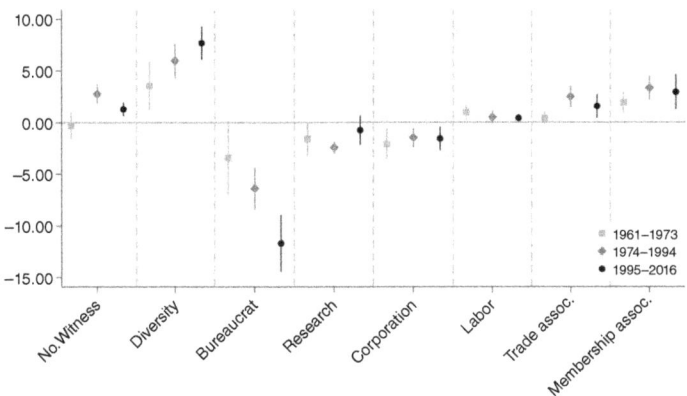

Figure 5.5 The effect of referral hearings on witness invitations by different periods – House
Notes: Each plot indicates the regression coefficient for each issue area (x-axis). The y-axis shows the regression coefficients (the percentage). Group witnesses include labor union, trade association, and membership association. The plots are presented with 95 percent confidence interval.

particular, given the results presented in Figures 5.3 and 5.4, and use the shares of these two categories of witnesses as outcomes. We follow the categories in Deering and Smith (1997) and focus on two types of committees: policy committees (Ways and Means, Finance, Education and Labor, Energy and Commerce, Foreign Affairs, Judiciary, and Government Operations) and constituency committees (Agriculture, Armed Services, Interior, Science, Small Business, and Veterans Affairs). While the Ways and Means Committee is deemed a "prestige committee" by Deering and Smith (1997), the other committees in this category (Appropriations, Budget, and Rules) are quite distinctive in their functions and norms. The Rules Committee writes and issues procedural rules as directed by the majority party leadership. The Appropriations and Budget Committees consider a fixed number of bills each year and follow a prescribed annual process for hearings and markups that does not allow for much variance. Given this, we consider the Ways and Means Committee in the category of policy committees for our analysis.

We investigate whether some committees invite more or fewer expert or group witnesses depending on whether it is a referral hearing, when they consider a particular bill. Table 5.1 shows the number of legislative hearings and the percentage of referral hearings by committee in the House of Representatives during 1961 to 2016. There are significant differences in both the number of legislative hearings and the proportion of referral hearings. For example, policy committees hold more legislative hearings and the average proportion of referral hearings is over

Table 5.1 *Number of legislative hearings and proportions of referral hearings by committee*

| Policy committee | | | Constituent committee | | |
|---|---|---|---|---|---|
| Name | No. Hearing | %Referral | Name | No. Hearing | %Referral |
| Education/labor | 2,360 | 41.0 | Agriculture | 1,428 | 38.1 |
| Energy/commerce | 3,336 | 41.1 | Armed service | 1,417 | 29.8 |
| Finance | 2,077 | 36.2 | Interior | 1,902 | 55.5 |
| Foreign affairs | 2,688 | 8.1 | Science | 2,003 | 18.7 |
| Judiciary | 2,435 | 54.2 | Small business | 1,153 | 17.4 |
| Gov. operation | 3,004 | 13.4 | Veterans affairs | 1,136 | 28.0 |
| Ways and means | 1,836 | 29.3 | | | |

*Notes: No. Hearing* indicates the total number of legislative hearings in each committee in the House of Representatives. *%Referral* indicates the percentage of referral hearings among legislative hearings.

30 percent, although there is significant variation within each type of committee.

We run the same regression as in Eq. (5.1), except we drop the committee fixed effects. We run separate regressions for each committee and present the results by committee type to determine if a committee chair's intent to attach a bill to a hearing affects the invitation patterns of expert and group witnesses differentially.

Figure 5.6 shows the results for policy committees for two outcomes: the proportion of expert witnesses and the proportion of group witnesses out of the total number of witnesses invited. The *Committee Intent Hypothesis* states that when a committee holds a referral hearing, we expect to see fewer invitations of expert witnesses and more invitations of group witnesses. The *Committee Intent Hypothesis* is clearly supported in policy committees: A referral hearing was associated with more invitations of group witnesses, and hearings with a bill attached were less likely to invite expert witnesses. There are obvious patterns across all seven committees and the coefficients are precisely estimated.

Figure 5.7 shows how a referral hearing is associated with invitations of expert and group witnesses for constituent committees. The Committees on Agriculture, Science, Small Business, and Veterans Affairs show an unambiguous, expected pattern of witness invitations as a function

## 5.3 Variation across Time, Committees, and Issues

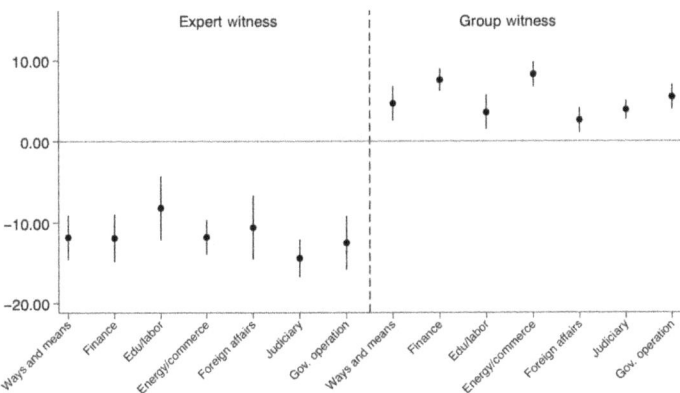

Figure 5.6 The effect of referral hearings on witness invitations in policy committees
Notes: Each plot indicates the regression coefficient for each outcome measure (x-axis). The y-axis shows the regression coefficients (the percentage). The plots are presented with 95% confidence interval.

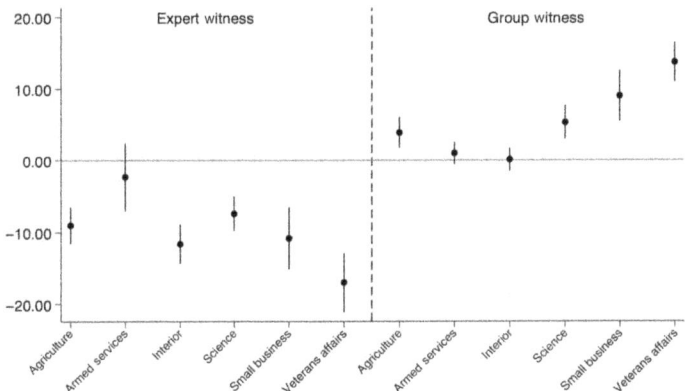

Figure 5.7 The effect of referral hearings on witness invitations in constituent committees
Notes: Each plot indicates the regression coefficient for each outcome measure (x-axis). The y-axis shows the regression coefficients (the percentage). The plots are presented with 95% confidence interval.

of committee intent, while the Armed Services and Interior Committees show less precise estimates.

The results across committee types suggest that a committee's intent to gather different types of information by inviting different types of witnesses is most evident in policy committees. In the other types of committees, other considerations – such as inviting committee members' constituents – may also play an important role in determining whom they invite to testify. In policy committees, however, our results suggest that informational concerns play a stronger role than other considerations, leading to a robust relationship between a committee's intent and its witness invitation patterns.

Table 5.2 *Number of legislative hearings and proportions of referral hearings by issue*

| Issue | No. Hearing | %Referral | Issue | No. Hearing | %Referral |
|---|---|---|---|---|---|
| Macroeconomics | 1,039 | 24.5 | Law and crime | 1,448 | 40.9 |
| Civil rights | 815 | 36.5 | Social welfare | 736 | 33.2 |
| Health | 2,177 | 27.4 | Housing | 755 | 28.6 |
| Agriculture | 1,178 | 36.3 | Domestic commerce | 2,882 | 37.9 |
| Labor | 1,140 | 39.3 | Defense | 2,661 | 25.0 |
| Education | 1,190 | 35.1 | Technology | 1,468 | 24.5 |
| Environment | 1,761 | 36.7 | Foreign trade | 905 | 26.0 |
| Energy | 1,641 | 30.8 | International affairs | 2,734 | 12.3 |
| Immigration | 344 | 36.3 | Government operation | 3,055 | 33.6 |
| Transportation | 1,590 | 34.7 | Public land | 1,770 | 55.6 |

Notes: *No. Hearings* indicates the total number of legislative hearings in each issue area. *%Referral* indicates the percentage of referral hearings among legislative hearings.

Next, we examine heterogeneous effects by issue area. Following the issue coding of the Comparative Policy Agenda Project, each hearing has a major issue code. There are twenty-one major issue areas, but we drop hearings on "culture" because there were only 3 hearings on this issue in the House during the 1961–2016 period. This leaves twenty major issue areas. Table 5.2 shows the total number of legislative hearings and the proportion of referral hearings across issue areas. The number of legislative hearings reveal that issues such as government operations, international affairs, domestic trade, and defense were most frequently addressed. The lowest proportion of referral hearings concerned international affairs and the highest proportion of referral hearings considered public lands.

Issues show significant variation in both the number of legislative hearings and the proportion of referral hearings. Would we expect to see consistent patterns across issue areas for the effect of referral hearings on the composition of witnesses? We use the proportion of expert witnesses and group witnesses as outcomes and run the same regression as Eq. (5.1) but include only Congress fixed effects. We run separate regressions for each issue area and present the results by issue area to understand whether a committee chair's intent to attach a bill has different effects on the invitation patterns of expert and group witnesses. Figure 5.8 shows the results for the effect of a referral hearing on the

## 5.3 Variation across Time, Committees, and Issues

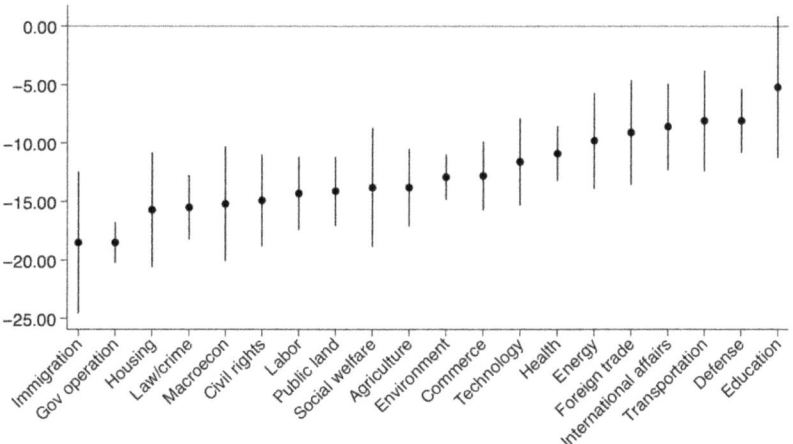

Figure 5.8 Referral hearings and inviting expert witnesses by issue areas
Notes: Each plot indicates the regression coefficient for each issue area (x-axis). The y-axis shows the regression coefficients (the percentage). Group witnesses include labor union, trade association, and membership association. The plots are presented with 95% confidence interval.

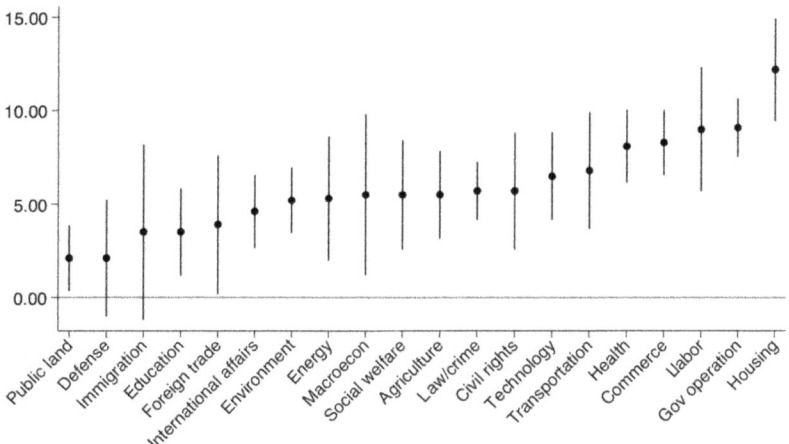

Figure 5.9 Referral hearings and inviting group witnesses by issue areas
Notes: Each plot indicates the regression coefficient for each issue area (x-axis). The y-axis shows the regression coefficients (the percentage). Group witnesses include labor union, trade association, and membership association. The plots are presented with 95% confidence interval.

proportion of expert witnesses. We sort the issues by the (absolute) size of the coefficient on the variable "referral hearing," but this does not necessarily indicate the absolute effect size, since the baseline invitation rates of expert and group witnesses vary by issue area, as Table A5 shows. One thing is evident: Regardless of issue area, when a committee holds a hearing with a bill attached, the committee is less likely to invite bureaucrats or think tank/university and corporate witnesses. The only issue area that fails to achieve 95 percent statistical significance is education.

Figure 5.9 summarizes the coefficients of the variable "referral hearing" on the proportion of group witnesses out of the total number of invited witnesses. We sort the issue areas by the size of the coefficients. Across all issue areas, a referral hearing is associated with more frequent invitations of witnesses from labor unions, trade associations, and membership associations.

## 5.4 SUMMARY

In this chapter, we examine how a committee's intention to hold a hearing is related to the composition of the witnesses the committee invites to testify. We argue that committees, guided by the partisan goals of the committee chair, seek different types of information depending on whether they are considering specific bills in hearings. When the committee chair has not yet advanced a bill through the committee process – and therefore committee members do not need to defend or promote a particular position in the draft legislation – it gives the committee more political flexibility to hear from those who can provide expertise in policy development. Consistent with our argument, we show that committees turned to think tanks, universities, and bureaucrats – witnesses who can provide more analytical information – at higher rates for hearings without a bill, when committees use hearings to learn about an issue area or to prepare for future legislation.

Committees tended to invite witnesses from mass-based groups, such as labor unions, trade associations, and membership associations, at higher rates for hearings on a specific bill. Committees and the committee chair use these referral hearings and testimony to assess the likely impact of the legislation and build support for the bill under consideration. These patterns are most pronounced in policy committees. Taken together, the results demonstrate that committees invite different groups of witnesses to testify depending on whether the committee intends to hold a hearing with a bill attached. Different witness compositions between referral and nonreferral hearings suggest strategic choices of the identities of witnesses and thus the types of information that the committee hearing generates.

## NOTES

1. Note that Talbert, Jones, and Baumgartner (1995) consider all types of hearings without a bill attached and call them "nonlegislative hearings." In this book, we use the term "legislative hearing" to distinguish hearings that are not oversight, investigative, or nomination hearings and then distinguish between

## 5.4 Summary

    legislative hearings that have a referred bill attached – referral hearings – and legislative hearings that do not have a referred bill attached – nonreferral hearings.
2. "The Global Investment in American Jobs Act of 2013," Hearing before the Subcommittee on Commerce, Manufacturing, and Trade of the Committee on Energy and Commerce, April 18, 2013. www.govinfo.gov/content/pkg/CHRG-113hhrg82185/pdf/CHRG-113hhrg82185.pdf
3. Issues $i$ represent the twenty-one major issues from the Policy Agendas Project.
4. Additional committee-level time-varying controls are the absolute difference in the DW-NOMINATE scores between the Democrats and Republicans on the committee, and the absolute difference in the DW-NOMINATE scores between the committee median and the floor median.
5. Table A3 presents the results examining the effects of committee intent on witness invitation patterns.
6. Table A4 shows the results examining the effect of committee intent on witness invitation patterns.
7. Given the number of different types of witnesses and the number of committees in our data set, grouping both witnesses and committees into broader categories on theoretical grounds allows us to uncover and interpret patterns.

# 6

## How Control of Government Shapes Information Exchange

For reasons which are not altogether clear, bureaucracies associated with executive offices have more efficiently collected and processed information than have legislatures. Not only is Congress unprepared to obtain independent information about the world through its own resources, but it must rely on data collected by the executive.

– James A. Robinson (1962)

In January 2011, a new Republican majority took control of the House of Representatives – the first time that Republicans had control of a chamber during Barack Obama's presidency. They immediately attempted to repeal the Affordable Care Act (ACA), passing H.R. 2: "Repealing the Job-Killing Health Care Law Act." The Democratic majority in the Senate launched a countercampaign by holding a series of hearings in the Senate Committee on Health, Education, Labor, and Pensions to defend the ACA and proclaim its success. Chairman Tom Harkin (D-IA) opened the first hearing on January 27, 2011, stating:

> Today we meet for the first in a series of hearings that this committee will hold on The Affordable Care Act; hearings that will focus not on the politics of Health Care Reform nor on the rhetoric that surrounds it, but rather on the tangible, positive impact that reform is having on Americans' lives. I think we can all agree that what this debate needs is more light and less heat.

The key witness called to testify at this hearing was Secretary of HHS Kathleen Sebelius, an Obama appointee. The beginning of her testimony clearly emphasized the executive branch's continued commitment to health-care reform under the ACA:

> The law is a key part of the Administration's effort to win the future by out-innovating, out-educating and out-building the rest of the world. It gives Americans more freedom in their health care choices, from greater freedom to change jobs or start a business without worry that they'll lose coverage to greater freedom from skyrocketing premiums.

Secretary Sebelius' testimony detailed the benefits of the ACA's preexisting condition provisions and explained how executive agencies have implemented the ACA. Throughout the hearing, the president's policy priorities and defense of the ACA against repeal efforts loomed large, highlighting how interbranch relationships shape committees' strategic behavior in holding hearings and inviting witnesses. This example shows how bureaucrats – in this case, a cabinet-level appointee – are strategically invited to legislative hearings, particularly on issues that presidents prioritize. In defending the Democratic president's signature legislation from the threat of the Republican House, the Democratic Senate deliberately opened its committee hearings to bureaucrats who brought their executive influence from the Democratic-controlled White House into the hearing rooms.

The informational advantage that bureaucrats enjoy over their legislative counterparts is a central theme in the literature on interbranch politics. Congressional uncertainty about agency actions and policy implementation prompts Congress to develop means of controlling the bureaucracy. An extensive literature has developed to explain the degree of oversight and delegation that Congress exercises on itself and grants to its agents.

As seen in the descriptive patterns in Chapter 3, bureaucrats comprise a substantial number of the witnesses called to testify at hearings, and our analysis in Chapter 4 shows that bureaucrats provide the relatively highest levels of analytical information. Additionally, the analysis in Chapter 5 shows that bureaucrats are invited to testify more often at the early stages of the legislative process – before a bill is attached to a hearing or the committee stakes out a position – which could give bureaucrats more opportunities to shape policy.

Given executive agencies' informational advantage, we investigate how the politics of legislative – executive relations unfold in congressional hearings. Committee chairs face trade-offs when deciding how much input to seek from bureaucrats during the hearing process. On the one hand, bureaucrats' informational advantages imply that their input could lead to better-informed politicians. This, in turn, could lead to better legislation by reducing uncertainties in the implementation of policies and their consequences.

On the other hand, because bureaucrats could provide information favoring the executive branch's policy preferences, hosting more of them during the policymaking process could shift legislation toward the executive branch's position. This trade-off becomes particularly salient when the preferences of the legislative branch diverge from those of the executive branch.

## How Control of Government Shapes Information Exchange

In this chapter, we examine how the politics of interbranch relations between the legislative and executive branches affect the invitation of bureaucratic witnesses to hearings and how Congress can use hearings to control the legislative influence of the executive branch. In particular, we focus on the presence of divided government – when the party controlling Congress is not the party that controls the White House – a central feature studied in interbranch politics (e.g., Epstein and O'Halloran, 1999). Divided government creates challenges for legislative control over the implementation process. Thus, Congress has created numerous legislative and procedural solutions to increase its influence over the behavior of the executive branch.

Scholars reveal that congressional strategic behavior also applies to investigative oversight of the president and executive agencies. Divided government is associated with congressional investigative activity, especially when the majority party in Congress is homogeneous (Kriner and Schwartz, 2008; Kriner and Schickler, 2016). Congressional committees also conduct more oversight hearings when the ideological preferences between the committee and the executive agencies are more divergent (McGrath, 2013). We investigate whether the partisan logic of oversight hearings applies to legislative hearings, where the goal is more focused on information acquisition.

We focus on legislative hearings because they are a prime representation of how members of Congress must balance their lawmaking responsibilities with their political roles. In legislative hearings, committees consider potential or current bills. They pursue knowledge about what is needed in legislation, what to include in policy, and what effects to anticipate. This technical lawmaking role occurs within a political context where each member is highly likely to be sensitive to how the details of bills or framing of legislation may support or hinder their party's goals. Therefore, information revealed in committees may assist in developing policy, play a partisan role, or both.

Given bureaucrats' informational advantage in policy implementation, we argue that they are less likely to be invited to legislative hearings when the preferences of the legislative and executive branches diverge. By strategically adjusting the frequency of bureaucrats' appearances in legislative hearings under divided government, committees can control executive branch input. However, this creates a dilemma for committees: Limiting executive branch input may keep policy outcomes closer to the committee's ideal, but the lack of bureaucratic input creates an informational void that could lead to inferior policy outcomes. To overcome this, under divided government, committees substitute for bureaucratic input by shifting to two types of witnesses whose testimony also contains a

## 6.1 Bureaucratic Expertise

high degree of analytical information: (1) congressional support agencies, such as the Congressional Research Service or the Congressional Budget Office, and (2) witnesses from research organizations, such as think tank affiliates and academics.

Moreover, we show that the patterns of committee invitations to bureaucrats reflect a strategic element of response to president's issue priorities. While there are many career civil servants in the bureaucracy, the president heads the executive branch and selects political appointees who supervise and directly manage career bureaucrats. Given the informational advantages of bureaucrats, committee chairs can strategically use bureaucratic witnesses to help or hurt the president's policy agenda. If the majority in the committee is of the same party as the president, inviting more bureaucrats to testify at legislative hearings helps ensure that policy outcomes will reflect more input from the executive branch. If the majority in Congress is not of the same party as the president, committee chairs have a stronger incentive to limit executive branch input that reflects the president's preferences. This pattern is even more likely to occur when the president prioritizes an issue. Using presidential State of the Union addresses, we estimate the president's issue priorities and show that committee chairs strategically invite bureaucrats to oppose or support the president's issue priorities depending on their preference alignment with the executive branch.

### 6.1 CONGRESSIONAL CONTROL OF THE BUREAUCRACY AND BUREAUCRATIC EXPERTISE

The relationship between Congress and the executive branch is a canonical application of the principal–agent problem to politics (Miller, 2005). If formal authority is in the hands of Congress (the principal) but bureaucrats (the agents) have an informational advantage, how does Congress persuade bureaucrats to act in accordance with Congress's preferences? Pioneering work by Weingast and Moran (1983) and Weingast (1984) introduced the idea that Congress can create incentives for bureaucrats to make decisions that are consistent with the legislative body's preference through the means of budget appropriations and congressional influence over the top bureaucrat in the agency. Their work implies that the absence of oversight does not necessarily mean that oversight is ineffective.

McCubbins and Schwartz (1984) develop this argument further by modeling two techniques of oversight: (1) police patrol oversight, in which Congress directly examines a sample of executive agency activities, and (2) fire-alarm oversight, in which Congress creates a decentralized system allowing interest groups and individual citizens to examine agency actions, with Congress intervening when complaints are reported. The authors argue that fire-alarm oversight is more effective because it reduces the burden on Congress to examine a large number of agency actions that may result in no detection of violations. According to McCubbins and Schwartz (1984), a key requirement for effective fire alarm oversight is to design procedures and rules that allow for smooth transitions of feedback from citizens and organized interests to Congress.

Since McCubbins and Schwartz (1984)'s seminal work, an extensive literature has developed on the political control of the bureaucracy through procedural processes, especially the degree of delegation to executive agencies. The question of how much Congress would delegate its authority to executive agencies has been central to the discussion of congressional control of the bureaucracy (Bendor, Glazer, and Hammond, 2001; Huber and McCarty, 2004), and the key question is under what conditions Congress can delegate its authority to bureaucrats to take advantage of their policy expertise (Gailmard and Patty, 2012a).

The literature treats this expertise in two ways. First, expertise has been treated as a binary variable. Gailmard and Patty (2012a) summarize the binary nature as follows:

Typically, an agent is an expert if he or she is completely aware of the state of the world, $\omega$, whereas a nonexpert agent is presumed to have the same information about $\omega$ as the principal. In other words, an expert agent can completely foresee the outcome of any policy choice, and a nonexpert agent cannot, in isolation, make a policy choice that leaves the principal better off than if the principal simply set policy on his or her own behalf.

This approach treats bureaucratic expertise as a fixed stock, often using bureaucrats' demographic background information or perceptions of their skills as measurements. For example, Clinton et al. (2012) measure the policy expertise of federal bureaucrats in each agency by calculating the proportion of technical and professional employees. Richardson, Clinton, and Lewis (2018) use federal bureaucrats' opinions about the workforce to measure the skill level and competence of agencies. Their analysis shows considerable variation in the perceived skills of agency employees, even within the same department. For example, out of ninety-seven sub-agencies within fifteen executive departments, the National Institutes of Health (NIH) within the Department of Health and Human Services (HHS) ranked first, while the Indian Health Service, also within HHS, ranked ninety-fourth out of the ninety-seven agencies surveyed.

Alternatively, the literature proposes bureaucratic expertise as a dynamic concept in which the acquisition of expertise is endogenous, depending on other parameters, such as the degree of discretion given to bureaucrats, their career goals, and interactions with regulated interest

## 6.1 Bureaucratic Expertise

groups (e.g., McCarty [2017]). Gailmard and Patty (2012b) provide a detailed definition of the endogenous acquisition of expertise within a bureaucratic agency:

> The notion of expertise we adopt rests on the presumption that most individuals' preferences about policy decisions are induced by the "state of the world" prevailing in society at the time (and, perhaps, those expected to prevail in the future) ... We define policymaking expertise as the knowledge of facts of this type. In other words, expertise is the ability to choose the government policy that best suits the prevailing conditions in the real world to achieve a particular policy outcome. In our theory, bureaucrats "acquire expertise" only if they invest individual effort in obtaining it, and this investment gives them knowledge of the facts whenever they are asked to make policy decisions in the future.

This leads us to the questions of what factors influence bureaucrats' willingness to acquire expertise. Andersen and Moynihan (2016) directly test the theoretical implication from Gailmard and Patty (2012b) using a field experiment conducted among school principals in Denmark. They show that greater discretion in the allocation of personal resources increases the amount of knowledge principals acquire about school performance. Using a survey of federal executives, Richardson (2019) shows that the politicization of the agency and an ideological divergence between a civil servant and the agency she works for leads to less investment in acquiring policy expertise. Bertelli and Lewis (2013) examine the relationship between expertise acquisition and bureaucrats' career choices and show that acquiring agency-specific human capital reduces federal bureaucrats' intention to leave their jobs.

Given the literature's definition of expertise and bureaucrats' incentives to acquire it, theories of delegation largely examine changes in how much authority Congress delegates to the bureaucracy using three factors: preference alignment, policy uncertainty, and risk aversion (Bendor, Glazer, and Hammond, 2001). Increased policy uncertainty leads Congress to delegate more to bureaucrats to take advantage of their policy expertise. When the principal's risk aversion increases, delegation also increases because it can reduce uncertain policy outcomes. The alignment of preferences between Congress and executive agencies has received so much attention because the policy preferences of bureaucrats play an important role in their policy implementation decisions. The intuitive comparative static is that as preferences between Congress and bureaucrats converge, Congress delegates more discretion to bureaucrats (Gailmard and Patty, 2012a).

Divided government is often used as an indicator of divergent policy preferences when operationalizing the alignment of preferences between Congress and the bureaucracy. Under divided government, the majority party in Congress is not from the same party as the president – the head of the executive branch – who is likely to have different policy preferences and issue priorities than Congress. Thus, divided government presents potential obstacles to legislative control over the implementation process. Congress has created numerous legislative and procedural solutions to increase its control over the executive agencies responsible for implementing its legislation. For example, Congress can design agencies to be more insulated from presidential influence, or it can write more detailed laws (Huber, Shipan, and Pfahler, 2001) to reduce the amount of discretion delegated to the bureaucracy (Lewis, 2003). We turn, however, to focus on one way Congress can control the bureaucracy's input in Congress: hearings.

## 6.2 HEARINGS AS A MEANS OF CONTROLLING EXECUTIVE BRANCH INFLUENCE IN CONGRESS

Most of the literature on the principal–agent relationship between Congress and the bureaucracy focuses on administrative structures and rules that check the actions of the executive branch. However, Congress also has a more direct, public tool that the legislative majority can use with the executive branch: congressional hearings. Two types of hearings are specifically designed to check the behavior of the executive branch: oversight hearings and investigative hearings. These can be used to review, monitor, and oversee the implementation of public policy. Committees can hold oversight hearings to review ongoing programs or policies that agencies are implementing, or when programs need to be evaluated for renewal (Heitshusen, 2017). Congress may hold investigative hearings against executive branch officials when there are allegations of misconduct. Investigative hearings are generally more confrontational than oversight hearings (Heitshusen, 2017). Institutional designs, such as decisions about the degree of delegation, are *ex ante* congressional controls over the bureaucracy; oversight and investigative hearings are more likely to be *ex post* control mechanisms, since hearings usually occur after the action(s) in question have occurred.

The existing literature shows that the majority party in Congress strategically uses oversight hearings to control the executive branch and reap political benefits. By examining the number of oversight hearings between 1946 and 2006, McGrath (2013) finds that the ideological relationship between congressional standing committees and the executive branch determines the volume of hearings: The number of oversight hearings is significantly lower when committees are controlled by the president's party than when they are controlled by the opposing party.

## 6.2 Hearings to Control Executive Influence

A review of investigative hearings shows a similar pattern of ideological alignment and oversight intensity. Kriner and Schwartz (2008) collect detailed information on the scope and intensity of high-profile investigations in Mayhew's analysis (Mayhew, 2005) and examine how divided government is associated with the frequency and intensity of congressional investigations. They find strong empirical evidence that divided government increases the number of investigative hearings, the number of days of investigative hearings, and the media coverage of investigations, especially when the majority party in Congress is more internally unified. Additionally, Kriner and Schickler (2016) examine investigative hearings held in the House and Senate from 1898 to 2014 and show that divided government is strongly correlated with the intensity of congressional investigative activity of the executive branch. For example, the House spent an average of 31 days on investigative activity under unified government, compared to 88.6 days under divided government. The authors also find that investigative activity undermines presidential approval ratings, demonstrating that there are clear partisan and electoral motivations behind congressional investigations.

Compared to fighting the president legislatively, hearings may be a more advantageous strategy for Congress to control the power and influence of the executive branch. As Kriner and Schickler (2016) argue, if Congress were to choose to engage the president legislatively, it would face several disadvantages: collective action problems among members, transaction costs associated with building coalitions within a chamber or between chambers, and institutional tools that the president possesses (e.g., the presidential veto) or that the president's allies in Congress possess (e.g., the Senate filibuster). By contrast, Congress can use hearings as public opportunities to air information that is politically unfavorable to the executive branch without having to deal with the aforementioned disadvantages.

Another critical factor in this setting is the information asymmetry between Congress and the executive branch. As noted, one way to manipulate the balance of power in policymaking between Congress and the bureaucracy is the amount of discretion Congress grants to the executive branch (Huber, Shipan, and Pfahler, 2001); another way is to control information. In theory, the advantage in this power struggle goes to the institution with more information about the costs and consequences of policy implementation: the "informational advantage" (Banks and Weingast, 1992; Bendor, Taylor, and van Gaalen, 1985; Miller and Moe, 1983).

Given the prominent role of bureaucrats in legislative hearings, we argue that the partisan logic motivating many investigative and oversight hearings can be applied to legislative hearings. Legislative hearings are the most common type of hearing; their stated purpose is gathering information related to pending or potential legislation (Heitshusen, 2017). The informational advantage and policy expertise that bureaucrats possess forces committee chairs to judge carefully whether to invite them to testify at legislative hearings. Inviting bureaucrats could improve the quality of the legislation they produce (e.g., more accurate predictions about the consequences of a new law or less risk of litigation against the law). However, allowing more bureaucratic input could tilt legislation toward the policy preferences of the executive branch.

This trade-off is particularly pronounced during divided government when policy disagreements between the legislative and executive branches are more likely. When the majority party in Congress differs from the party of the president, committees are faced with the potential of bureaucratic witnesses representing the opposing party. Therefore, committees may prefer to use other sources of information, such as nonbureaucratic witnesses or internal congressional sources. This leads to our first hypothesis about interbranch relations and legislative hearings:

*Interbranch Relations Hypothesis 1: Committees will invite relatively fewer bureaucrats to testify at legislative hearings during periods of divided government than during periods of unified government.*

Assuming that bureaucrats will express views that reflect the president's policy preferences, whether committees invite them to testify in legislative hearings also depends on the president's issue priorities. The president's role in setting the policy agenda is well recognized. For example, Kingdon writes, "No other single actor in the political system has quite the capacity of the president to set agendas in given policy areas for all who deal with these policies" (Kingdon, 1995). Baumgartner and Jones (1993) make a similar point. Presidential agenda setting affects executive agencies through the president's control of the bureaucracy using such tools as political appointments and executive orders. Presidential issue priorities also affect how Congress allocates its attention to its legislative agenda. Studies show that the president's legislative program – "a comprehensive set of requests for new or modified laws, typically in the form of draft bills, submitted to Congress for its consideration" (Cameron and Park, 2007) – affects the congressional agenda (Rudalevige, 2002) and that presidents are strategic in their choice of legislative program (Gelman, Wilkenfeld, and Adler, 2015).

For example, the first congressional hearing held by the House Ways and Means Committee in February 2001, immediately after George W. Bush's inauguration, was on President Bush's tax relief proposals

## 6.2 Hearings to Control Executive Influence

(the "Bush Tax Cut").[1] During the 2000 presidential campaign, candidate Bush stressed that the US federal government's budget surplus in the late 1990s should be returned to the people through tax cuts. This was a central campaign point and one of his top priorities. Wasting no time, House Ways and Means Committee Chairman Bill Thomas, a Republican congressman from California, added congressional support for President Bush's policy goal by holding a hearing on February 6, 2001, in anticipation of President Bush submitting a package of tax relief proposals to Congress. The specific topic of the hearing was the change in the income tax code proposed by the president two days later. In his opening statement, Chairman Thomas declared:

> ... today the subject is the Income Tax Code of the United States and changes to that Code offered by the President. There are many reasons to amend the Code. It is too complex. It is unfair. Its current structure collects more money than is needed to fund the government. Some are asking that our examination of the IRS Code should wait until we have a more complete budgetary picture of where we are on the projected surplus so that we could examine all the competing demands on our resources. And there are some, I have a hunch, who just want to stall because they don't want to reduce the income tax burden on Americans.

Clearly, the chairman intended to use the hearing to support his co-partisan president's key policy proposal. He invited Treasury Secretary Paul O'Neill to testify, along with three economists: Kevin A. Hassett of the American Enterprise Institute, Robert Greenstein of the Center on Budget and Policy Priorities, and Martin Feldstein of Harvard University. In his prepared statement to the committee members, Secretary O'Neill obviously supported the views of President Bush. Following are some excerpts from Secretary O'Neill's testimony:

> It is a great pleasure for me to be here this morning in this first of your meetings and my first opportunity as Secretary of the Treasury to speak to you ... about the President's proposals for changing our Income Tax Code and giving the American people, however you might stylize it, a tax reduction or a pay raise which would go to every Federal taxpayer ...
>
> And so we have the President's proposal in front of you. It is a proposal not fashioned in the last few weeks or in the last few months, but created out of his ideas of what he thought would be a fair system for the American people as he went around the country and campaigned for office over the last two years ...
>
> The President has proposed tax relief that reinforces the values that make America great – opportunity, entrepreneurship, strong families and individual success ...

This anecdote illustrates the president's ability to influence congressional attention to issues. It also shows how bureaucrats represent the president's viewpoint when they testify in legislative hearings. And it illustrates how the partisan distribution between the legislative and executive branches can shape the strategic behavior of committee chairs. Given the president's agenda-setting power and its potential impact on the congressional agenda, the logic of strategically inviting bureaucrats to legislative hearings may be more salient for issues that presidents prioritize.

During divided government, when committees hold hearings on issues that the president prioritizes, committee chairs should be less likely to invite bureaucrats who would represent the views of the executive branch. In contrast, during unified government, committee chairs should be more likely to invite bureaucrats to testify at legislative hearings on issues the president prioritizes to garner support for the president's policy agenda. For issues that are not presidential priorities, the difference between unified and divided governments in the frequency of inviting bureaucrats should be less pronounced. This leads to our second hypothesis regarding interbranch relations and legislative hearings:

*Inter-Branch Relations Hypothesis 2: For issues that presidents prioritize, committees will invite relatively fewer (more) bureaucrats to testify in legislative hearings during periods of divided (unified) government. For issues that presidents do not prioritize, the difference between divided and unified government in the invitation rate of bureaucrats will be smaller.*

## 6.3 BUREAUCRATS AT LEGISLATIVE HEARINGS

Before empirically testing our theoretical expectation, we present the descriptive statistics on bureaucratic appearances in legislative hearings in detail. First, Figure 6.1 plots the ratio of bureaucratic witnesses to the total number of witnesses invited in a given Congress over time for each chamber from the 87th Congress to the 114th Congress (1961–2016).[2] The trends are similar in both chambers: the proportion of bureaucratic witnesses gradually declined until the early 1990s, and then increased. The House had a higher ratio of bureaucratic witnesses, on average, through the 101st Congress, but the pattern reversed in the early 1990s. Since then, the average ratio of bureaucratic witnesses has been higher in the Senate.

Figure 6.2 shows the proportion of bureaucratic witnesses by issue area in ascending order. We merge the issue areas of each hearing from the Policy Agenda Project's database of congressional hearings. There are 21 major issue areas, and there was considerable variation in the invitation of bureaucratic witnesses across issue areas. Clearly, bureaucrats were more frequently invited to testify at hearings on defense and foreign policy issues. Issues related to culture, education, and social welfare have a lower proportion of bureaucratic witnesses. This pattern is consistent

## 6.3 Bureaucrats at Legislative Hearings

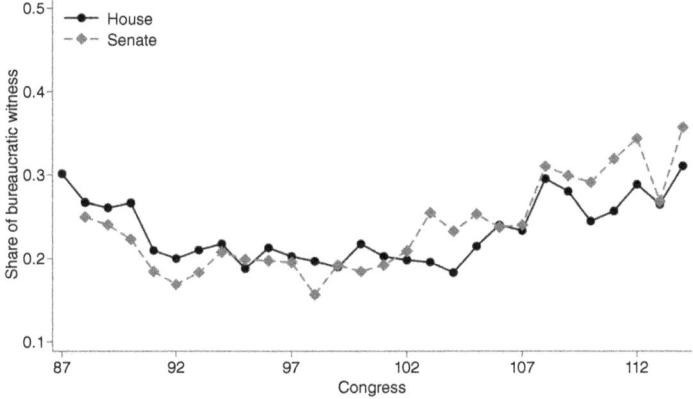

Figure 6.1 Ratio of bureaucratic witness over time
Notes: The lines in this graph depict the ratio of bureaucratic witnesses in the House and Senate.

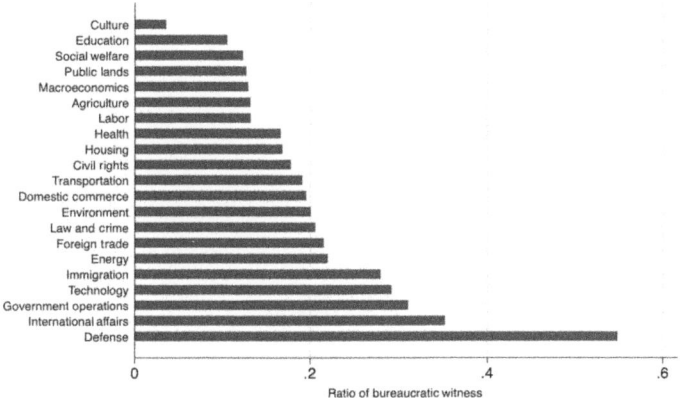

Figure 6.2 Ratio of bureaucratic witness across issues
Notes: This figure shows the ratio of bureaucratic witnesses in hearings under each issue area.

with the summary statistics we present in Chapter 3 regarding the ratio of bureaucrats across congressional committees. The Armed Services and Foreign Affairs Committees invited a higher proportion of bureaucratic witnesses. The Committee on Oversight and Reform also had a higher ratio of bureaucratic witnesses. The fact that bureaucrats are invited to testify on issues related to "government operations" is closely related to this pattern.

Among the many agencies in the federal government, which are most likely to be featured in legislative hearings? Figures 6.3 and 6.4 show the number of hearings by executive department and by independent agency, respectively. We aggregate the total number of legislative hearings in both the House and Senate for the 1961–2016 period. For independent

## How Control of Government Shapes Information Exchange

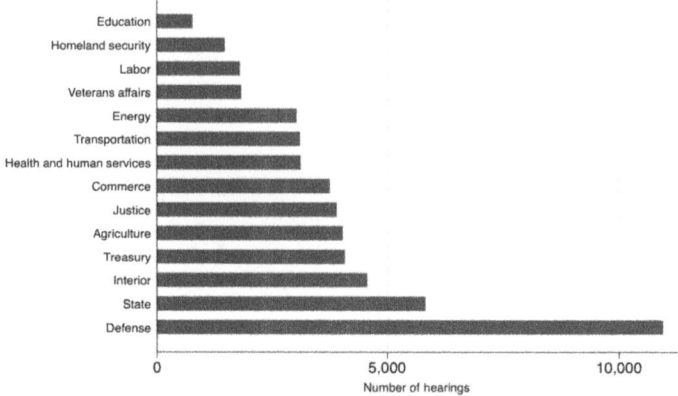

Figure 6.3 Number of legislative hearings by executive departments
Notes: This figure shows the total number of hearings in which bureaucratic witnesses from each executive department testified in the House and Senate for the period 1961–2016.

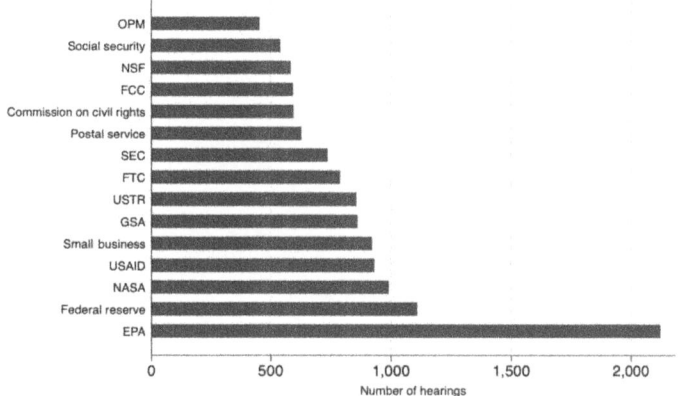

Figure 6.4 Number of legislative hearings by independent agencies
Notes: This figure shows the total number of hearings in which bureaucratic witnesses from each independent agency testified in the House and Senate for the period 1961–2016. We present the top fifteen agencies in terms of total number of appearances in legislative hearings.

agencies, we present the top fifteen agencies in terms of total number of appearances in legislative hearings. Consistent with the patterns shown in Figure 6.2, witnesses from executive departments with foreign policy and defense responsibilities – the Department of State and the Department of Defense – appeared frequently in congressional hearings. Witnesses from the Department of the Interior, responsible for the management and conservation of federal lands and natural resources, also appeared at high rates. Among independent agencies, witnesses from the Environmental Protection Agency (EPA) outnumbered other agencies in appearances at congressional hearings.

## 6.4 Divided Government and Bureaucrats as Witnesses

Table 6.1 *Bureaucratic witnesses under divided vs. unified government*

|  | Divided | | Unified | |
| --- | --- | --- | --- | --- |
|  | No. Witness | Bureaucrat ratio | No. Witness | Bureaucrat ratio |
| House | 9.9 | 0.37 | 9.7 | 0.40 |
| Senate | 9.8 | 0.36 | 9.9 | 0.39 |

*Notes:* This table shows the average number of witnesses (*No. Witness*) and the mean ratio of bureaucratic witnesses per hearing (*Bureaucratic Ratio*) under divided and unified government in the House and Senate.

Before moving on to the statistical analysis of the relationship between divided government and the invitation patterns of bureaucratic witnesses, we present simple summary statistics. Table 6.1 presents a summary of the average number of witnesses and the ratio of bureaucratic witnesses per hearing in divided vs. unified government in each chamber.

In both chambers, the number of witnesses invited per hearing did not change depending on whether the majority party in Congress was unified with the president. In terms of the ratio of bureaucratic witnesses, unified government shows a 3-percent increase in the ratio of bureaucratic witnesses compared to divided government in both chambers. Given the average value of the ratio of bureaucratic witnesses, this represents a 10-percent difference between divided and unified government. Table 6.1 suggests that there are differences in the frequency of bureaucratic appearances in legislative hearings depending on the structure of government. However, these differences potentially could be driven by the issues that committees address through legislative hearings or the different intensity of holding legislative hearings across committees between divided vs. unified government. In Section 6.4, we test our theoretical expectations, controlling for the above potential explanations, and systematically examine whether fewer bureaucrats are invited to testify during divided government.

### 6.4 DIVIDED GOVERNMENT AND BUREAUCRATS AS WITNESSES

To understand the effect of interbranch relations on witness invitation patterns, we compare them during periods of divided government compared to periods of unified government. To test our *Interbranch Relations Hypothesis 1*, we use the following regression and ordinary least squares estimation:

$$Y_{hict} = \beta \text{Hearing Characteristics}_{hict} + \gamma \text{Committee Characteristics}_{ct} + \delta \text{Congress Characteristics}_t + \alpha_i + \alpha_c + \alpha_p + \varepsilon_{hict},$$

where the subscripts indicate hearing $h$, issue $i$, committee $c$, Congress $t$, and president $p$. *Congressional Characteristics* includes *Divided Government* and *Democratic Majority*. The main explanatory variable, *Divided Government*, equals 1 if the majority party in the House (Senate) is different from the party of the president, and 0 otherwise. *Democratic Majority* equals 1 if the Democratic Party holds the majority in the House (Senate) and 0 if the Republican Party holds the majority. Both *Divided Government* and *Democratic Majority* are at the Congress level; to estimate the effects of these variables that differ by Congress while controlling for time trends, we include president fixed effects ($\alpha_p$). Committee-level and hearing-level control variables (i.e., the number of witnesses in a hearing) are included as controls, as before. The outcome variable $Y_{hict}$ measures the number of witnesses, the diversity of witnesses, and the percentage of witnesses in a given hearing who are of a given affiliation type.

We focus on legislative hearings from the 87th through the 114th Congresses (1961–2016), when there were 32,134 legislative hearings in the House and 19,772 in the Senate. The unit of analysis is the hearing. Table A6 presents summary statistics for the main outcomes and key variables used in the statistical analysis. In the House, 65 percent of the legislative hearings in our dataset occurred divided government. In the Senate, 49 percent of the legislative hearings were held during divided government. The average number of bureaucratic witnesses per hearing was 34.8 percent in the House and 32.6 percent in the Senate.

First, we present the coefficient estimates of the effect of the *Divided Government* variable on a selected set of outcome variables in the House. The full results, including the outcomes of all affiliation types and all control variables, are available in Table A7. Figure 6.5 shows the effects of divided government on witness invitation patterns. Our analysis shows no relationship between divided government and the number or diversity of witnesses testifying at a hearing.

However, our results show that divided government has a negative, statistically significant effect on the percentage of bureaucratic witnesses a committee invites compared to periods of unified government. This supports the idea that during divided government, committees are faced with the choice of whether to invite bureaucratic witnesses who may represent the opposing party's views. Specifically, our results show that divided government is associated with a 2.6-point decrease in the percentage of witnesses who were bureaucrats, a magnitude equal to 7.5 percent of the average percentage of bureaucrats testifying before committees. The direction of this result is particularly noteworthy and has implications for the information that committees seek and receive during periods of

## 6.4 Divided Government and Bureaucrats as Witnesses

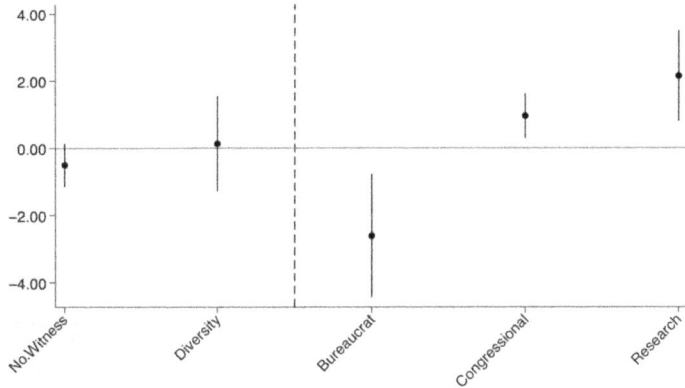

Figure 6.5 The effect of divided government on witness invitations – House
Notes: Each plot indicates the regression coefficient for each outcome measure (x-axis). The y-axis shows the regression coefficients; "No.Witness" is the number of witnesses, "Diversity" is one minus the Herfindahl index, and the others are the percentage shares of witnesses. The plots are presented with 95% confidence interval.

divided government because bureaucrats, on average, provide relatively more analytical information than other types of witnesses.

Committees compensate for the lower proportion of bureaucratic witnesses during divided government by inviting a higher proportion of witnesses from think tanks and universities. The coefficient plots for the "Congressional" and "Research" variables in Figure 6.5 show a two percentage point increase in the percentage of witnesses from think tanks and universities. Since the mean percentage of such witnesses appearing in hearings is 9.3 percent, a two-percentage-point increase represents just over 20 percent of the mean percentage of such witnesses – a significant change. Similarly, divided government is associated with an increase of about one-percentage point in the percentage of witnesses who are internal congressional staff, an effect size that represents 12.5 percent of the mean percentage of witnesses of this type appearing in hearings.

Figure 6.6 shows the regression results for different time periods. As we explain in Chapter 5, there were two major reforms to the congressional committee system during our period of study. We divide the entire period into three subsets based on the reform years and examine how the effect of divided government varied by time period. The patterns we present in Figure 6.5 are most evident for the period after 1995: Divided government was associated with fewer invitations to bureaucratic witnesses and more invitations to witnesses from internal congressional organizations and research institutes. This could be partly explained by the fact that partisan competition between the legislative and executive

*How Control of Government Shapes Information Exchange*

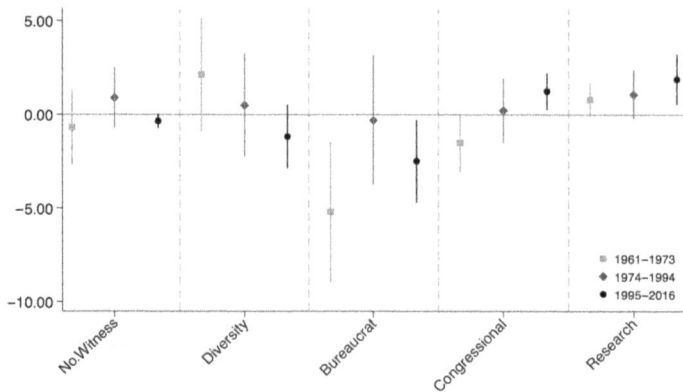

Figure 6.6 The effect of divided government on witness invitations – House
Notes: Each plot indicates the regression coefficient for each outcome measure (x-axis) in each period. The Y-axis shows the regression coefficients; "No.Witness" is the number of witnesses, "Diversity" is one minus the Herfindahl index, and the others are the percentage shares of witnesses. The plots are presented with 95% confidence interval.

branches became more aggressive after the new Republican majority in the House in 1995 and the Republicans' partisan war with the Clinton administration. Additionally, divided government has occurred more frequently in recent years than in previous periods and some bureaucratic agencies, such as the Environmental Protection Agency (EPA), received criticism for their partisan leanings, which resulted in a decline in their reputation along party lines (Bellodi, 2023).

Next, we examine strategic committee behavior under divided government in the Senate. Full results, including results for all types of affiliation and all control variables, are presented in Table A8. Figure 6.7 shows that Senate hearings during periods of divided government had a slightly lower number of witnesses, but there is no discernible effect on the diversity of witness affiliations. There is an obvious effect of divided government on the frequency of bureaucratic witness appearances. Our analysis shows that divided government is associated with a three-percentage-point decrease in bureaucratic witnesses; since the average percentage of such witnesses appearing in hearings is 32.5 percent, this decrease represents almost 10 percent of the average percentage of executive branch witnesses. The magnitude of the divided government effect on bureaucratic invitations is similar to that in the House.

However, unlike the House, the Senate did not substitute congressional or research witnesses for bureaucrats during divided government. Instead, there was a significant increase – 7.2 percent – in the number of corporate witnesses under divided government in the Senate. Given that the average

## 6.4 Divided Government and Bureaucrats as Witnesses

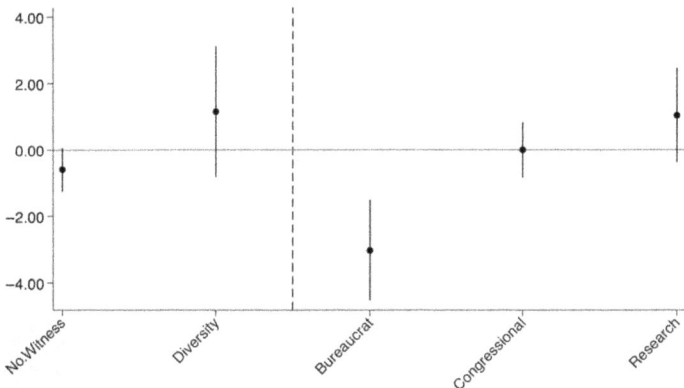

Figure 6.7 The effect of divided government on witness invitations – Senate
Notes: Each plot indicates the regression coefficient for each outcome measure (x-axis). The y-axis shows the regression coefficients; "No.Witness" is the number of witnesses, "Diversity" is one minus the Herfindahl index, and the others are the percentage shares of witnesses. The plots are presented with 95% confidence interval.

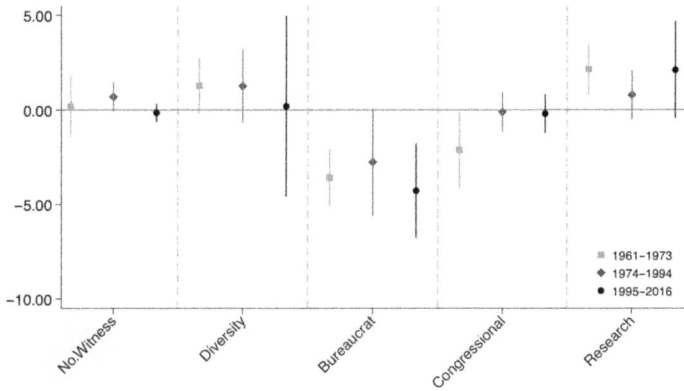

Figure 6.8 The effect of divided government on witness invitations by different periods – Senate
Notes: Each plot indicates the regression coefficient for each outcome measure (x-axis) in each period. The y-axis shows the regression coefficients; "No.Witness" is the number of witnesses, "Diversity" is the Herfindahl index, and the others are the percentage shares of witnesses. The plots are presented with 95% confidence interval.

percentage of corporate witnesses in a given hearing was 9 percent, this increase is noteworthy.

Figure 6.8 shows the regression analysis for the effect of divided government on Senate witness invitation patterns for three different periods. Across all periods, Congress was less likely to invite bureaucratic witnesses and more likely to invite witnesses from research organizations under divided government. In the Senate, the substitution effect is not observed for witnesses from internal congressional organizations.

Including president fixed effects instead of Congress fixed effects allows us to examine the influence of the majority party in Congress on witness patterns.[3] As Table A7 shows, a Democratic majority in the House did not affect the number of witnesses or the diversity of witnesses invited, nor did it affect the invitation patterns of congressional witnesses, bureaucrats, or witnesses from think tanks or universities. However, a Democratic majority was associated with an increase in the percentage of witnesses from labor unions and a decrease in the percentage of witnesses from trade associations, confirming the close relationship between the Democratic Party and organized labor (Schlozman, 2015). We see a similar pattern in the Senate, although the effect is only weakly statistically significant (at the 10-percent level). After controlling for issue and committee, a Democratic majority was not strongly associated with any particular type of witness. The only exception is a decrease in invitations to witnesses from trade associations.

## 6.5 PRESIDENTIAL ISSUE PRIORITIES AND BUREAUCRATIC PRESENCE AT HEARINGS

In this section, we test our *Interbranch Relations Hypothesis 2* how divided government and presidential issue priorities interact with respect to executive agency invitations. To measure presidential issue priorities, we follow existing work (e.g., Krause and O'Connell, 2016; Ballard and Curry, 2021) and leverage data from the Comparative Agenda Project's State of the Union Address (SOTU) dataset. This dataset provides issue information for each statement made during the president's speeches. The unit of analysis is "a quasi-statement [which] simply refers to the text between periods, semicolons, and other punctuation (e.g., question marks)," and each entry is coded by major issue area.[4] Cohen (1995) shows that issues mentioned more frequently by presidents during SOTU addresses increase public attention, suggesting that the frequency of mentions has a significant impact on public opinion and, potentially, the legislative agenda. We aggregate the number of issues by Congress and assign a decile to each issue area to identify the relative issue priorities of each president. We then merge this information with our hearings dataset to determine whether a hearing was held on an issue prioritized by the president.

Table 6.2 presents the list of top presidential issues aggregated by each Congress from the 87th through the 116th Congresses. The share for the top issue is calculated by dividing the number of quasi-sentences in each issue by the total number of quasi-sentences. Across the years, issues related to international affairs, defense, and the economy have

## 6.5 Presidential Issue Priorities

Table 6.2 *Top issue in the State of the Union address by Congress*

| Congress | President | Top issue | Share |
|---|---|---|---|
| 87 | Kennedy | International affairs | 0.24 |
| 88 | Johnson | International affairs | 0.31 |
| 89 | Johnson | Defense | 0.28 |
| 90 | Johnson | Defense | 0.21 |
| 91 | Nixon | Macroeconomics | 0.18 |
| 92 | Nixon | Government operations | 0.35 |
| 93 | Nixon | Government operations | 0.16 |
| 94 | Ford | Macroeconomics | 0.23 |
| 95 | Carter | Macroeconomics | 0.23 |
| 96 | Carter | International affairs | 0.42 |
| 97 | Reagan | Macroeconomics | 0.40 |
| 98 | Reagan | Macroeconomics | 0.31 |
| 99 | Reagan | Macroeconomics | 0.26 |
| 100 | Reagan | International affairs | 0.26 |
| 101 | H. W. Bush | International affairs | 0.19 |
| 102 | H. W. Bush | Defense | 0.29 |
| 103 | Clinton | Health | 0.23 |
| 104 | Clinton | Government operations | 0.18 |
| 105 | Clinton | Education | 0.16 |
| 106 | Clinton | International affairs | 0.15 |
| 107 | W. Bush | International affairs | 0.25 |
| 108 | W. Bush | International affairs | 0.42 |
| 109 | W. Bush | International affairs | 0.27 |
| 110 | W. Bush | International affairs | 0.30 |
| 111 | Obama | Macroeconomics | 0.37 |
| 112 | Obama | Macroeconomics | 0.20 |
| 113 | Obama | Macroeconomics | 0.16 |
| 114 | Obama | Defense | 0.14 |
| 115 | Trump | Defense | 0.16 |
| 116 | Trump | Law and crime | 0.17 |

often earned the top spot in presidential State of the Union addresses. Other topics, such as health care, government operations, education, and law and crime, also ranked high, depending on the president's particular issue priorities.

We examine whether congressional committees changed their patterns of inviting bureaucrats as a function of presidential issue priorities. To do so, we include an issue decile based on the frequency of the issue mentioned in the SOTU and an interaction term between divided government and issue decile. To simplify the analysis, we also include a dummy variable for issues with higher salience. Higher salience issues are those in the top 50 percent and lower salience issues are those in the bottom

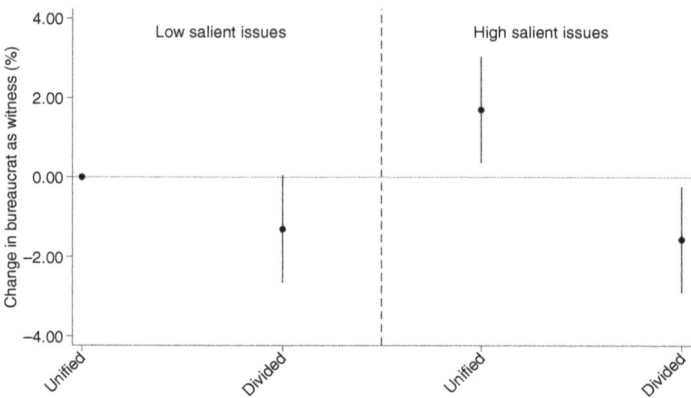

Figure 6.9 The effect of divided government on inviting bureaucrats as witnesses by presidential issue priorities – House
Notes: Plots indicate the changes in the percent of witnesses who are bureaucrats during unified/divided government, by the president's issue priorities. The plots are presented with 95% confidence intervals.

50 percent in terms of their frequency of appearance in presidential State of the Union addresses in each Congress.

Figure 6.9 presents the result for the House.[5] When committees held hearings on issues that the president did not prioritize, there was little difference in the frequency of inviting bureaucrats to testify during periods of unified vs. divided government. However, when committees held hearings on issues that the president prioritizes ("higher salience issues"), there was an evident divergent pattern: Committees invited relatively more bureaucrats to hearings during unified government; they invited relatively fewer bureaucrats to testify when there was divided control.

In the previous analysis, we show that divided government led to fewer invitations to bureaucrats in both the House and the Senate. Figure 6.10 shows the effect of divided government in the Senate on bureaucratic invitations and whether the relationship varied by the president's issue priorities.[6] When committees held hearings on issues that were less salient in the SOTU address, bureaucrats were less likely to be invited under divided government compared to unified government. Committees invited more bureaucrats to hearings on the president's higher salience issues under unified government, but the difference compared to divided government is not statistically significant.

There are two possible explanations for the chamber differences. First, the partisan logic we outline in our hypothesis is stronger in the House of Representatives than in the Senate, which explains why we see clearer empirical evidence for *Interbranch Relations Hypothesis 2*. Kriner and Schickler (2016) show that the effect of divided government on

## 6.5 Presidential Issue Priorities

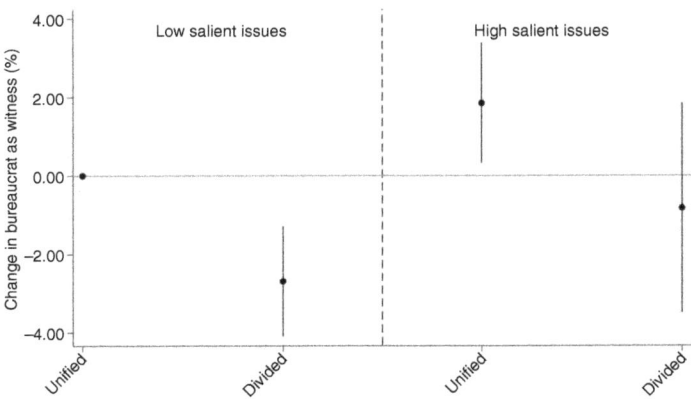

Figure 6.10 The effect of divided government on inviting bureaucrats as witnesses by presidential issue priorities – Senate
Notes: Plots indicate the changes in the percent of witnesses who are bureaucrats during unified/divided government by the president's issue priorities. The plots are presented with 95% confidence interval.

congressional investigative activity of the executive branch is most robust in the House of Representatives. The authors explain why the effect of divided government on investigative hearings may be weaker in the Senate (p. 18):

Because the Senate affords the majority party leadership considerably weaker procedural tools – and accordingly grants much greater prerogatives to individual senators – divided government has little influence on the sheer volume of investigative activity in the aggregate.

Although our results show that divided government has a clear impact on the frequency of inviting bureaucrats as witnesses in both the House and the Senate, a similar logic could be applied to heterogeneity by presidents' issue priorities. The partisan logic of controlling executive branch input in legislative hearings – especially on issues that presidents prioritize – is stronger in the House than in the Senate.

Second, we show that there is a clear substitution effect of inviting more congressional and research witnesses under divided government in the House when committees reduce the presence of bureaucrats in legislative hearings. However, we do not find a similar substitution effect in the Senate. This suggests that the strategy of the congressional majority party facing a nonpartisan president may depend on the chamber, especially for highly salient issues. In the House, the congressional majority may simply substitute bureaucrats with other witnesses who could provide analytical information that could fill the information gap Congress faces when it limits bureaucratic input. In the Senate, under both unified and divided government, the majority party invites bureaucrats on highly salient issues. However, the types of questions and information they seek from bureaucrats may differ. During unified government, senators may invite input from bureaucrats to help them craft legislation that advances the president's agenda. During divided government, the majority party may seek information that will help it avoid a presidential veto.

## 6.6 SUMMARY

This chapter shows that committees' incentives to manage interbranch relations have a significant impact on witness invitation patterns. We find that during periods of divided government, committees invited relatively fewer bureaucrats to testify; instead, they invited relatively more witnesses from think tanks, universities, and within Congress itself. Moreover, this result is particularly pronounced when hearings were held on issues that the president prioritized. These results are substantively important, especially given how the existing literature has characterized bureaucrats' advantages in information and expertise in policy implementation vis-à-vis Congress (Gailmard and Patty, 2012a). Our findings provide evidence that under divided government, committees limited the amount of expert information from the executive branch that could be favorable to a president from the opposing party. Instead, they welcomed outsiders, such as those from think tanks and universities, to compensate for the relative loss of information from bureaucrats (Banks and Weingast, 1992).

This link between divided government and lower bureaucrat invitation rates sheds light on a new mechanism for how divided government affects interbranch relations through information transmission. The partisan divide between the legislative and executive branches may do more than cause obstacles for the congressional majority in getting its legislation signed into law, as is commonly understood. It also may have implications for the extent to which Congress incorporates input from the executive branch in formulating legislation. This would have significant consequences for the content of legislation as well as its implementation by federal agencies (McCarty, 2019b).

### NOTES

1. www.govinfo.gov/content/pkg/CHRG-107hhrg74198/pdf/CHRG-107hhrg74198.pdf
2. The ratio of bureaucratic witnesses in the Senate in the 87th Congress is 0.66, which was exceptionally high, so we drop that observation for the graphical purpose.

## 6.6 Summary

3. The majority party rarely varies within a Congress, so including Congress fixed effects does not allow us to estimate the majority party effect.
4. State of the Union Address. The Policy Agendas Project at the University of Texas at Austin, 2017. https://urldefense.com/v3/__http://www.comparativeagendas.net__;!!Mih3wA!B6CqgoQ1Ms2bJhMdszppQSyTo1deZn2ctm78eneolWZmP1P6qRJGMe7O-ToAI1J6mqX57fjtM3S39aY$ (accessed July 29, 2021).
5. Table A9 presents the regression results, and Figure 6.9 visualizes the results in column (3). The reference category is a hearing on lower salience issues under unified government.
6. Table A10 presents the regression results, and Figure 6.10 visualizes the results in column (3). The reference category is a hearing on lower salience issues under unified government.

# 7

## Congressional Capacity and the Search for Specialized Information

When OTA was disbanded, Congress gave itself a lobotomy. Our national policies have suffered ever since. In the years since the demise of the Office of Technology Assessment [OTA], no group or combination of groups has been able to assume OTA's place as the provider of scientific and technical assessment and advice to Congress.
– Representative Rush Holt (D-NJ12)'s Statement on the Office of Technology Assessment, 2009

I think we've all been embarrassed by the way Congress fails to understand technology. OTA needs to come back in some form.
– Former Congressman Vic Fazio (D-CA3) during the Committee on the Modernization of Congress Hearing, 2019

On July 25, 2006, the Science Committee held a hearing entitled, "Scientific and Technical Advice for the U.S. Congress," to focus on specific ideas to improve the mechanisms through which Congress receives scientific advice.[1] Five distinguished witnesses testified at the hearing, the first four of whom were eminent scientists: Dr. Jon M. Peha, Professor in the Departments of Engineering and Public Policy and of Electrical and Computer Engineering at Carnegie Mellon University; Dr. Albert H. Teich, Director of Science and Policy Programs at the American Association for the Advancement of Science; Dr. Peter D. Blair, Executive Director in the Division of Engineering and Physical Sciences of the National Academy of Sciences; and Dr. Catherine T. Hunt, President-Elect of the American Chemical Society. The fifth witness was the committee's own colleague, Representative Rush Holt, a fourth-term Democratic congressman from New Jersey's 12th District. Holt's inclusion on the witness list reflected his atypical career path to Capitol Hill: He earned a PhD in physics from New York University in 1981, served on the faculty of Swarthmore College from 1980 to 1988 and then became Associate Director of the Princeton Plasma Physics Laboratory at Princeton University.

When Representative Holt joined the US House in 1998, he was only the second research scientist to be elected to Congress, following Vern Ehlers (R-MI), who had a PhD in nuclear physics from the University of California, Berkeley, and was elected to Congress in 1993. During Representative Holt's tenure in Congress from 1999 to 2014, he was a strong advocate for the creation of in-house congressional professional offices dedicated to providing scientific and technical assessment services. He went further and created several congressional caucuses within the US House, such as the Research and Development Caucus and the Biomedical Research Caucus.

Appearing before his fellow members of Congress at the July 2006 hearing, Representative Holt lamented the loss of the congressional support agency, the Office of Technology Assessment (OTA). Congress created the OTA in 1972 to study emerging technologies and advise Congress on these and other scientific matters. This in-house congressional support agency provided technical assessment services and regular reports on legislative issues ranging from agricultural technology to international relations in technology transfer. In his testimony, Representative Holt stated:

... Congress decided in 1995 that we didn't need an in-house body dedicated to technological assessment. The technological assessment could come, we told ourselves – this was before my time here – could come through committee hearings, through CRS [Congressional Research Service] reports, through experts in our district, through think tanks, through the National Research Council and the National Academies ... We do not suffer from a lack of information here on Capitol Hill, but from a lack of ability to glean the knowledge and to gauge the validity, the credibility, and the usefulness of the large amounts of information and advice that we receive.

Congressman Holt explicitly described why in-house, permanently staffed organizations are critical to keeping members of Congress informed about the economic, social, and political impacts of scientific and technological advances. Members of Congress are politicians and generally unfamiliar with the details of science and technology issues. They lack sufficient time to analyze technical information and its ramifications for various sectors of the country, yet they make important decisions involving technical and scientific components. Holt's testimony underscores that in-house organizations such as the OTA could help members understand "the validity, credibility, and usefulness of the vast amounts of information and advice" that members of Congress receive.

Representative Holt's testimony and the hearing above suggest a link between a particular type of internal congressional resource – congressional support agencies such as the OTA – and Congress's ability comprehend large amounts of information, particularly scientific and expert information. More broadly, this example raises an important question about the role of *congressional capacity*, which scholars define as Congress's own resources, expertise, knowledge, and technology that it uses to fulfill its constitutional role (LaPira, Drutman, and Kosar, 2020; Bolton and Thrower, 2021).

Scholars point to the declining number of policy and committee staff along with the lack of internal resources as signs of weakened congressional capacity over time. They have concerns about Congress's ability to fulfill its institutional duty, especially with the diminished or eliminated roles of congressional support agencies, such as the Congressional Budget Office and the OTA (Kosar, 2020). Making matters worse, the number of staff and officials employed to support legislative research declined (Baumgartner and Jones, 2015) while the workload and fundraising pressures on members of Congress have increased significantly (Curry, 2015; Lee, 2016). As a result, scholars express concern that lobbyists and outside groups would step in to take on the role of information providers (LaPira and Thomas, 2017; Kosar, 2020).

In this chapter, we consider how the internal capacity of Congress affects the ways members are informed through the channel of witness testimony. We focus on one of the primary sources of congressional capacity: congressional support agencies. The Congressional Budget Office, the Congressional Research Service, the Government Accountability Office, and the former OTA comprise the set of internal support agencies that were created to assist members and committees in their work (Kosar, 2020). In general, these internal support agencies supply Congress with information that helps the identify issues, arms them with specialized information, and helps rebalance intrabranch information asymmetries (Baumgartner and Jones, 2015).

This form of congressional capacity received a shock in 1995 when the Republicans gained majority status in the House of Representatives for the first time since 1955. A key agenda of House Speaker Newt Gingrich's "Contract with America" platform was to reduce the size of government. The legislative branch was not immune to these changes. The Republican majority in the House eliminated funding for the OTA and cut funding for the other internal congressional support agencies as part of its reform (Bimber, 1996). Committees with a particular need for scientific and technical advice often requested information from the OTA as a source of information and expert in-house staff. Committees that relied on the OTA reported the benefits of both internal information and trusted relationships with OTA staff, who helped committees navigate scientific research and sort through the large amount of available expertise and competing expert opinions (Tudor and Warner, 2019; Johnson, 2019). When the OTA was eliminated in 1995, these committees suffered an immediate reduction in their access to internal information and staff to liaise between committees and the scientific community.

We examine how two committees that relied heavily on the OTA for scientific and technical advice – the Committee on Energy and Commerce and the Committee on Science, Space, and Technology – changed the way they invited witnesses to hearings after the partisan elimination of the OTA. In particular, we focus on the invitation rates of research-oriented witnesses, such as individuals from think tanks and universities, who tend to provide high levels of analytical and technical information in their testimonies. We generate two contrasting hypotheses about how defunding the OTA would change the frequency of invitations of research-oriented witnesses.

The first hypothesis reflects a *substitution* effect, which expects committees that relied more heavily on the OTA to invite relatively more witnesses from think tanks and research organizations to legislative hearings after the OTA was eliminated. This theoretical expectation tests whether Congress can successfully substitute external witnesses to provide high levels of analytical information when it experiences a cut to its internal capacity.

The second hypothesis reflects an alternative *amplifying* effect of the loss of congressional capacity, expecting these two committees to invite fewer research-oriented witnesses after the elimination of the OTA. Under this theoretical expectation, the cut to Congress's capacity is amplified. It cannot compensate for the loss of internal expertise and does not expend effort to seek witnesses to provide specialized information such as analytical information.

Using a difference-in-differences design, we show that the committees relying most heavily on information produced internally within Congress suffered a drastic reduction in the number of technical and scientific witnesses they invited in the wake of the OTA's abolition – a result that supporting the amplifying effect of the loss of congressional capacity. This implies that those committees did not compensate for this loss of information through outside witnesses. The partisan cuts in congressional capacity resulted in a void of technical and scientific witnesses testifying before Congress.

Our findings underscore the importance of a strong congressional capacity to bring research-based witnesses to hearings. As Representative Holt noted, congressional support agencies help legislators understand the validity and usefulness of large amounts of information. Our analysis in this chapter shows that without these resources and support, legislators' abilities and incentives to identify and process important scientific and technical information are significantly diminished.

## 7.1 DECLINING CONGRESSIONAL CAPACITY

When the 116th Congress began in January 2019, it quickly passed House Resolution 6 that authorized the creation of the House Select Committee on Congressional Modernization. The goal of the Modernization Committee was, and remains, to examine ways to improve the operations of the legislative branch and identify areas for reform.[2] This was not Congress's first attempt to reform its internal operations. The Congressional Research Service report, "Reorganization of the House of Representatives: Modern Reform Efforts," provides detailed descriptions of the history of internal reforms within the House.[3] As examples, Congress passed the Legislative Reorganization Act in 1946, which increased legislators' pay and hired nonpartisan professional committee staff. In 1965, Congress established the Joint Committee on the Organization of Congress to handle proposals aimed at reforming committee structures, such as limiting the power of committee chairs and giving the minority party more power in committee activities. There were several reforms in the 1970s and 1980s, mostly focused on committee jurisdiction and updating procedures such as scheduling and the legislative calendar. It was not until 1992 that Congress, faced with the increasing need to keep pace with ever-accelerating technological change and the emergence of new issue areas, agreed to establish the Joint Committee on the Organization of Congress to review Congress's internal organization. Although the Legislative Reorganization Act of 1994 was introduced in both chambers, it did not pass Congress. However, some of the proposals contained in the legislation were adopted by the new Republican majority in the 104th Congress, including measures to strengthen the power of committee chairs and party leaders.

## 7.2 1995 REFORM AND ELIMINATION OF THE OTA

For forty years, beginning in 1955, the Republican Party was the minority party in the House of Representatives. That tenure ended on the night of the November 8, 1994 midterm elections, when the Republicans gained 54 seats in the House, which moved them from a 176-seat minority party to a 230-seat majority party. In the Senate, the Republican Party picked up ten seats, a gain that also made them the majority party. This Republican takeover during the 1994 midterm elections followed Newt Gingrich's "Contract with America" campaign platform. Gingrich,

## 7.2 1995 Reform and Elimination of the OTA

then the Republican House Minority Whip representing Georgia's 6th district, and Dick Armey, a Texas politician who was chairman of the House Republican Conference, had developed a platform around ten major legislative proposals (Green and Crouch, 2022). The "Contract with America" centered on issues such as a balanced budget, tax cuts, and anti-crime initiatives, as well as operational reforms in Congress to downsize government and cut budgets.[4]

Once the Republicans became the majority party in 1995, they quickly worked to implement their "Contract with America" platform and began slashing the budgets of federal agencies across Capitol Hill (Wolfenberger, 2001). The OTA was a major casualty; the new Republican majority defunded it, ending its existence in September 1995. Even though the OTA accounted for only 1% of the legislative branch's appropriations budget and its permanent staff was capped at 150, the OTA's elimination played a symbolic role. Republicans boasted that they had eliminated an entire federal agency in fulfilling the downsizing of government promised in their "Contract with America" (Blair, 2013).

The OTA had been created by Congress in 1972 through the Office of Technology Assessment Act. The office's purpose was to study emerging technologies and provide advice exclusively to Congress on these technologies and other scientific matters. The creation was in recognition that emerging technologies could have significant economic and social impacts, and that lawmakers needed a better understanding of these impacts to implement policy responses (Sargent, 2020). At the time of the OTA's creation, Congress was considering major technological issues such as US investment in supersonic transport, the anti-ballistic missile system, and the Trans-Alaska Pipeline (Blair, 2013). Moreover, members of Congress were motivated to create an in-house think tank to provide independent information and policy analysis to help them compete with the executive branch (Bimber, 1996). The federal executive branch had been greatly expanded in the wake of World War II and was beginning to accumulate a clear advantage of information and expertise over Congress. For example, the creation of the Office of Management and Budget (OMB) within the White House in 1970 was a concrete threat to Congress in terms of its policy expertise vis-à-vis that of the president. Thus, the ability to keep pace with the executive branch and to match the president in terms of information and expertise – especially on technical and scientific matters – was a secondary motivation for the creation of the OTA. This was plainly stated by Charles Mosher, a congressman from Ohio, during the debates over the creation of the OTA (Sargent, 2020):

> Let us face it, Mr. Chairman, we in the Congress are constantly outmanned and outgunned by the expertise of the executive agencies. We desperately need a

stronger source of professional advice and information, more immediately and entirely responsible to us and responsive to the demands of our own committees, in order to more nearly match those resources in the executive agencies.

The Technology Assessment Act of 1972 categorized the OTA's functions and duties as "identifying existing or probable effects of technologies or technical programs" and "ascertaining cause-and-effect relationships, where possible" (Sargent, 2020). The OTA was also designed to have close ties to the academic and scientific communities. It maintained a liaison with the National Science Foundation, particularly for grants and contracts related to technology assessment. In addition, the OTA had a Technology Assessment Advisory Council (TAAC), which included the Comptroller General of the General Accounting Office, the Director of Congressional Research Service, and ten members from the public who were to be persons "eminent in one or more fields of the physical, biological, or social sciences or engineering" (Sargent, 2020). Figure 7.1 is the first page of the OTA's annual report to Congress, submitted in 1974. Its advisory board consisted of prominent scientists, including Dr. Frederick C. Robbins, who shared the 1954 Nobel Prize in Physiology or Medicine with John F. Enders and Thomas H. Weller "for their discovery of the ability of poliomyelitis viruses to grow in cultures of various types of tissue," which paved the way for the development of polio vaccines.[5]

The OTA began producing technology assessments in 1974, and they became one of its signature products. This exchange of information

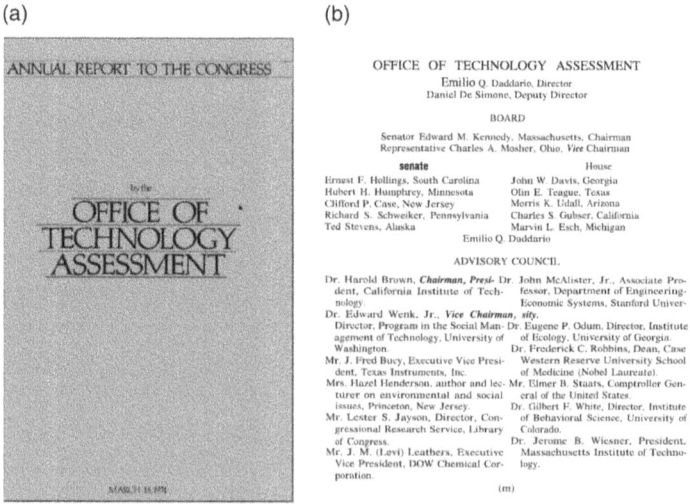

Figure 7.1 OTA Annual Report to the Congress, 1974
Notes: These images show the front page of the OTA annual report submitted to the Congress in 1974 (a) and the page that shows the leadership, board members, and advisory council members of the OTA (b).

## 7.2 1995 Reform and Elimination of the OTA

between the OTA and Congress was channeled through congressional committees – specifically, through committee chairs who requested assessments for themselves or on behalf of ranking minority members or a majority of committee members. Thus, unlike requests to CRS, an individual member of Congress – except committee chairs – could not request a study or report from the OTA. From 1974 until its end in 1995, the OTA not only produced an annual report to Congress summarizing its assessment activities, it also produced around 750 assessments, papers, memoranda, and case studies, according to a count by Sargent (2020).

There were three main divisions within the OTA: (1) energy, materials, and international security; (2) health and life sciences; and (3) science, information, and natural resources. The topics of the OTA's reports were diverse and covered a wide range of topics within agricultural research and technology, environmental technology, medical services, and energy efficiency. As an illustrative example, Figure 7.2 shows the list of publications by the division of "Energy, Materials, and International Security Division" in 1992. While earlier reports did not systematically indicate who had requested the publication, reports from 1990 to 1995 indicate the requesting committee. During this period alone, the OTA produced 523 reports. We extract request data to gain insight into which committees actively sought information from the OTA.

Figure 7.3 shows the distribution of technology assessment requests to the OTA by House committees from 1990 to 1995. It is immediately apparent that certain committees – such as Small Business, Budget, and Rules – very rarely requested reports from the OTA. On the other hand, two committees – Energy and Commerce and Science, Space, and Technology – with policy jurisdictions covering technology and science-related issues, frequently requested reports at rates that far outpaced other committees during this time period. Even though the OTA was created to support Congress as a whole, the data in Figure 7.3 show that the OTA's work fell along a practical division that reflected demand: the two committees with the most topical overlap with the OTA and whom availed themselves of the vast majority of the OTA's resources, and everyone else. For the Energy and Commerce Committee and the Science, Space, and Technology Committee in particular, the elimination of the OTA in 1995 meant a sharp, immediate reduction in internal information and resources, as well as the disappearance of a group of OTA staff who had served as liaisons between the committees and the scientific community.

Committee and floor debates during the OTA repeal discussion revealed a sharp partisan divide. Republicans argued that other congressional support agencies, such as the General Accounting Office (GAO) and the Congressional Research Service (CRS), could replace

ISC has concentrated on arms control, strategic defense, weapons trade and proliferation, and space research and development. Most recently, work on defense conversion has helped redefine the defense industrial base required to support future force structure needs.

ITE has analyzed numerous industries and their competitive posture in a global economy. The training and retraining needs of the U.S. workforce also has been studied at length. In addition, the program has analyzed the technology and trade policies of the United States' global competitor nations. Most recent work has concentrated on the need to address the conversion of assets in the U.S. dedicated to defense, which must now be productively refocused to the peacetime economy of the U.S.

This division will continue to address some of the most difficult technology-driven issues facing the U.S Congress, the Nation and the global community of nations.

**Monitoring Limits on Sea-Launched Cruise Missiles, September 1992**
Requested by:
Senate Foreign Relations Committee
House Foreign Affairs Committee

**U.S.-Mexico Trade: Pulling Together or Pulling Apart?, September 1992**
Requested by:
House Committee on Education and Labor

**Green Products by Design: Choices for a Cleaner Environment, September 1992**
Requested by:
House Committee on Science, Space, and Technology
House Committee on Energy and Commerce

**Police Body Armor Standards and Testing: Volume I, August 1992**
Requested by:
Senate Committee on the Judiciary
House Committee on the Judiciary
House Committee on Rules

**Police Body Armor Standards and Testing: Volume II Appendixes, August 1992**
Requested by:
Senate Committee on the Judiciary
House Committee on the Judiciary
House Committee on Rules

**Building Future Security: Strategies for Restructuring the Defense Technology and Industrial Base, July 1992**
Requested by:
House Committee on Government Operations
Senate Committee on Labor and Human Resources
Senate Committee on Commerce, Science, and Transportation
Senate Committee on Armed Services

**Retiring Old Cars: Programs to Save Gasoline and Reduce Emissions, July 1992**
Requested by:
House Committee on Energy and Commerce

**Lessons in Restructuring Defense Industry: The French Experience—Background Paper, June 1992**
Requested by:
House Committee on Government Operations
Senate Committee on Labor and Human Resources
Senate Committee on Commerce, Science, and Transportation
Senate Committee on Armed Services

**Fueling Development: Providing Energy Services for Developing Countries, May 1992**
Requested by:
House Committee on Energy and Commerce
House Committee on Foreign Affairs
House Committee on Banking, Finance and Urban Affairs
House Select Committee on Hunger
Congressional Competitiveness Caucus
Senate Committee on Governmental Affairs
Senate Committee on Environment and Public Works

**Trade and Environment: Conflicts and Opportunities—Background Paper, May 1992**
Requested by:
House Committee on Foreign Affairs
House Committee on Energy and Commerce
Senate Committee on Finance

**Building Energy Efficiency, May 1992**
Requested by:
House Committee on Energy and Commerce
House Committee on Science, Space, and Technology
Senate Committee on Governmental Affairs
Senate Committee on Energy and Natural Resources

**After the Cold War: Living with Lower Defense Spending, February 1992**
Requested by:
House Committee on Interior and Insular Affairs
House Committee on Government Operations
Senate Committee on Labor and Human Resources
Senate Committee on Commerce, Science, and Transportation
Senate Committee on Foreign Relations
Senate Committee on Armed Services

**Performance Standards for the Food Stamp Employment and Training Program, February 1992**
Mandated Study

**Technology Against Terrorism: Structuring Security, January 1992**
Requested by:
Senate Committee on Governmental Affairs
Senate Committee on Commerce, Science, and Transportation

**Competing Economies: America, Europe, and the Pacific Rim, November 1991**
Requested by:
Senate Committee on Finance

**American Military Power: Future Needs, Future Choices—Background Paper, October 1991**
Requested by:
House Committee on Government Operations
Senate Committee on Commerce, Science, and Transportation
Senate Committee on Foreign Relations
Senate Committee on Armed Services

**Improving Automobile Fuel Economy: New Standards, New Approaches, October 1991**
Requested by:
Senate Committee on Energy and Natural Resources

**U.S. Oil Import Vulnerability: The Technical Replacement Capability, October 1991**
Requested by:
House Committee on Energy and Commerce
Senate Committee on Energy and Natural Resources

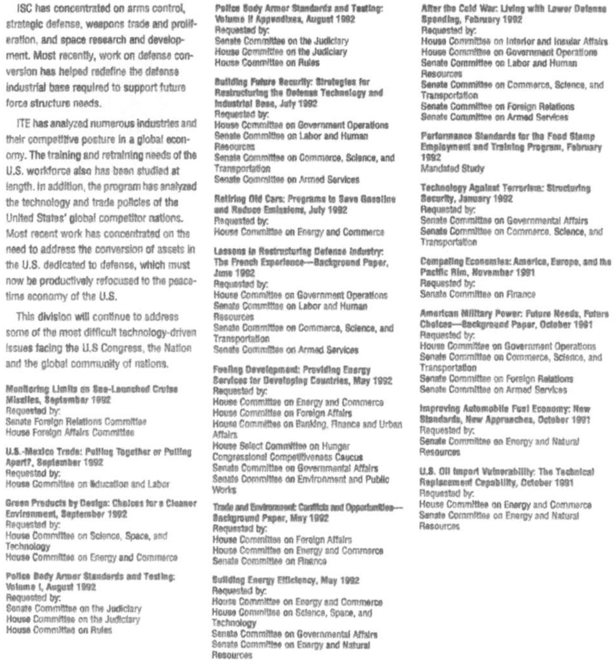

Figure 7.2 OTA Annual Report to Congress, 1992
Notes: This image shows a list of reports issued by the OTA's Energy, Materials, and International Security Division in 1992 and the names of the committees that requested each report.

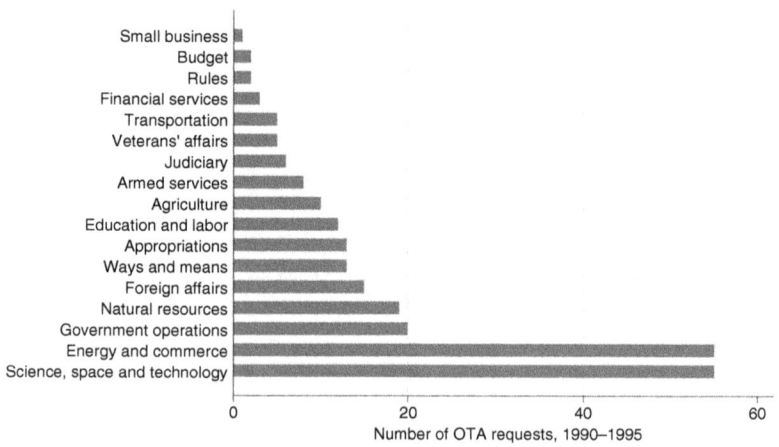

Figure 7.3 Number of OTA request by House committees, 1990–1995
Notes: This figure shows the total number of technology assessment requests made to OTA by the standing committees of the House of Representatives for the years 1990–1995.

the OTA and that outside scientific organizations could provide technical assessments. Democrats strongly disagreed, emphasizing the OTA's uniqueness as an internal congressional resource (Bimber, 1996). During the Senate debate on the 1996 Legislative Branch Appropriations Act, Democratic Senator Daniel Inouye of Hawaii stated (Sargent, 2020):

> Some of my colleagues have suggested that we don't need an OTA .... How many of us are able to fully grasp and synthesize highly scientific information and identify the relevant questions that need to be addressed? The OTA was created to provide the Congress with its own source of information on highly technical matters. Who else but a scientifically oriented agency, composed of technical experts, governed by a bipartisan board of congressional overseers, and seeking information directly under congressional auspices, [can give] the Congress and the country accurate and essential information on new technologies?

Congressman George Brown (D-CA), a ranking member of the House Science Committee, criticized the action to defund the OTA as removing Congress's "defense against the dumb" (Sargent, 2020). Although Republican members hoped that other agencies would fill the role of the OTA, analyses of the use of other agencies for technical matters after the defunding of the OTA suggest that the void was not filled quickly (Blair, 2013). The partisan action of defunding the OTA clearly caused a shock to Congress's capacity to gather and process technical information, especially for those committees that had relied heavily on the OTA's services.

## 7.3 ELIMINATION OF THE OTA AND CHANGES TO WITNESS INVITATIONS

We examine how the elimination of the OTA in 1995 affected the invitation patterns of external witnesses to committees that previously relied on the OTA for information and expertise. In particular, we investigate changes in the invitation patterns of witnesses from think tanks and universities – who offer more analytical and technical information – to determine how the change in Congress's internal capacity might affect its use of expertise outside of Congress.

One perspective is that committees who relied heavily on internal sources of information might increase their efforts to hear from outside witnesses, especially research-based witnesses who provide technical and analytical information, to compensate for the loss of internal information from the OTA. This is explicitly stated in the House Appropriations Committee's report on the Legislative Branch Appropriations Act, 1996 (H.R. 1854) (Sargent, 2020):

> If any functions of OTA must be retained, they shall be assumed by other agencies such as Congressional Research Service or the General Accounting Office.

Alternatively, the National Academy of Sciences, university research programs, and a variety of private sector institutions will be available to supplement the needs of Congress for objective, unbiased technology assessments.

This viewpoint generates the following hypothesis that emphasizes the *substitution* effect:

*Congressional Capacity Hypothesis A: Committees that relied more heavily on the OTA will invite relatively more witnesses from think tanks and research organizations to legislative hearings after the elimination of the OTA.*

On the other hand, without the advice and guidance of the OTA, these committees might choose not to exert effort to seek out scientific witnesses or facilitate their invitation to testify. Selecting witnesses consumes time and resources to identify, research, and prepare them. Additionally, the 1995 reform drastically cut committee staff who are integral to the witness arrangement process. The elimination of the OTA, along with significant reductions in the number of committee staff, could result in a more drastic reduction in expert witnesses for those committees that relied more heavily on the OTA, even though the demand for these types of witnesses may have increased. This leads to the following hypothesis, which emphasizes the *amplifying* effect:

*Congressional Capacity Hypothesis B: Committees that relied more heavily on the OTA will invite relatively fewer witnesses from think tanks and research organizations to testify at legislative hearings after the elimination of the OTA.*

To examine how the elimination of the OTA in 1995 affected the witness invitation patterns of committees that relied on it, we exploit the considerable variations documented in Figure 7.3. For example, from 1990 to 1995 (the period for which report request data is available), the House Committee on Small Business requested only one report from the OTA, while the Energy and Commerce Committee and the Science, Space, and Technology Committee requested fifty-five reports. Certain committees, such as the latter two, demonstrated a particular reliance on internal information compared to other committees that made minimal use of the OTA. Thus, we assign the Energy and Commerce and the Science, Space, and Technology Committees as the treated group – the committees that would be experience the most impact from the elimination of the OTA.

Figure A7 shows the percentage of research witnesses in the treated and control groups over time, and Table 7.1 shows the summary statistics for the number of witnesses and the presence of research witnesses between the treated and control committees for a shorter time period:

## 7.3 Elimination of the OTA

Table 7.1 *Changes in witness invitations before and after the 1995 reform – House*

|  | Number of witnesses | | Research witnesses (%) | |
| --- | --- | --- | --- | --- |
|  | Before | After | Before | After |
| Treated | 8.9 | 7.4 | 13.1 | 10.8 |
|  | (6.6) | (6.2) | (18.3) | (16.6) |
| Control | 9.1 | 8.3 | 8.4 | 9.9 |
|  | (8.9) | (7.9) | (16.2) | (16.9) |

*Notes:* The unit of observation is the hearing level. *Treated* includes the Committee on Energy and Commerce and the Committee on Science, Space, and Technology. *Control* includes all other standing committees of the House. *Before* includes the three Congresses before the 1995 reform (101st, 102nd, and 103rd); *After* includes the three Congresses after the reform (104th, 105th, and 106th). The numbers in the parentheses are standard deviations.

three Congresses before the 1995 reform and three Congresses after the reform. There are slight declines in the number of witnesses in both the treated and control groups, but the pattern is similar. There is a significant decrease in the presence of research witnesses in the treated committees after the 1995 reform, but we do not observe a similar pattern in the control committees. By contrast, there is a slight increase in the proportion of research witnesses in the control group. This is consistent with the patterns we presented in Chapter 3: The share of witnesses from think tanks and universities has increased over time. It suggests that the elimination of the OTA may have had a significant negative impact on the presence of research-based witnesses in committees that relied heavily on the OTA.

To systematically examine the effect of eliminating the OTA after controlling for other factors, we focus on House legislative hearings for the Congresses before and after the 1995 reform. We estimate the following difference-in-differences model to examine whether witness invitation patterns differed in the treated committees relative to the control committees:

$$Y_{hict} = \beta \text{Treated}_c + \sum_{s=1}^{6} \gamma_s \text{Congress}_{100+s}$$
$$+ \sum_{s=1}^{6} \delta_t (\text{Treated}_c \cdot \text{Congress}_{100+s}) + \rho X_{hict} + \alpha_i + \epsilon_{hict}.$$

In this equation, $Y_{hict}$ indicates the outcome measures for witness characteristics at the hearing level (for hearing $h$, issue $i$, committee $c$, in Congress $t$). *Treated* indicates the two House committees that relied

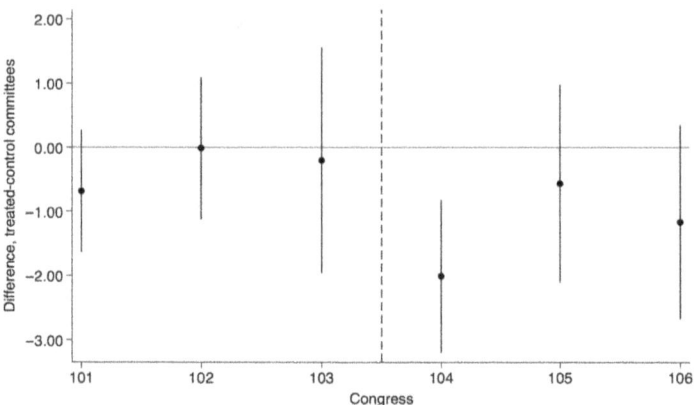

Figure 7.4 OTA elimination on the change in the number of witnesses
Notes: The reference Congress is the 100th Congress. The reform took place during the 104th Congress and the dashed vertical line indicates before and after the reform. The y-axis indicates the difference in the change in the number of witnesses between the treated and control committees. The plots are presented with 95% confidence intervals.

heavily on internal information: the House Committee on Energy and Commerce and the House Committee on Science, Space, and Technology. The variable, *Congress*, captures the lead time periods from the 100th Congress (1987–1988), which is the reference Congress. The main variable of interest is $\delta_t$, which indicates whether there were any significant differences in the witness invitation patterns between the treated and control groups before and after the reform during the 104th Congress. $X_{hict}$ includes other hearing level control variables. We include an issue fixed effect ($\alpha_i$), and standard errors are clustered at the committee level.

Figure 7.4 shows the results for the number of witnesses testifying at hearings, and Figure 7.5 shows the results for the percentage of witnesses from think tanks and universities.[6] In the figures, the reference Congress is the 100th Congress; the plots cover the time trends from the 101st to the 106th Congresses, a period that includes three terms before and three terms after the 1995 reform. Prior to 1995, there was no pre-trend in the number of witnesses invited and the number of witnesses from think tanks and universities. After the reform, however, there was a significant decline in the number of witnesses in the treated committees, although the pattern disappears in subsequent Congresses. The decline in the number of research-based witnesses in the treated group immediately after the reform was more substantial, and the pattern continued in subsequent Congresses. Given that the average percentage of research-based witnesses before the reform was 7.3 percent, the coefficients shown in Figure 7.5 suggest that there was at least a 24 percent decline in the invitation of research-based witnesses after the OTA was eliminated.

## 7.3 Elimination of the OTA

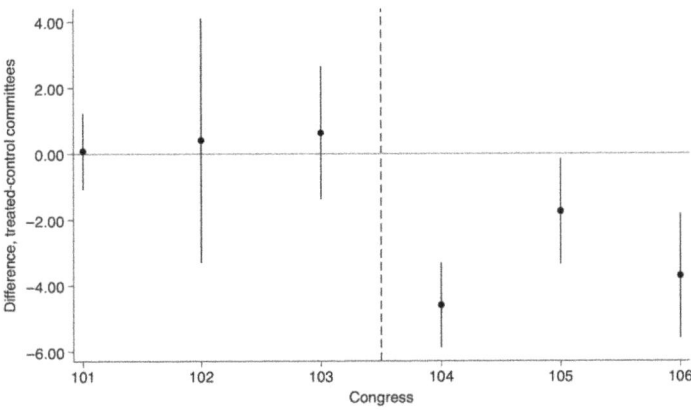

Figure 7.5 OTA elimination on the change in research witness share
Notes: The reference Congress is the 100th Congress. The reform took place during the 104th Congress, and the dashed vertical line indicates before and after the reform. The y-axis indicates the difference in the change in the share of research witnesses between the treated and control committees. The plots are presented with 95% confidence intervals.

These decreases confirm the expectation from *Congressional Capacity Hypothesis B*: Committees that relied more heavily on the OTA will invite relatively *fewer witnesses from think tanks and research organizations* after the elimination of the OTA. With the defunding of the OTA, committees that had relied heavily on internal sources of information indeed might be expected to increase their efforts to invite external witnesses, especially research-based witnesses who could provide technical and analytical information.

The result is contrary to the expectation in the opposing hypothesis *Congressional Capacity Hypothesis A*, which held that committees that had relied heavily on the OTA might be expected to increase their efforts to invite outside witnesses to compensate for the loss of internal information provided by the OTA. However, the process of selecting, inviting, and preparing witnesses – especially technical and scientific witnesses – requires knowledge and expertise. The ability of committees to invite and prepare these types of witnesses requires committee staff, and this may be why our findings support Hypothesis B rather than A.

Committee staff play a particularly important role in organizing and preparing witnesses for hearings. Prior to hearings, they identify potential witnesses, research their views, and interview them as necessary. This process takes time and resources, especially for the types of witnesses that require relatively more effort to identify, research, and prepare. For example, committee staff may need to devote more time and resources to understanding the views of witnesses who contribute a greater amount of

Table 7.2 *Number of committee staff and witness invitations, 95th–114th Congresses*

| Outcome = | (1) No.Witness | (2) Diversity | (3) Research (%) |
|---|---|---|---|
| Number of committee staff | 0.0204 | −0.0144 | 0.0359** |
|  | (0.0123) | (0.0201) | (0.0161) |
| Number of witness |  | 1.147*** | 0.0564 |
|  |  | (0.134) | (0.0331) |
| Mean outcome value | 8.82 | 54.09 | 10.67 |
| N | 23,215 | 23,206 | 23,206 |
| adj. $R^2$ | 0.171 | 0.305 | 0.115 |

Notes: *$p < 0.10$, **$p < 0.05$, ***$p < 0.01$. Congress, committee, issue FEs, and other control variables are included. Standard errors are clustered at the committee level. Data source: Congressional Research Service (2016), "House of Representative Staff Level in Member, Committee, Leadership, and Other Offices, 1977–2016."

analytical information, such as witnesses from academic institutions and think tanks.

Indeed, our analysis shows that the number of committee staff is strongly correlated with the proportion of witnesses from research-oriented institutions. Table 7.2 shows the relationship between the number of committee staff and patterns of witness invitations for the period 1977 to 2016, when systematic information on the number of committee staff is available. The analysis shows that there is no statistically significant relationship between the number of committee staff and the number of witnesses invited or the diversity of witness affiliations. However, more committee staff is strongly correlated with the number of research-based witnesses. The mean number of committee staff is 81 with a standard deviation of 28. Therefore, a one standard deviation increase in the number of committee staff is associated with a 1.01 ($\sim 28 \times 0.0359$) increase in the percentage of think tank/research witnesses, which is a 10-percent increase from the mean for the number of this witness type.

Figure 7.6, which depicts the patterns of committee staffing in each House standing committee over time, shows sharp declines in the number of committee staff from the 103rd to the 104th Congresses across the board. The average number of committee staff in treated committees fell from 89 to 69, and the average number of committee staff in control committees fell from 92 to 65.

The two committees that relied heavily on the OTA for technical and scientific expertise were not exempt from this decline in committee staff.

## 7.4 Summary

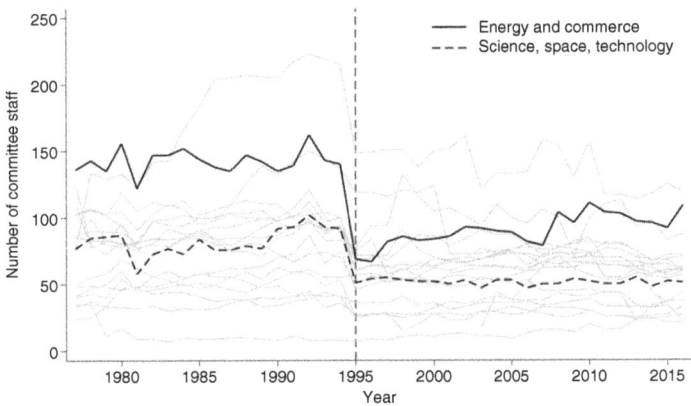

Figure 7.6 Changes in the number of committee staff in the House
Notes: This figure shows the number of committee staff on House standing committees for the period 1977–2016. The dashed vertical line indicates the 1995 Republican majority's reform. The two committees that requested the most reports from OTA – Energy and Commerce and Science, Space, and Technology – are labeled, and all other committees are indicated by thin lines.

The reduced number of committee staff is a possibly why these treated committees were unable to fill the resulting void with external witnesses. A committee's own staff were weaker substitutes for OTA staff – the chair of the Science, Space, and Technology Committee clearly stated in 2019 that "committee staff are not a replacement for OTA" (Johnson, 2019).

Taken together, internal congressional support agencies and congressional committee staff largely arm committees with the ability to gather and process information – these two types of internal capacity can be characterized as "tools" that committees possess to conduct information searches. The 1995 reform eliminated one internal source of information, the OTA, for the specific committees that relied on this internal information. Our difference-in-differences results show that these committees suffered a decline in the number of witnesses, especially research-based witnesses, as a result of the elimination of the OTA, and likely could not compensate for this loss of information because of the corresponding reduction in committee staff across Congress.

### 7.4 SUMMARY

The revival of the OTA has been at the center of discussions about congressional capacity and improving the legislative body's understanding of ever-evolving technology and science. It is easy to find calls to restore the OTA to better prepare and inform lawmakers, especially on scientific and technical issues such as climate change and global health crises such as the COVID-19 pandemic. For example, the American Political Science Association's 2019 Congressional Reform Task Force report recommended expanding existing congressional support agencies and adding new ones. The Task Force specifically points to the OTA as a model for how to create internal congressional support agencies.[7]

The final report of the Select Committee on the Modernization of Congress, issued in October 2020, devoted an entire chapter to strategies for modernizing and revitalizing the institutions of the House. Of the report's twelve recommendations, the very first is to "reestablish an improved Office of Technology Assessment (OTA)" to help members understand the impact of new technologies. Although a recommendation to reestablish an OTA was not included in the final bill (H.Res.756), committee members acknowledged that current support for understanding technological advances in Congress lags behind the private sector and the executive branch. The testimony of Vic Fazio, a former Democratic congressman from California succinctly captures this sentiment[8]:

> The Houses should reestablish what was called in the past the Office of Technology Assessment... Technology affects the work of every committee. And perhaps new ways of making a similar institution more responsive to the needs of each committee might allow for its restoration. It is far too obvious that Members are behind the curve on technology. That glaring weakness causes you to lose credibility with an increasingly large number of your constituents.

The recurring proposals to reinstate the OTA or create a similar internal institution are a clear indication of the problem Congress faces: how to process and use the abundance of information available. There is no lack of information; numerous outside groups, experts, and lobbyists are eager to provide information to members of Congress. What Congress lacks, however, is what Warner and Tudor (2019) calls "absorptive capacity," which allows Congress to evaluate the quality and relevance of complex and technical information when applying it to policy proposals and legislation.

If the quantity of technical information were the core issue in eliminating the OTA, its abolition would have led to more invitations of research-based witnesses to the committees that relied heavily on the OTA. However, our analysis in this chapter shows that when partisan actions lead to a reduction in congressional capacity, it amplifies the reduced interaction between committees and outside experts on technology: The committees that relied most heavily on information produced within Congress experienced a drastic reduction in the number of technical and scientific witnesses who testified in hearings as a result of the Republican leadership's elimination of the OTA.

## 7.4 Summary

Our analysis shows that in-house legislative support agencies play a critical role in helping members of Congress evaluate and use technical information for policymaking, and that partisan motivations could impede this process. Today's Congress faces issues that require a deep understanding of complex technical and scientific issues underlying society's problems. In May 2021, the Congressional Research Service released a report listing "Science and Technology Issues in the 117th Congress," highlighting nearly fifty issue areas ranging from "Advanced Battery Energy Storage" to "Federal Law Enforcement Use of Facial Recognition Technology."[9] This list alone demonstrates the demand and need for technical information in congressional policymaking. Given the importance of science and technology in solving the pressing problems facing Congress combined with the evidence we present in this chapter, enacting the Select Committee on Modernization's recommendation to reestablish nonpartisan in-house agencies similar to the OTA could have a significant impact on improving congressional lawmaking.

### NOTES

1. https://ota.fas.org/legislation/testimonyfull_7-25-06.pdf
2. https://modernizecongress.house.gov/
3. https://crsreports.congress.gov/product/pdf/RL/RL31835
4. https://web.archive.org/web/19990427174200/http://www.house.gov/house/Contract/CONTRACT.html
5. www.nobelprize.org/prizes/medicine/1954/robbins/biographical/
6. Regression results are presented in Tables A11 and A12.
7. www.cbcfinc.org/wp-content/uploads/2020/01/Congressional-Reform-Report-Final-Design.pdf
8. https://docs.house.gov/meetings/MH/MH00/20190501/109377/HHRG-116-MH00-Wstate-FazioV-20190501-U1.pdf
9. https://crsreports.congress.gov/product/pdf/R/R46787

# 8

## Conclusion
### A Partisanly Informed Congress

Members of Congress make laws to affect climate change, but they are not scientists. They make laws to fight pandemics, but they are not doctors. They make laws to regulate agriculture, but they are not farmers. To make policy, legislators rely on others for information and various outside interests compete to satisfy this demand, attempting to shape the content and framing of legislation. This exchange of information, however, takes place in a highly politicized arena. Members have a serious role in policymaking, a role that requires information, but do so while they are political actors incentivized by political forces.

In this book, we argue that as Congress, its committees, and its members face their dual roles of lawmakers and politicians, partisan incentives shape the amount and type of information they receive. These dynamics provide opportunities for party leaders and interest groups to control information flows and influence public policy. Marshaling extensive new data on hearings and witnesses from 1961 to 2018 and using new methodological approaches that quantify the quality of information, we offer the first comprehensive analysis of the ways partisan incentives and institutional conditions influence how and from whom members of Congress seek information.

Our main theoretical insight is how partisan incentives determine when committees seek out witnesses during the committee process who can provide analytical input to policy decisions. We argue that the public nature of hearings allows committees to use hearings and witness invitations to convey information that can advance their policy goals or legitimize their actions. This creates a constant tension over how members' political goals encourage and discourage the production and dissemination of policy-relevant information. We develop a theory of how, under certain conditions, committees are more likely to seek witnesses who can provide analytical information rather than purely political information. Our framework incorporates how partisan incentives within three categories of institutional conditions – committee intent, interbranch relations, and congressional capacity – can affect the choice of to whom committees turn for external information.

## 8.1 Challenges in Informing Congress

Throughout the book, we use our extensive data to deliver empirical evidence within these three categories. In the first category (committee intent), when there is no bill to champion, members have political flexibility to hear from those who can provide expertise in policy development. In the second (interbranch relations), when the majority party secures unified government, it is assured of control over the policymaking process from inception to implementation and thus is incentivized to obtain information from the executive branch to help it develop and implement effective legislation in its favor. And in the third (congressional capacity), when party leaders provide committees with more internal resources, committees have the ability to select expert witnesses who provide specialized information.

We show how legislators strategically use a central institution of Congress – committees and their hearings – to acquire and disseminate information, ultimately influencing the development of policy in American democracy. Information is currency for members of Congress, and the importance of committee hearings as a venue for members to gather information from interest groups, bureaucrats, and other actors has long been recognized by congressional scholars (Curry, 2015; Krehbiel, 1991; Leyden, 1995). Understanding this process is particularly important when coupled with the fact that information is the input to policy production. As our book details, committees show an interest in policy learning and the acquisition of analytical information under limited conditions due to partisan incentives.

Our findings have important implications for congressional deliberation (Quirk and Bendix, 2011) and Congress's capacity to acquire information. Our book explains *how* partisan motivations can dominate serious policymaking deliberation and when committees have reduced incentives to seek and acquire the information necessary for technical policy development. This is made even more salient when considered in the context of increasing polarization and intensifying competition for majority control (Lee, 2015, 2016). In this final chapter, we relate our arguments and findings to the recent challenges Congress faced in seeking information in its partisan environment. We propose new lines of research that build on our data and work in our book and emphasize the connections to long-standing issues in American democracy.

### 8.1 CHALLENGES IN INFORMING CONGRESS

Recent institutional trends in Congress coupled with the types of issues legislators must address make it more difficult to inform Congress in a

## Conclusion: A Partisanly Informed Congress

highly partisan environment. First, as we show in Chapter 3, the number of hearings has declined in recent years. This is particularly troubling because hearings are important channels for experts, bureaucrats, and other groups to effectively communicate valuable information to members of Congress. Of course, Congress can receive information through other avenues, such as meetings with lobbyists, communications sent to members' offices, briefings, or other private meetings. However, a member of Congress may receive a report from a think tank in the mail but never read it. A member can meet with a lobbyist hired by a trade association but might not acknowledge the lobbyist's input beyond their private conversation. A member can have a one-to-one telephone conversation with a bureaucrat from an executive agency but would not hear the bureaucrat's responses to questions from other members of Congress.

Hearings position the information supplier in the same place and time as members of Congress, allowing strategic displays of Congress's information searches to others. In a congressional hearing, members of Congress receive information from witnesses in their committee rooms where members must directly acknowledge, engage with, and hear from other committee members as they respond to the same information. Moreover, this information is broadcast in a way that is observable by others; the committee hearing is a venue for both the acquisition and dissemination of information from witnesses.

In the House, the 101st Congress (1989–1990) was the high point with 2,200 hearings. In the Senate, the 96th Congress (1979–1980) ranks as the Congress with the highest number of hearings (1,429 hearings). However, in the 115th Congress (2017–2018), the House held a total of only 1,179 hearings, half the number held at its peak, and the Senate held only 485 hearings, about 34 percent of its chamber's peak.

While our book is concerned with *who* Congress invites to these hearings, there could be several reasons for the downward patterns in the *number* of hearings Congress organizes, such as polarization (McCarty, 2019a), fundraising pressures to secure the majority (Lee, 2016), the shift of power from committee chairs to party leaders (Ban, Moskowitz, and Snyder, 2021), and the rise of the lobbying industry as an alternative source of information for members from outside groups (Baumgartner et al., 2009; Drutman, 2015). As we show in Chapter 7, internal congressional capacity may also be an important factor in the decline in congressional hearing activity. We illustrate how partisan cuts to congressional capacity result in a lasting reduction in the ability and incentives of legislators to identify and acquire key scientific and technical information; these cuts may have affected Congress's ability to gather information more broadly.

## 8.1 Challenges in Informing Congress

In particular, long-term trends of decline in the number of congressional staffers along with the levels of their compensation reveal serious problems with Congress's internal capacity (LaPira, Marchetti, and Thomas, 2020). According to the Brookings Institute's Vital Statistics on Congress, the total number of committee staff in the House and Senate was 3,475 in 1991. That number dropped to 2,115 in 2015, and other statistics on staffing show a similar pattern. The Congressional Research Service (CRS), a congressional support agency that produces informative reports at the request of congressional offices, also experienced a staffing deficit. In 1989, the CRS had more than 800 employees; by 2015, it had 600. Among members' personal staff, the percentage of those working in members' Washington, DC, offices declined from 70 percent in the late 1970s to only 50 percent in the 2010s (LaPira and Thomas, 2016). These statistics suggest a clear pattern: Legislative resources within Congress have declined significantly over time, often due to party decisions (Crosson et al., 2021).

Staff compensation is another challenge to congressional internal capacity. Congressional staff are highly educated: According to the Congressional Staff Survey, most full-time staff have a bachelor's degree, and 20 percent earned a JD or PhD (Shepherd and You, 2020). However, their compensation does not match that of their peers in other industries. When inflation is taken into account, the median salary for most congressional staff has declined over time. In particular, legislative staff – who are primarily responsible for a member's legislative activities, such as legislative directors – have experienced significant declines in their salaries. In the 103rd Congress (1993–1995), the median salary for a legislative director was $75,000. In the 116th Congress (2019–2020), that number dropped to nearly $55,000 (Furnas and LaPira, 2020). At the same time, rents in the Washington, DC, area have increased so dramatically it is one of the most expensive cities in the nation. According to an analysis conducted by the nonprofit organization Issue One, 13 percent of DC-based congressional staffers do not make a living wage, which is $42,610 for an adult without children in Washington, DC (Ratliff, Neikrie, and Beckel, 2022). The decline in real wages for congressional staff is often cited as a reason the lobbying industry, which pays much more for the same skills, is an attractive option and why Congress has a problem of high staff turnover (LaPira, Drutman, and Kosar, 2020). Our book shows that the lack of internal capacity – often the result of partisan initiatives – affects the information acquisition of members of Congress. Congress will face an uphill battle in finding information if recent declining trends in congressional staffing and compensation continue.

A second challenge to informing Congress is that, in recent years, the majority of hearings were oversight or investigations of the executive branch, rather than legislative hearings. Recent trends suggest that this is due, at least in part, to the majority party in Congress using hearings as a partisan tool to embarrass or grandstand against an opposing party in the White House. For example, after narrowly winning the majority in the 2022 midterm elections, House Republican Leader Kevin McCarthy (R-CA) promised to prioritize investigations of the Biden administration as part of the Republican House agenda for the 118th Congress. A letter sent to the Department of Justice by Congressman Jim Jordan (R-OH04) – who would become the chairman of the House Judiciary Committee in the 118th Congress – sent a clear signal that a new Republican-controlled Judiciary Committee would conduct extensive oversight hearings into the DOJ's raid on President Trump's residence and the DOJ's investigation of Project Veritas, a conservative group accused of stealing the diary of Ashley Biden, a daughter of President Biden (Brownstein, 2022).

The partisan shift toward more oversight and investigative hearings has coincided with a decline in the number of legislative hearings. In Chapter 3, we showed that the number of legislative hearings had steadily increased through the 1980s and surpassed the number of oversight hearings. In the House, for example, 85 percent of the hearings in the 96th Congress (1979–1980) were legislative. Since then, the share of legislative hearings has declined sharply; the ratio of legislative hearings to oversight or investigative hearings reached a historic low of 43 percent in the 113th Congress (2013–2014). A similar trend occurred in the Senate. This increase of oversight and investigative hearings, combined with our findings, suggests that the informational function of congressional hearings for legislation – particularly the acquisition of analytical information necessary for technical policy development – is likely to continue to decrease if parties continue to spend more time on oversight and investigations. Also, as noted in Chapter 6, during divided government, committees control executive branch input by strategically lowering the frequency of bureaucratic appearances in legislative hearings. This behavior is likely to accelerate as parties continue to struggle to control government. Fierce competition for control of the White House and congressional majorities makes it more likely that this partisan priority will overtake information gathering for policy development.

This is particularly troubling in light of the third challenge facing Congress: the types of issues that members of Congress must address are becoming more complex, requiring higher rates of information acquisition and knowledge. From climate change to coronaviruses to artificial intelligence, new complex issues are emerging quickly and society is

## 8.1 Challenges in Informing Congress

changing at a rapid pace. A Senate hearing on the use of consumer data by social media companies offers one example. On April 10, 2018, the Senate Judiciary Committee held a hearing, "Facebook, Social Media Privacy, and the Use and Abuse of Data," with Facebook CEO Mark Zuckerberg as the main witness. The hearing was called by the committee's Democratic majority after news broke of Cambridge Analytica's possible exploitation of Facebook users' personal information during the 2016 presidential election. Noting growing criticism of how tech companies, such as Facebook, handle the personal information of their users, Chairwoman Senator Dianne Feinstein (D-CA) opened the hearing by remarking that the hearing is "the first step toward learning how this happened, who knew about these tactics, what can be done to prevent this in the future, and what else we can do to protect individual privacy and the integrity of our elections."

However, the news headlines did not focus on the committee's efforts to mitigate future election interference or regulate the potential misuse of users' social media data. Instead, they stressed the Senate's complete lack of knowledge about the underlying issue and highlighted partisan attacks on how social media companies did or did not help conservative campaign platforms. Coverage of this hearing was dominated by the following exchange between Senator Orrin Hatch (R-UT) and Mark Zuckerberg, in which Hatch exhibited his lack of knowledge about how social media platforms work:

Hatch: If a version of Facebook will always be free, how do you sustain a business model in which users don't pay for your service?
Zuckerberg: Senator, we run ads.

Understanding the influence of Big Tech – Apple, Amazon, Facebook, and Google – on Americans' daily lives, market competition, the spread of misinformation, and how to oversee them is one of the most pressing issues facing Congress. A hearing that could have informed members of Congress about how to protect the personal information of social media users or how the business of Big Tech differs from traditional business models went awry because legislators did not know – or were not incentivized to prepare – the right questions to ask (Ovide, 2020).

Issues such as climate change and global warming also require rapid government action, and members of Congress need analytical information for policy development. Since the release of the First Assessment Report in 1990 by the International Panel on Climate Change (IPCC), an international body established by the World Meteorological Organization (WMO) and the United Nations Environment Programme (UNEP) to assess the science of climate change, calls for action to reduce greenhouse gases and mitigate climate change have increased. However, the number of hearings on climate change remained low until the catastrophic event of Hurricane Katrina in 2005 (Weiner, 2007). In the 110th Congress, the number of hearings on climate change increased dramatically, largely driven by the newly created Select Committee on Energy Independence and Global Warming (later renamed the Select Committee on Climate Crisis). When the Democratic Party became the majority after the 2006 midterm elections, the newly elected Speaker of the House, Nancy Pelosi (D-CA), announced the plan to create the Select Committee on Global Warming, and Representative Edward J. Markey (D-MA) chaired the committee. Hearings held during the 110th and 111th Congresses, under the Democratic majority in the House, account for 47 percent of all climate change hearings held in Congress during the 100th–115th Congresses (1987 to 2018).

However, climate change is one of the most contentious issues that illustrates the stark partisan difference in opinions between Democrats and Republicans (Egan and Mullin, 2017). According to a Pew Research report released in April 2022, 71 percent of Democrats believed that human activities, such as burning fossil fuels, contribute a great deal to global climate change, while only 17 percent of Republicans believed the same. Congress showed a similar pattern of polarization regarding the frequency of hearings on climate change, as well as the types of witnesses invited to testify.

For example, on March 29, 2017, Lamar S. Smith (R-TX), chairman of the House Committee on Science, Space, and Technology, opened a hearing entitled, "Climate Change: Assumptions, Policy Implications, and the Scientific Method." Smith stated that, "Far too often, alarmist theories on climate science originate with scientists who operate outside of the principles of the scientific method … In the field of climate science, there is legitimate concern that scientists are biased in favor of reaching predetermined conclusions … Much of climate science today appears to be based more on exaggerations, personal agendas, and questionable predictions than on the scientific method." Chairman Smith's skepticism about the science behind climate change was reflected in the three witnesses invited to testify at the hearing. They all argued that climate science overemphasizes the human causes of global warming and that there was little scientific basis for concluding that greenhouse gases increase extreme weather events because of the uncertainties and complexities involved in climate science. The Democratic minority was able to secure a seat for one witness: Dr. Michael Mann, Distinguished Professor of Atmospheric Science at The Pennsylvania State University. Professor Mann's testimony highlighted the stark contrast between the consensus among scientists about climate change and the views presented by the Republican majority's invitees.

After all the witnesses delivered their prepared statements, each member of the committee asked questions that reflected close alignment with their partisan affiliations. For example, Chairman Smith dismissed Professor Mann's testimony by saying that "the 97 percent was derived from a small sample of a small sample" and Congressman Clay Higgins (R-LA03) asked if Professor Mann was "affiliated or associated with an organization called the Union of Concerned Scientists" inferring that Mann's testimony and assessment were politically motivated.

Under the Democratic majority, committee hearings on climate change often featured witnesses who emphasized human contributions to global warming and political interference (mostly by the Republican president and his political appointees) in the scientific process at the Environmental Protection Agency, the primary government agency regulating carbon emissions in the United States.[1] The story of the climate change hearing we present here summarizes the main message of our book: A committee's partisan incentives determine the witnesses who are invited to testify in hearings, which ultimately determines the types of information Congress gathers and disseminates to other stakeholders during hearings. The increasing polarization of issues intensifies challenges to Congress's ability to become informed in a timely manner and to develop effective policy responses.

## 8.2 HOW CAN CONGRESS BECOME BETTER INFORMED?

The US Congress is one of the most important collective decision-making bodies in the world, choosing outcomes with extensive scope and consequences that ripple throughout the globe. Thus, how and from whom members of Congress seek information in making those decisions is a matter of broad interest.

Congress can become better informed in various ways, but many possible reforms are nearly impossible, or at best limited, given the realities of partisan politics. In this final section, we briefly discuss two ideas that factor in a partisan environment. These ideas have the potential to help Congress and its members become better informed and more equipped to address the pressing, polarized issues facing society today.

First, *internal* congressional capacity matters. As our analysis of the defunding of the Office of Technology Assessment shows, when resources such as congressional support agencies or congressional staff are cut due to partisan incentives, congressional information-seeking is outsourced to outside groups and the lobbying industry, and the flow of information between Congress and the research community, particularly the scientific research community, diminishes. This is particularly problematic as the top issues Congress must consider, such as climate change and artificial intelligence, require expertise and experience in understanding scientific, technological, and other research findings.

Recently, demands to reform Congress and increase its internal capacity to prepare for these legislative issues have increased. Perhaps because congressional capacity has reached critically low levels and most Americans believe the US Congress is dysfunctional (Binder, 2015), these calls for reform have come from both sides of the partisan aisle. As an initial response, the 116th Congress established the House Select Committee on Congressional Modernization in 2019 with overwhelming bipartisan support. This bipartisan committee is composed of twelve members – six Democrats and six Republicans – whose mandate is to "investigate, study, make findings, hold public hearings, and develop recommendations on modernizing Congress" (H.Res.6, 116th Congress).

From its inception through 2022, this Select Committee has held 39 hearings and generated more than 200 recommendations. Hearing topics included "Strengthening the Lawmaking Process: How Data Can Inform and Improve Policy"; "Congressional Staff Capacity: Improving Staff Professional Development, Increasing Retention and Competing for Top Talent"; and "Modernizing the Congressional Support Agencies to Meet the Needs of an Evolving Congress." These titles indicate the committee's focus on building internal capacity; effectively recruiting talented congressional staff; retaining experienced congressional staff; and improving the functionality of existing congressional support agencies, such as the CRS. The committee's consistent focus on the role of technology and data in the policymaking process reveals that Congress itself recognizes the need to stay current and modernize its information-seeking resources.

A key policy recommendation in one of the committee's 2019 reports is the creation of an improved OTA: "The new OTA should be renamed the Congressional Technology and Innovation Lab and is intended to keep the House on the cutting edge of technology."[2] The recommendation states that the new OTA would serve as a liaison between Congress and experts in the scientific community, so members could receive expertise and advice from outside perspectives efficiently. Congress has not enacted this recommendation, but discussions about reestablishing the OTA continue and other measures to improve congressional capacity have been authorized.

The Select Committee also issued recommendations to improve staff retention and recruitment. As examples, they recommended that the Chief Administrative Office (CAO) of the House of Representatives regularly

## 8.2 How Can Congress Become Better Informed?

survey staff to gather information about their pay and benefits. This data would inform adjustments to compensation and benefits, thereby increasing staff retention. They recommended increasing the maximum pay rates for House staff and bringing congressional salaries up to levels competitive with the rest of the federal workforce. Speaker Nancy Pelosi took immediate action on those recommendations.

Second, the issue of witness diversity has begun to attract congressional lawmakers' attention. In 2019, the chairs of the Congressional Tri-Caucus – which includes the Congressional Hispanic Caucus, the Congressional Black Caucus, and the Congressional Asian Pacific American Caucus – announced a new initiative to increase diversity among witnesses. Following the announcement, the House Office of Diversity and Inclusion recently began tracking the geographic, racial, and sexual orientation of witnesses, albeit in broad and aggregate terms, beginning with witnesses in 2021. The *representation* of diverse voices in the transmission of information from outside groups to Congress is important. Because policymaking relies on information, then, normatively, representational concerns in policymaking are related to who exactly are the information providers and the racial, ethnic, gender, and geographic diversity of those information providers. In Chapter 3, we examined the gender ratio of congressional witnesses over time. Although the proportion of female witnesses in the House of Representatives increased from 8 percent in the late 1960s to 24 percent in the 2010s, there is still a significant gender gap in witness representation. If background or lived experience influences the information a witness can offer Congress, then increasing the diversity of those called to testify can bring a critical diversity of perspectives and opinions to the policymaking table.

The Tri-Caucus initiative brings this to the foreground and calls for an increase in the number of women and minority witnesses to reflect the demographic changes in American society itself. Existing research examines how a member's own gender and race, or the demographics of the member's district, may affect legislative activity, such as constituent service, public funding provisions, and committee participation rates (e.g., Broockman, 2013; Grose, 2011; Gamble, 2007). If a member's own identity or constituency influences these legislative activities, these factors also might influence how a member seeks out witnesses. Therefore, the ways a member's style or form of *representation* affects information-seeking behavior is a promising area for future research.

This is especially true in light of recent election results. After the 2022 midterm elections, it became clear that the 118th Congress would be the most racially and ethnically diverse Congress to date, with 124 members identifying as Black, Hispanic, Asian/Pacific Islander, or Native

## Conclusion: A Partisanly Informed Congress

American. A record number of women would also serve in the 118th Congress. As the composition of Congress becomes more demographically diverse, it may affect the types of witnesses that Congress invites or the types of information that members elicit from witnesses. Additionally, because congressional staff play an important role in organizing hearings and inviting witnesses, the diversity of staff may play a similar role. Women make up more than half of the staff on Capitol Hill, but comprise lower percentages in the top ranks of staff positions (Ritchie and You, 2021). Non-white individuals make up a very small percentage of congressional staff, currently less than 15 percent; they comprise even lower percentages moving up the ranks. The Select Committee on Modernization has held several hearings to discuss methods to diversify the pool of congressional staff. These conversations and efforts also may impact Congress's information-seeking behavior and bring new perspectives to the legislative process.

Another important dimension of representing diverse voices in informing Congress is the geographic location of witnesses. Given the vastly different experiences and economic conditions throughout the US, it is important for lawmakers to hear viewpoints from across the country. Although geographic representation is an important issue in congressional politics (e.g., Lee and Oppenheimer, 1999; Lee, 2000), it has received little scholarly attention regarding sources of information for policymaking. The public often expresses concern that politicians are susceptible to the culture of the Washington, DC establishment; this could lead to disconnection from ordinary Americans' perspectives on key policies.

One source of this concern is the disproportionately high representation of inside-the-Beltway witnesses in DC. Given that numerous influential trade associations, nonprofits, and think tanks are based in DC, it is not surprising that many witnesses live in the DC area. And, witnesses often pay for their own transportation to testify on Capitol Hill, which could increase the geographic and economic inequality of the witnesses who testify before Congress. Under House rules, travel expenses are reimbursed only if approved by the committee chair, but committees rarely support reimbursable transportation costs. Potential witnesses who live far from Capitol Hill, or do not have sufficient organizational financial resources to supplement or cover their travel there, face challenges in appearing at hearings.

A recent development in response to the COVID-19 pandemic offers a potential solution. Concerned about the transmission of COVID-19, Congress switched from in-person to virtual hearings during the height of the pandemic. On April 30, 2020, the Senate Homeland Security &

## 8.2 How Can Congress Become Better Informed?

Government Affairs Permanent Subcommittee on Investigations held the Senate's first virtual hearing; on May 15, 2020, the House of Representatives passed a rules change that allowed for virtual or hybrid hearings in which most witnesses would appear remotely. These virtual hearings have significantly reduced the financial burden of travel to Capitol Hill for witnesses living outside DC. This shift to virtual hearings provides an opportunity for researchers to examine how a reduction in the financial costs of testifying before Congress affected the witness types in geographic terms. The change in the hearing format also could increase the appearance rate of witnesses from organizations with lower levels of economic resources, which is often correlated with advocacy for minority interests.

As we note in the introduction, good public policy in a democracy depends on efficient and accurate information flows between those who have firsthand, substantive expertise and our elected legislators. We have shown how partisan and institutional conditions can affect to whom, why, and how often legislators turn to outsiders for information. By revealing the extent to which external groups are invited to testify at congressional hearings, understanding the partisan drivers of these invitation patterns, and showing how the type of information presented varies by group affiliation, our book highlights crucial ways in which external groups shape legislative processes. The debates described in this chapter are continuing in Congress. The exchange of information between external groups and politicians and how partisan politics and institutions shape this exchange are important considerations that Congress and American society must continue to address. Our book, empirical evidence, and accompanying analyses promote a new understanding of the dynamics underlying the acquisition and dissemination of information in Congress and, we hope, will stimulate further inquiry into the role of information in shaping public policy in a democracy.

### NOTES

1. www.govinfo.gov/content/pkg/CHRG-110hhrg62923/pdf/CHRG-110hhrg62923.pdf
2. From the committee report "Recommendations to Streamline House Human Resources, Overhaul the Onboarding Process, Improve Member Continuing Education Opportunities, Modernize House Technology, and Improve Accessibility" of the Select Committee on the Modernization of Congress, US House, issued on July 25, 2019.

# Appendix A

## A.1 APPENDIX FOR CHAPTER 3

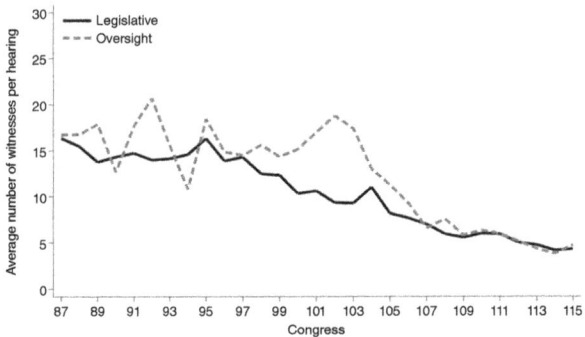

Figure A1 Number of hearings by type of hearing – House
Notes: Figure shows the average (mean) number of witnesses per hearing by hearing type in the House.

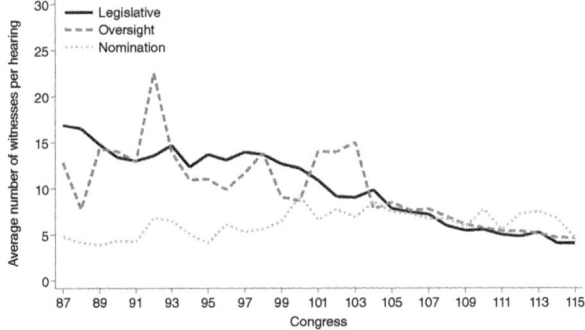

Figure A2 Number of hearings by type of hearing – Senate
Notes: Figure shows the average (mean) number of witnesses per hearing by hearing type in the Senate.

## Appendix A

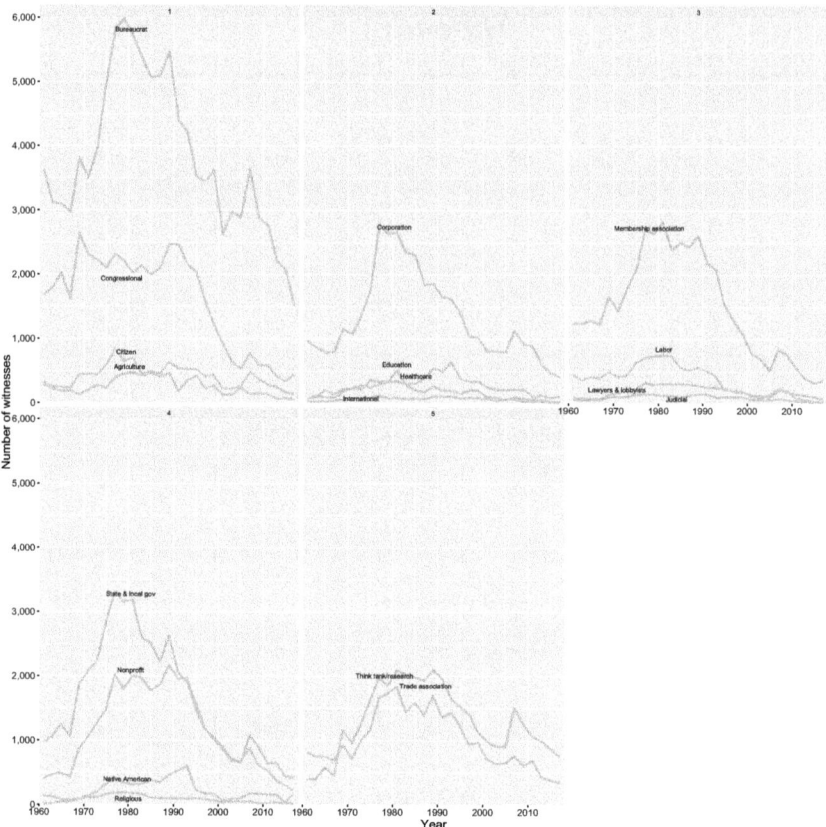

Figure A3 Number of witnesses by type – House
Notes: These figures show the number of witnesses in each type in the House for the period 1961–2018.

## A.1 Appendix for Chapter 3

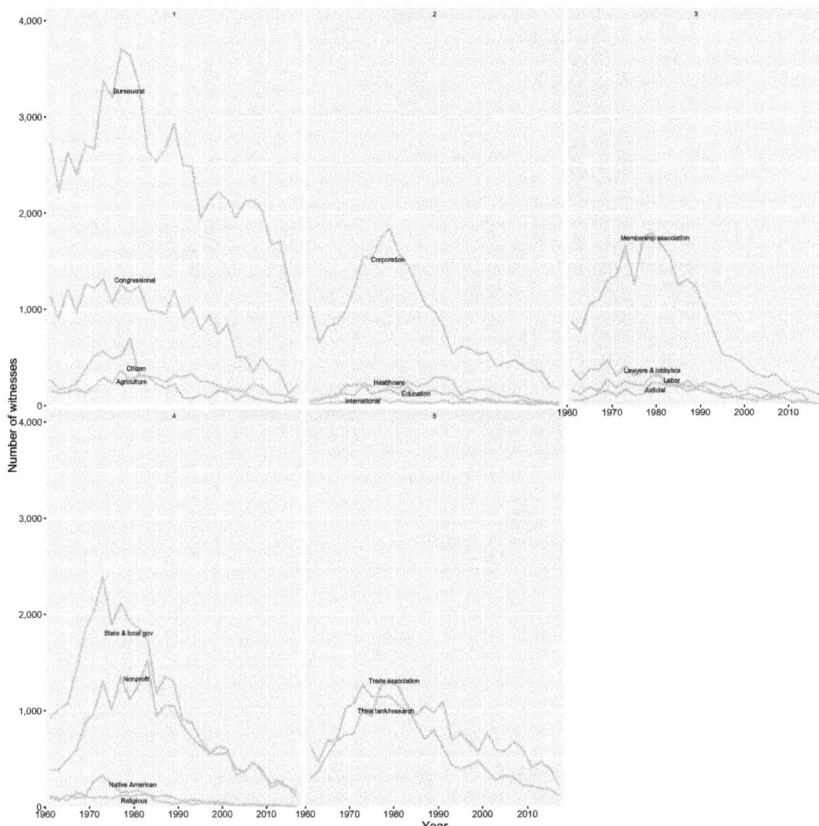

Figure A4 Number of witnesses by type – Senate
Notes: These figures show the number of witnesses in each type in the Senate for the period 1961–2018.

## Appendix A

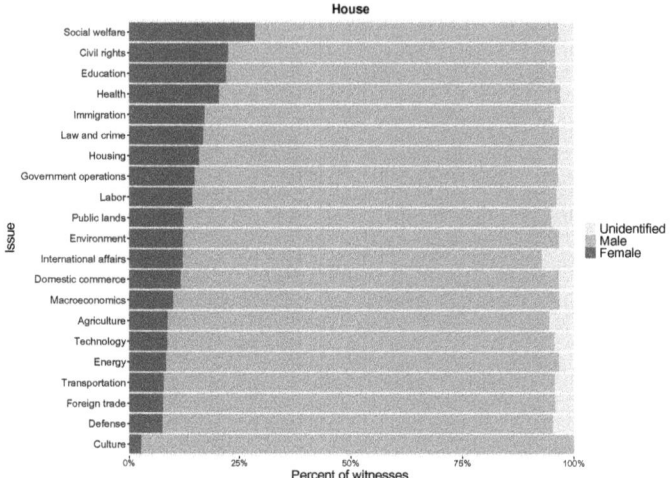

Figure A5 Witness gender composition by issue areas – House
Notes: This figure shows the gender composition of witnesses across hearing issue areas in the House.

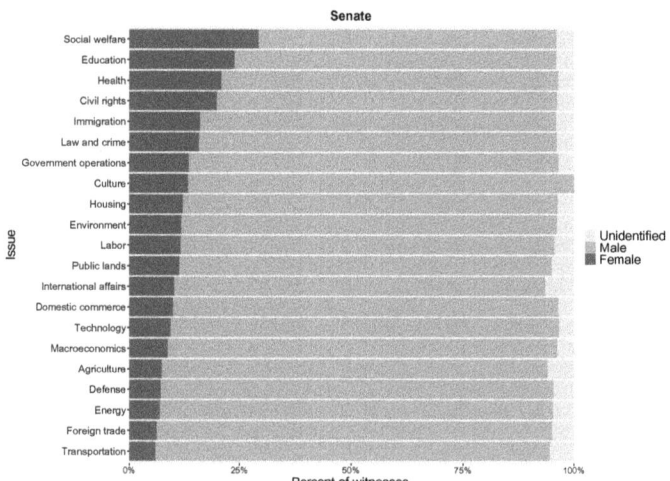

Figure A6 Witness gender composition by issue areas – Senate
Notes: This figure shows the gender composition of witnesses across hearing issue areas in the Senate.

## A.2 Appendix for Chapter 4

### A.2.1 The List of the 134 Keyword Stems

$, %, address, analit, analysi, analyt, answer, approxim, assess, associ, author, averag, awar, benefit, better, bill, budget, calcul, case, caus, chang, classif, classifi, comment, compar, comparison, consequ, consid, content, contrast, contribut, correct, correl, cost, criteria, data, decid, decis, decreas, degre, determin, determinist, diagnosi, diagnost, differ, discuss, disproportion, dollar, effect, empir, equival, estim, evid, examin, explain, fact, factor, feasibl, fund, higher, impact, implaus, imposs, improv, increas, indic, influenc, inform, interest, investig, laboratori, law, legisl, less, letter, level, list, lower, mean, measur, necessari, need, number, object, odd, percent, percentag, plan, plausibl, point, polici, possibl, predict, probabl, process, product, project, propos, rais, rank, rate, reason, recommend, record, reduc, refer, relat, report, requir, research, respond, respons, result, review, rise, risk, scienc, scientif, solut, solv, specif, standard, statement, statist, studi, substanti, survey, technolog, test, testifi, understand, unit, wors, yield

### A.2.2 The Most and Least Analytical Testimony
*With the Length Limit to Include 50 to 150 Words*
*The Most Analytical Statements*

1. "When projects are authorized, when there is a Chief's Report and the Congress authorizes a project, the economic analysis that is done on that calculates a benefit to cost ratio. And that benefit to cost ratio is based on a 3.125 discount rate. When the Office of Management and Budget evaluates projects for funding, including in the President's budget, that benefit to cost ratio is evaluated at a 7-percent discount rate. So the budgeting discount rate is different from the authorization discount rate that's used."
2. "We found that the differences are primarily – and this is a big amount of – the biggest chunk was in the estimate of labor costs associated with the subcontractors. There were costs also associated – of $1.2 billions – associated with engine cost that was a difference in the estimate; also $1 billion in terms of the production cost reduction plans, and also $800 million difference in terms of what the Air Force's plans for – relating to productivity investments."
3. "In terms of offsetting the costs and benefits, we did offset those costs, so the benefits are reduced by the amount of those costs in terms of attributing – and that's in the cost/benefit analysis, but in

# Appendix A

analyzing the costs and in analyzing the benefits, we did reduce the benefits by those costs."

*The Least Analytical Statements*

1. "Now, the access through public lands is, again, a heated debate. The President just drew an Executive Order declaring much of the border area and New Mexico as a monument, wilderness, whatever. They are all the same. Is the Organ Pipe National Monument, has that still got the signs up there requesting people not to go in there, American citizens, saying you should not go in there because it is too dangerous?"
2. "I guess we mistakenly believed that it was a secret location, and the only people who knew about it were the EOD staff from both SFPD, the FBI and the Sheriff's Office. Unbeknownst to us, this particular individual, and I won't say too much, but was a plumber in that area and apparently had seen the officers going into that area and perhaps followed them in."
3. "And don't forget by the way, sir, that we have right now – and the senator gets upset about this, but you have time to do this. We should do it this year. But we should adjust the system so that we get ready for 2017 when more money is going out than coming in, and we can do it."

*Without the Length Limit*
*The Most Analytical Statements*

1. "Well, when you say higher costs, higher costs overall or higher costs——-"
2. "It would increase confidence, lower expected tax rates, and lower real interest rates."
3. "That is correct. The President's budget proposes a funding level of $100 million."

*The Least Analytical Statements*

1. "Thank you. I am going to ask my colleague, Mike Connor, to take that question."
2. "Thank you very much, Mr. Souder, and your staff for helping to deal me in today. I found out about this yesterday morning, and I'm pleased to be here. I am a former college administrator and teacher. My name is Dean, but I was one once."
3. "If Congress would like to do that, I would be absolutely thrilled."

## A.2 Appendix for Chapter 4

### A.2.3 Topic Model Analysis

Table A1 *The featured words of each topic*

| Topic label | Highest probability words | Most frequent and exclusive words |
|---|---|---|
| Virus | vaccin, virus, year, cdc, blood, diseas, flu, influenza, immun, anthrax, dose, infect, mercuri, pandem, manufactur, season, protect, anim, case, use | vaccin, plasma, cjd, virus, thimeros, amalgam, chiron, flu, measl, influenza, mmr, tamiflu, antivir, h5n1, anthrax, mercuri, vaer, nile, season, midlothian |
| Lawmaking | issu, process, review, specif, recommend, believ, polici, standard, comment, meet, discuss, agenc, requir, regul, rule, decis, appropri, author, propos, concern | comment, rule, statut, criteria, advisori, commiss, draft, review, recommend, guidanc, board, input, specif, opinion, meet, standard, app, polici, process, expert |
| Inspection | medicar, provid, payment, program, plan, servic, contract, beneficiari, cms, manag, fee, claim, chang, requir, system, project, fraud, part, process, also | hcfa, cms, contractor, audit, bid, fraud, fee, contract, appeal, payment, beneficiari, oig, claim, construct, icd, y2k, hcfas, overpay, adjust, improp |
| Health insurance | insur, health, plan, coverag, busi, employ, benefit, cost, small, care, market, afford, employe, premium, compani, privat, pay, tax, peopl, state | insur, coverag, deduct, credit, employ, erisa, premium, aca, afford, subsidi, reinsur, busi, tax, uninsur, underwrit, medigap, fehbp, employe, ahp, small |
| Drug | drug, treatment, abus, use, program, state, enforc, substanc, addict, communiti, law, counti, problem, also, prevent, campaign, crimin, year, alcohol, methamphetamin | methamphetamin, meth, heroin, ecstasi, hidta, oxycontin, addict, traffick, buprenorphin, marijuana, offend, opioid, methadon, dea, naloxon, cocain, crime, pseudoephedrin, jail, prison |
| Analysis | data, report, studi, use, test, inform, risk, devic, evid, effect, base, safeti, result, clinic, collect, medic, assess, evalu, show, event | devic, data, reprocess, sampl, collect, advers, analysi, valid, test, analyz, studi, report, databas, survey, legionella, evid, analys, error, assess, event |
| Medication | drug, product, fda, market, compani, manufactur, price, prescript, state, pharmaci, industri, approv, consum, pharmaceut, generic, inspect, import, regul, safeti, suppli | counterfeit, generic, pharmaci, wholesal, brand, awp, heparin, formulari, inspect, cosmet, pharmacist, pbms, patent, antitrust, pharmaceut, ftc, fdas, adulter, chain, pedigre |

## Appendix A

### Table A1 (*continued*)

| Topic label | Highest probability words | Most frequent and exclusive words |
|---|---|---|
| Crisis management | health, state, work, public, depart, nation, respons, feder, local, need, effort, program, develop, new, system, secur, emerg, also, communiti, plan | dhs, homeland, disast, biowatch, prepared, local, secur, depart, capabl, infrastructur, katrina, fema, hhs, biosurveil, emerg, threat, partner, capac, terrorist, strateg |
| Veteran | veteran, servic, care, mental, health, medic, center, facil, program, militari, provid, need, member, famili, support, injuri, dod, nation, disabl, thank | servicememb, warrior, polytrauma, veteran, dav, legion, pva, tbi, armi, reed, visn, vet, vha, ptsd, prosthet, oefoif, marin, vas, soldier, cboc |
| Medicare & medicaid | percent, cost, year, program, state, medicar, medicaid, increas, million, rate, fund, budget, spend, 000, pay, dollar, billion, number, save, money | medicaid, spend, billion, budget, dollar, expenditur, cap, financ, revenu, cbo, averag, growth, per, estim, cut, senior, formula, debt, gdp, percentag |
| Disease | diseas, ill, brain, condit, caus, effect, symptom, can, disord, exposur, peopl, war, gulf, treat, problem, chronic, studi, use, one, treatment | mrsa, antibiot, resist, gulf, tuberculosi, staph, symptom, anabol, ill, asthma, brain, adhd, chelat, epilepsi, syndrom, nerv, respiratori, neurolog, fluid, receptor |
| Stem cell research & women's health | women, cell, prevent, american, human, suicid, diabet, health, organ, research, minor, transplant, stem, risk, death, rate, popul, clone, depress, donat | clone, embryo, embryon, abort, hpv, pregnanc, preterm, transplant, reproduct, postpartum, accutan, stem, cervic, smear, pap, african, hispan, racial, women, somat |
| Procedural | chairman, thank, bill, committe, law, question, member, hear, inform, record, offic, today, testimoni, ask, legisl, congress, statement, answer, act, protect | privaci, senat, letter, bill, hipaa, whistleblow, disclosur, file, constitut, statement, written, record, complaint, alleg, wit, apolog, page, legal, retali, memo |
| Youth health | children, famili, school, educ, parent, life, child, live, program, help, kid, young, need, student, age, autism, work, today, adult, peopl | footbal, parent, school, teacher, athlet, student, nfl, sport, boy, kid, child, children, pediatrician, coach, player, concuss, son, welfar, girl, church |

## A.2 Appendix for Chapter 4

### Table A1 (*continued*)

| Topic label | Highest probability words | Most frequent and exclusive words |
|---|---|---|
| Medical research | research, develop, new, institut, scienc, technolog, nih, diseas, fund, year, health, scientif, innov, import, invest, public, clinic, tobacco, support, need | smokeless, nanotechnolog, tobacco, nih, scienc, obes, genom, research, discoveri, biomed, irb, biotech, biotechnolog, pathway, innov, smoke, institut, acceler, dietari, cigarett |
| Medical practice | care, health, patient, hospit, physician, provid, system, medic, qualiti, servic, access, practic, nurs, improv, home, need, communiti, rural, primari, area | telemedicin, nurs, specialti, hospit, physician, rural, ehr, care, qualiti, primari, deliveri, electron, practic, practition, telehealth, home, dental, readmiss, access, reward |
| Medical treatment | patient, cancer, treatment, therapi, screen, medic, treat, medicin, breast, diseas, pain, year, clinic, hepat, imag, surgeri, altern, prostat, mani, test | prostat, radiat, chemotherapi, oncologist, oncolog, tumor, cancer, breast, imag, therapi, brachytherapi, scan, biopsi, screen, convent, imclon, mammogram mammographi, colon, surgeri |
| Experiential (Junk 1) | year, time, day, said, just, month, doctor, one, know, back, got, get, went, week, last, never, came, call, come, everi | went, cruis, told, came, knew, guy, got, night, gave, hour, took, day, never, said, walk, week, sat, noth, saw, room |
| Response (Junk 3) | can, get, make, know, right, sure, work, yes, abl, now, back, inform, number, want, need, take, come, put, give, actual | sure, yes, sir, exact, right, make, get, abl, absolut, folk, back, put, piec, correct, can, send, tell, give, whatev, check |
| Opinion (Junk 2) | think, one, thing, peopl, look, just, know, say, realli, way, need, lot, like, differ, talk, see, tri, kind, problem, want | think, realli, thing, kind, lot, sort, someth, say, probabl, talk, bit, look, tri, way, pretti, just, mayb, obvious, everybodi, idea |

# Appendix A

## A.2.4 Divided Government and Democratic Majority on Witness Testimonies

Table A2 *Regression results for divided government and Democratic majority*

|  | Dependent variable | | |
|---|---|---|---|
|  | Words (1) | Keywords (2) | Keywords/words (3) |
| Divided government | −72.055*** | −3.668*** | 0.0001 |
|  | (12.399) | (0.739) | (0.0003) |
| Democratic majority | 65.410*** | 2.574*** | −0.0002 |
|  | (12.777) | (0.762) | (0.0003) |
| Number of members | 5.649*** | 0.155** | 0.00000 |
|  | (1.054) | (0.063) | (0.00002) |
| Number of witnesses | −28.957*** | −1.659*** | −0.0001*** |
|  | (0.988) | (0.059) | (0.00002) |
| Female witness | −125.999*** | −5.323*** | 0.0004** |
|  | (10.636) | (0.634) | (0.0002) |
| Number of statements | 67.239*** | 3.443*** | −0.0001*** |
|  | (0.337) | (0.020) | (0.00001) |
| Bill | −91.697*** | −3.252*** | 0.001** |
|  | (10.806) | (0.644) | (0.0002) |
| Subcommittee hearing | −46.824*** | −0.146 | 0.001** |
|  | (13.708) | (0.817) | (0.0003) |
| \|Comm. Dem-Comm. Rep\| | −736.588*** | −43.934*** | −0.003 |
|  | (113.770) | (6.781) | (0.002) |
| \|Floor Median-Comm. Chair\| | −217.128*** | −12.908*** | −0.001 |
|  | (49.673) | (2.961) | (0.001) |
| \|Floor Median-Comm. Median\| | −594.310*** | −14.156** | 0.009*** |
|  | (107.088) | (6.383) | (0.002) |
| Prop. of female members | 436.711*** | 27.261*** | 0.005* |
|  | (132.822) | (7.916) | (0.003) |
| Avg. LES of committee | 7.403* | 0.366 | −0.00003 |
|  | (4.417) | (0.263) | (0.0001) |
| Constant | 2,310.755*** | 122.264*** | 0.052*** |
|  | (96.818) | (5.771) | (0.002) |
| Witness type FE | Yes | Yes | Yes |
| Issue FE | Yes | Yes | Yes |
| Committee FE | Yes | Yes | Yes |
| President FE | Yes | Yes | Yes |
| Observations | 32,512 | 32,512 | 32,512 |
| $R^2$ | 0.657 | 0.608 | 0.144 |
| Adjusted $R^2$ | 0.657 | 0.608 | 0.142 |

Notes: *$p < 0.1$; **$p < 0.05$; ***$p < 0.01$.

# A.3 APPENDIX FOR CHAPTER 5

Table A3 *Committee intent and witness invitation patterns – House*

**Panel A**

| Outcome = | (1) No.Witness | (2) Diversity | (3) Bureau | (4) Research | (5) Corp. | (6) Labor | (7) Trade | (8) Membership |
|---|---|---|---|---|---|---|---|---|
| Bill | 2.123*** | 6.460*** | −7.605*** | −1.919*** | −1.551*** | 0.578** | 1.939*** | 3.056*** |
|  | (0.314) | (0.522) | (0.765) | (0.365) | (0.385) | (0.247) | (0.497) | (0.490) |
| Subcommittee | −0.896 | 6.228*** | −5.019*** | 0.593 | 1.216*** | 0.0450 | 0.0750 | 0.838** |
|  | (0.548) | (0.736) | (1.682) | (0.830) | (0.414) | (0.173) | (0.530) | (0.382) |
| No. Comm. Members | 0.0403 | −0.0778 | −0.0234 | −0.00754 | 0.0100 | 0.0202 | 0.0526** | 0.0917 |
|  | (0.0448) | (0.0592) | (0.0994) | (0.0424) | (0.0336) | (0.0202) | (0.0204) | (0.0551) |
| \|Floor Median − Comm. Median\| | −0.112 | 6.150 | 1.592 | −5.113 | −4.653*** | 1.176 | 5.060*** | 6.209* |
|  | (4.393) | (3.831) | (8.129) | (4.155) | (1.608) | (1.413) | (1.688) | (3.272) |
| \|Comm. Dem − Comm. Rep\| | 5.022* | −6.330* | 6.439 | 4.844* | −0.660 | 1.322 | −0.267 | −3.379 |
|  | (2.887) | (3.351) | (4.951) | (2.397) | (1.665) | (0.986) | (1.326) | (2.025) |
| \|Floor Median − Comm. Chair\| | 2.243 | −0.194 | 4.686 | −1.854 | −0.0650 | 0.544 | −0.212 | −2.980 |
|  | (1.645) | (3.043) | (3.770) | (1.616) | (0.863) | (0.531) | (0.900) | (1.908) |
| Number of witness |  | 1.045*** | −1.009*** | 0.0668** | 0.119*** | 0.0285*** | 0.105*** | 0.145*** |
|  |  | (0.0988) | (0.0909) | (0.0267) | (0.0229) | (0.00702) | (0.0205) | (0.0216) |
| N | 30,994 | 30,983 | 30,983 | 30,983 | 30,983 | 30,983 | 30,983 | 30,983 |
| Adj. $R^2$ | 0.157 | 0.318 | 0.288 | 0.128 | 0.130 | 0.166 | 0.161 | 0.224 |
| Mean outcome var. | 9.8 | 53.6 | 34.8 | 9.3 | 8.1 | 2.2 | 5.7 | 7.8 |

Table A3 (continued)

*Panel B*

| Outcome = | (9) Agri. | (10) Cong. | (11) Judicial | (12) Local Gov. | (13) Lawyer | (14) Nonprofit | (15) Healthcare | (16) Other |
|---|---|---|---|---|---|---|---|---|
| Bill | −0.106 | 6.194*** | 0.222 | −1.216*** | 0.153 | 0.775*** | −0.0612 | −0.459* |
|  | (0.0869) | (0.518) | (0.185) | (0.316) | (0.116) | (0.245) | (0.102) | (0.222) |
| Subcommittee | 0.155 | 0.901** | 0.0196 | 0.559 | −0.0799 | 1.551*** | 0.181 | −1.034 |
|  | (0.0994) | (0.352) | (0.0860) | (0.486) | (0.143) | (0.402) | (0.154) | (1.084) |
| No. Comm. Members | −0.0142* | −0.0726* | 0.00255 | 0.00787 | −0.0149 | −0.0176 | −0.0162* | −0.0185 |
|  | (0.00783) | (0.0387) | (0.00510) | (0.0284) | (0.00996) | (0.0202) | (0.00885) | (0.0175) |
| \|Floor Median – Comm. Median\| | 0.496 | 0.0771 | −1.714 | −3.551 | −0.648 | 0.715 | −0.578 | 0.932 |
|  | (0.633) | (3.126) | (1.114) | (2.442) | (0.903) | (1.714) | (0.685) | (1.022) |
| \|Comm. Dem – Comm. Rep\| | −0.742 | −4.718* | 0.550 | −1.133 | −0.259 | −0.680 | 0.305 | −1.622 |
|  | (0.601) | (2.702) | (0.659) | (0.980) | (0.718) | (1.396) | (0.573) | (1.267) |
| \|Floor Median – Comm. Chair\| | 0.521 | −1.496 | −0.173 | 0.485 | −0.213 | −0.420 | 0.154 | 1.023 |
|  | (0.482) | (1.462) | (0.224) | (1.116) | (0.290) | (0.952) | (0.410) | (1.185) |
| Number of witness | 0.0358** | 0.0946** | −0.00596 | 0.200*** | 0.000859 | 0.120*** | 0.0196*** | 0.0789*** |
|  | (0.0170) | (0.0351) | (0.00541) | (0.0283) | (0.00287) | (0.0172) | (0.00384) | (0.0107) |
| N | 30,983 | 30,983 | 30,983 | 30,983 | 30,983 | 30,983 | 30,983 | 30,983 |
| Adj. $R^2$ | 0.332 | 0.146 | 0.087 | 0.175 | 0.065 | 0.091 | 0.253 | 0.074 |
| Mean outcome var. | 1.0 | 7.7 | 0.6 | 8.5 | 1.4 | 6.7 | 1.4 | 4.1 |

*Notes:* *$p < 0.1$; **$p < 0.05$; ***$p < 0.01$. Congress, committee, and issue FEs are included. Standard errors are clustered at the committee level.

Table A4 Committee intent and witness invitation patterns – Senate

Panel A

| Outcome = | (1) No.Witness | (2) Diversity | (3) Bureau | (4) Research | (5) Corp. | (6) Labor | (7) Trade | (8) Membership |
|---|---|---|---|---|---|---|---|---|
| Bill | 1.961*** | 6.264*** | −4.623*** | −2.458*** | −1.797*** | 0.510*** | 2.198*** | 2.784*** |
|  | (0.438) | (1.289) | (1.399) | (0.268) | (0.273) | (0.139) | (0.414) | (0.548) |
| Subcommittee | −0.462 | 4.769*** | −4.990*** | 0.816 | 1.462*** | −0.128 | −0.138 | 1.088*** |
|  | (0.536) | (0.654) | (1.087) | (0.621) | (0.285) | (0.170) | (0.264) | (0.302) |
| No. Comm. Members | 0.184* | −0.272* | 0.214 | 0.0322 | −0.0732* | −0.0147 | −0.119* | −0.0654 |
|  | (0.104) | (0.153) | (0.271) | (0.0907) | (0.0422) | (0.0166) | (0.0604) | (0.0517) |
| \|Floor Median − Comm. Median\| | 0.190 | −1.791 | 0.190 | −0.705 | −1.922 | 3.152 | −2.594 | −1.926 |
|  | (2.708) | (4.965) | (4.987) | (3.998) | (2.701) | (1.866) | (2.208) | (1.978) |
| \|Comm. Dem − Comm. Rep\| | 1.856 | 2.312 | −4.535 | 3.929 | −0.563 | −0.336 | −0.134 | 1.191 |
|  | (2.260) | (4.670) | (6.812) | (3.339) | (1.791) | (0.973) | (1.128) | (1.912) |
| \|Floor Median − Comm. Chair\| | −2.321 | 5.356 | −4.848 | 1.509 | 0.782 | −1.132** | 0.812 | −1.790 |
|  | (2.818) | (3.114) | (3.645) | (1.611) | (1.344) | (0.459) | (0.975) | (1.239) |
| Number of witness |  | 1.036*** | −0.946*** | 0.0676*** | 0.123*** | 0.0290** | 0.102*** | 0.161*** |
|  |  | (0.118) | (0.0928) | (0.0235) | (0.0275) | (0.0105) | (0.0214) | (0.0245) |
| N | 19,010 | 18,997 | 18,997 | 18,997 | 18,997 | 18,997 | 18,997 | 18,997 |
| Adj. $R^2$ | 0.156 | 0.329 | 0.301 | 0.109 | 0.143 | 0.188 | 0.163 | 0.168 |
| Mean outcome var. | 10.2 | 56.7 | 32.5 | 9.0 | 9.0 | 1.9 | 6.1 | 7.8 |

Table A4 (continued)

| Panel B<br>Outcome = | (9)<br>Agri. | (10)<br>Cong. | (11)<br>Judicial | (12)<br>Local Gov. | (13)<br>Lawyer | (14)<br>Nonprofit | (15)<br>Healthcare | (16)<br>Other |
|---|---|---|---|---|---|---|---|---|
| Bill | −0.0119 | 4.131*** | 0.397 | −1.138* | 0.648 | 1.188** | −0.0430 | −1.784*** |
|  | (0.103) | (0.607) | (0.262) | (0.568) | (0.402) | (0.473) | (0.0780) | (0.523) |
| Subcommittee | 0.161 | −0.231 | −0.0359 | 0.473 | 0.155 | 0.886*** | 0.121 | 0.361 |
|  | (0.0933) | (0.554) | (0.112) | (0.437) | (0.129) | (0.268) | (0.146) | (0.293) |
| Num. Comm. Member | −0.0439* | 0.0349 | 0.00611 | −0.0133 | 0.0217 | −0.00513 | −0.00751 | 0.0327 |
|  | (0.0241) | (0.0650) | (0.00866) | (0.0482) | (0.0179) | (0.0516) | (0.0190) | (0.0576) |
| \|Floor Median − Comm. Median\| | 0.269 | 2.657 | −0.582 | 2.817 | 1.657* | −3.711* | 0.284 | 0.413 |
|  | (0.746) | (2.040) | (0.592) | (1.963) | (0.916) | (2.025) | (0.967) | (2.232) |
| \|Comm. Dem − Comm. Rep\| | −0.879 | 0.658 | 1.042*** | −5.279** | 0.524 | 0.330 | 0.549 | 3.502 |
|  | (1.067) | (2.171) | (0.274) | (2.210) | (0.584) | (1.229) | (0.686) | (2.912) |
| \|Floor Median − Comm. Chair\| | 0.849* | −2.252 | −0.206 | 2.015 | 0.530 | 2.284** | 0.832* | 0.617 |
|  | (0.418) | (1.741) | (0.241) | (1.223) | (0.549) | (0.818) | (0.404) | (1.118) |
| Number of witness | 0.0380** | −0.0295 | 0.000817 | 0.239*** | −0.00196 | 0.103*** | 0.0180*** | 0.0968*** |
|  | (0.0151) | (0.0245) | (0.00245) | (0.0261) | (0.00578) | (0.0169) | (0.00506) | (0.0116) |
| N | 18,997 | 18,997 | 18,997 | 18,997 | 18,997 | 18,997 | 18,997 | 18,997 |
| Adj. $R^2$ | 0.339 | 0.098 | 0.132 | 0.146 | 0.077 | 0.085 | 0.273 | 0.061 |
| Mean outcome var. | 1.2 | 7.0 | 0.8 | 9.7 | 1.6 | 6.9 | 1.5 | 4.3 |

Notes: *$p < 0.1$; **$p < 0.05$; ***$p < 0.01$. Congress, committee, and issue FEs are included. Standard errors are clustered at the committee level.

## A.4 Appendix for Chapter 6

Table A5 *Mean share of expert and group witnesses by issue*

| Issue | Expert (%) | Group (%) | Issue | Expert (%) | Group (%) |
|---|---|---|---|---|---|
| Macroeconomics | 52 | 16 | Law and crime | 44 | 9 |
| Civil rights | 44 | 15 | Social welfare | 38 | 16 |
| Health | 44 | 16 | Housing | 43 | 19 |
| Agriculture | 40 | 20 | Domestic commerce | 52 | 23 |
| Labor | 37 | 31 | Defense | 70 | 12 |
| Education | 41 | 14 | Technology | 71 | 12 |
| Environment | 46 | 13 | Foreign trade | 58 | 21 |
| Energy | 60 | 15 | International affairs | 66 | 5 |
| Immigration | 52 | 10 | Government operation | 52 | 15 |
| Transportation | 50 | 23 | Public land | 36 | 11 |

*Notes:* Numbers indicate the average (mean) share (in percent) of expert witnesses (bureaucrat, think tank/research, and corporation) and group witnesses (labor union, trade association, and membership association) in legislative hearings in each issue area.

## A.4 APPENDIX FOR CHAPTER 6

Table A6 *Summary statistics of the variables*

| Variable | House Mean | SD | Min. | Max. | Senate Mean | SD | Min. | Max. |
|---|---|---|---|---|---|---|---|---|
| Number of witness | 9.88 | 10.58 | 0 | 99 | 10.23 | 10.35 | 0 | 97 |
| Witness diversity | 53.61 | 28.20 | 0 | 89.45 | 56.71 | 27.25 | 0 | 90 |
| Bureaucrat witness (%) | 34.83 | 33.82 | 0 | 100 | 32.59 | 32.39 | 0 | 100 |
| Congressional witness (%) | 7.79 | 16.10 | 0 | 100 | 7.03 | 13.78 | 0 | 100 |
| Research witness (%) | 9.37 | 17.62 | 0 | 100 | 9.04 | 16.44 | 0 | 100 |
| Bill attached | 0.32 | 0.47 | 0 | 1 | 0.41 | 0.49 | 0 | 1 |
| Subcommittee hearing | 0.83 | 0.37 | 0 | 1 | 0.59 | 0.49 | 0 | 1 |
| Number of committee members | 44.37 | 10.76 | 9 | 80 | 19.41 | 4.60 | 7 | 37 |
| |Floor Median – Comm. Median| | 0.07 | 0.06 | 0 | 0.43 | 0.07 | 0.06 | 0 | 0.33 |
| |Comm. Dem – Comm. Rep| | 0.67 | 0.15 | 0.20 | 1.08 | 0.62 | 0.12 | 0.26 | 0.97 |
| |Floor Median – Comm. Chair| | 0.21 | 0.12 | 0 | 0.75 | 0.16 | 0.11 | 0 | 0.57 |
| Democratic majority | 0.72 | 0.45 | 0 | 1 | 0.68 | 0.46 | 0 | 1 |
| Divided government | 0.65 | 0.48 | 0 | 1 | 0.49 | 0.50 | 0 | 1 |
| Number of hearings | 32,124 | | | | 19,772 | | | |

*Notes:* The table shows the summary statistics of the key variables that are used in the empirical analysis in Chapter 6.

Table A7 *Institutional characteristics and witness invitation patterns – House*

Panel A

| Outcome (%) = | (1) No.Witness | (2) Diversity | (3) Bureau | (4) Cong. | (5) Research | (6) Agri. | (7) Corp. | (8) Trade |
|---|---|---|---|---|---|---|---|---|
| Divide government | −0.468 | 0.313 | −2.613** | 0.965** | 2.151*** | 0.161* | 0.238 | −0.0239 |
|  | (0.340) | (0.766) | (0.941) | (0.344) | (0.691) | (0.0818) | (0.405) | (0.272) |
| Democratic majority | 0.150 | 0.450 | −1.421 | −0.375 | 1.374* | −0.379** | 0.486* | −1.172*** |
|  | (0.319) | (1.152) | (1.217) | (0.438) | (0.727) | (0.137) | (0.272) | (0.341) |
| Bill | 2.149*** | 6.422*** | −7.533*** | 6.188*** | −1.943*** | −0.106 | −1.574*** | 1.926*** |
|  | (0.317) | (0.540) | (0.785) | (0.522) | (0.362) | (0.0842) | (0.376) | (0.501) |
| Bubcommittee | −0.909 | 6.131*** | −4.961*** | 0.854** | 0.580 | 0.147 | 1.199*** | 0.0621 |
|  | (0.545) | (0.732) | (1.660) | (0.341) | (0.834) | (0.0976) | (0.415) | (0.526) |
| No. Comm. Members | 0.0352 | −0.0166 | −0.0507 | −0.0765* | 0.00658 | −0.0142* | 0.0151 | 0.0527** |
|  | (0.0402) | (0.0551) | (0.0910) | (0.0390) | (0.0389) | (0.00698) | (0.0302) | (0.0203) |
| \|Floor Median − Comm. Median\| | −0.187 | 6.737 | 0.984 | 0.251 | −4.310 | 0.369 | −4.667*** | 5.078*** |
|  | (4.287) | (4.797) | (8.459) | (3.074) | (4.120) | (0.532) | (1.564) | (1.591) |
| \|Comm. Dem − Comm. Rep\| | 5.418* | −6.674* | 6.445 | −5.356** | 4.514* | −0.746 | −0.211 | −0.0954 |
|  | (2.741) | (3.445) | (4.890) | (2.614) | (2.290) | (0.610) | (1.544) | (1.330) |
| \|Floor Median − Comm. Chair\| | 1.974 | −0.812 | 4.409 | −1.565 | −1.564 | 0.475 | −0.308 | −0.209 |
|  | (1.629) | (3.241) | (3.682) | (1.495) | (1.515) | (0.466) | (0.978) | (0.933) |
| Number of witness |  | 1.043*** | −1.005*** | 0.0965** | 0.0650** | 0.0355** | 0.119*** | 0.105*** |
|  |  | (0.0987) | (0.0910) | (0.0351) | (0.0267) | (0.0169) | (0.0229) | (0.0205) |
| N | 30,994 | 30,983 | 30,983 | 30,983 | 30,983 | 30,983 | 30,983 | 30,983 |
| Adj. $R^2$ | 0.154 | 0.316 | 0.287 | 0.145 | 0.128 | 0.332 | 0.130 | 0.161 |
| Mean outcome var. | 9.8 | 53.6 | 34.8 | 7.7 | 9.3 | 1.0 | 8.1 | 5.7 |

| Panel B Outcome (%) = | (9) Judicial | (10) Local Gov. | (11) Lawyer | (12) Labor | (13) Nonprofit | (14) Healthcare | (15) Membership | (16) Other |
|---|---|---|---|---|---|---|---|---|
| Divided government | −0.0387 | 0.108 | 0.290* | −0.410*** | −0.224 | −0.214 | −0.659 | 0.271 |
| | (0.0504) | (0.270) | (0.152) | (0.135) | (0.278) | (0.163) | (0.396) | (0.365) |
| Democratic majority | 0.0723 | −0.287 | 0.361** | 0.340*** | 0.572 | −0.0582 | −0.114 | 0.601 |
| | (0.0993) | (0.457) | (0.172) | (0.100) | (0.531) | (0.162) | (0.484) | (0.564) |
| Bill | 0.223 | −1.212*** | 0.152 | 0.584** | 0.774*** | −0.0632 | 3.057*** | −0.475** |
| | (0.185) | (0.320) | (0.116) | (0.245) | (0.246) | (0.103) | (0.493) | (0.215) |
| Subcommittee | 0.0210 | 0.558 | −0.0684 | 0.0518 | 1.577*** | 0.176 | 0.842** | −1.041 |
| | (0.0848) | (0.481) | (0.141) | (0.173) | (0.403) | (0.152) | (0.369) | (1.075) |
| Num. Comm. Members | 0.00256 | 0.0176 | −0.0131 | 0.0176 | −0.0137 | −0.0137 | 0.0861* | −0.0162 |
| | (0.00510) | (0.0283) | (0.00923) | (0.0187) | (0.0196) | (0.00837) | (0.0491) | (0.0183) |
| \|Floor Median − Comm. Median\| | −1.707 | −3.758 | −0.579 | 0.877 | 0.902 | −0.436 | 6.057* | 0.938 |
| | (1.110) | (2.494) | (0.979) | (1.284) | (1.618) | (0.676) | (3.150) | (1.043) |
| \|Comm. Dem − Comm. Rep\| | 0.445 | −0.644 | −0.297 | 1.456 | −0.860 | −0.0215 | −3.424* | −1.205 |
| | (0.632) | (0.963) | (0.650) | (1.030) | (1.409) | (0.604) | (1.957) | (1.124) |
| \|Floor Median − Comm. Chair\| | −0.112 | 0.596 | −0.135 | 0.449 | −0.399 | 0.174 | −2.894 | 1.084 |
| | (0.196) | (1.182) | (0.327) | (0.508) | (0.926) | (0.406) | (1.982) | (1.078) |
| Number of witness | −0.00611 | 0.200*** | 0.000304 | 0.0286*** | 0.119*** | 0.0192*** | 0.145*** | 0.0781*** |
| | (0.00528) | (0.0284) | (0.00290) | (0.00723) | (0.0172) | (0.00383) | (0.0213) | (0.0107) |
| N | 30,983 | 30,983 | 30,983 | 30,983 | 30,983 | 30,983 | 30,983 | 30,983 |
| Adj. $R^2$ | 0.087 | 0.175 | 0.065 | 0.165 | 0.090 | 0.253 | 0.225 | 0.074 |
| Mean outcome var. | 9.6 | 8.5 | 1.4 | 2.2 | 6.7 | 1.4 | 7.8 | 4.1 |

Notes: *$p < 0.1$; **$p < 0.05$; ***$p < 0.01$. President, committee, and issue FEs are included. Standard errors are clustered at the committee level.

Table A8 *Institutional characteristics and witness invitation patterns – Senate*

| Panel A<br>Outcome (%) = | (1)<br>No. Witness | (2)<br>Diversity | (3)<br>Bureau | (4)<br>Cong. | (5)<br>Research | (6)<br>Agri. | (7)<br>Corp. | (8)<br>Trade |
|---|---|---|---|---|---|---|---|---|
| Divided government | −0.595* | 1.157 | −3.025*** | −0.00285 | 1.042 | 0.0388 | 0.736** | 0.623* |
|  | (0.337) | (1.010) | (0.775) | (0.432) | (0.726) | (0.108) | (0.328) | (0.359) |
| Democratic majority | −0.0806 | 0.789 | 1.270 | −0.272 | −0.313 | −0.187* | −0.658 | −1.207*** |
|  | (0.221) | (0.930) | (0.781) | (0.462) | (0.655) | (0.0931) | (0.424) | (0.283) |
| Bill | 1.964*** | 6.304*** | −4.678*** | 4.111*** | −2.434*** | −0.0135 | −1.741*** | 2.211*** |
|  | (0.417) | (1.264) | (1.357) | (0.589) | (0.268) | (0.101) | (0.287) | (0.412) |
| Subcommittee | −0.449 | 4.763*** | −4.941*** | −0.233 | 0.775 | 0.168* | 1.454*** | −0.146 |
|  | (0.529) | (0.668) | (1.075) | (0.565) | (0.610) | (0.0958) | (0.298) | (0.266) |
| Num. Comm. Member | 0.143** | −0.157 | 0.0670 | 0.0423 | 0.0340 | −0.0282 | −0.0312 | −0.0749 |
|  | (0.0552) | (0.110) | (0.153) | (0.0499) | (0.0658) | (0.0166) | (0.0326) | (0.0451) |
| \|Floor Median − Comm. Median\| | 0.120 | −3.149 | −0.730 | 1.705 | 1.224 | 0.0408 | −3.237 | −2.321 |
|  | (2.676) | (5.594) | (4.588) | (2.115) | (4.434) | (0.753) | (2.447) | (2.113) |
| \|Comm. Dem − Comm. Rep\| | 1.515 | 3.139 | −5.965 | 0.293 | 4.749 | −0.850 | −0.160 | −0.00290 |
|  | (2.098) | (4.875) | (6.297) | (2.239) | (3.148) | (1.017) | (2.054) | (1.196) |
| \|Floor Median − Comm. Chair\| | −1.894 | 5.424* | −4.754 | −1.666 | 0.874 | 0.901* | 0.506 | 1.013 |
|  | (3.002) | (2.871) | (4.017) | (1.658) | (1.715) | (0.433) | (1.293) | (0.861) |
| Num. witness |  | 1.037*** | −0.943*** | −0.0282 | 0.0676*** | 0.0379** | 0.122*** | 0.101*** |
|  |  | (0.120) | (0.0933) | (0.0244) | (0.0232) | (0.0152) | (0.0280) | (0.0214) |
| N | 19,010 | 18,997 | 18,997 | 18,997 | 18,997 | 18,997 | 18,997 | 18,997 |
| Adj. $R^2$ | 0.153 | 0.329 | 0.300 | 0.096 | 0.107 | 0.339 | 0.142 | 0.163 |
| Mean outcome var. | 10.2 | 56.7 | 32.5 | 7.0 | 9.0 | 1.2 | 9.0 | 6.1 |

| Panel B<br>Outcome (%) = | (9)<br>Judicial | (10)<br>Local Gov. | (11)<br>Lawyer | (12)<br>Labor | (13)<br>Nonprofit | (14)<br>Healthcare | (15)<br>Membership | (16)<br>Other |
|---|---|---|---|---|---|---|---|---|
| Divided government | 0.121 | −0.281 | 0.00635 | −0.0307 | 0.374 | 0.126 | −0.0950 | 0.367 |
|  | (0.124) | (0.437) | (0.0861) | (0.136) | (0.304) | (0.222) | (0.392) | (0.300) |
| Democratic majority | 0.0197 | 0.0613 | 0.115 | 0.340* | 0.404 | 0.301* | −0.112 | 0.237 |
|  | (0.0785) | (0.459) | (0.209) | (0.187) | (0.369) | (0.147) | (0.505) | (0.348) |
| Bill | 0.377 | −1.139* | 0.636 | 0.519*** | 1.202** | −0.0502 | 2.759*** | −1.759*** |
|  | (0.257) | (0.556) | (0.404) | (0.140) | (0.463) | (0.0769) | (0.538) | (0.525) |
| Subcommittee | −0.0331 | 0.498 | 0.152 | −0.127 | 0.883*** | 0.122 | 1.075*** | 0.354 |
|  | (0.112) | (0.438) | (0.125) | (0.172) | (0.264) | (0.147) | (0.304) | (0.298) |
| Num. Comm. Member | −0.000685 | 0.0269 | −0.00131 | −0.0133 | 0.0164 | −0.00107 | −0.0656 | 0.0297 |
|  | (0.00772) | (0.0329) | (0.0171) | (0.0151) | (0.0343) | (0.0136) | (0.0418) | (0.0331) |
| \|Floor Median − Comm. Median\| | −0.636 | 2.726 | 2.348** | 3.168 | −3.497 | 0.236 | −1.424 | 0.396 |
|  | (0.618) | (1.773) | (1.030) | (1.916) | (2.044) | (0.988) | (2.054) | (2.250) |
| \|Comm. Dem − Comm. Rep\| | 1.215** | −5.147** | 0.683 | −0.643 | 0.828 | 0.549 | 1.333 | 3.119 |
|  | (0.434) | (2.204) | (0.519) | (0.889) | (1.073) | (0.648) | (1.985) | (2.892) |
| \|Floor Median − Comm. Chair\| | −0.447 | 2.132* | 0.491 | −0.992** | 2.302*** | 0.837* | −1.851 | 0.654 |
|  | (0.359) | (1.138) | (0.603) | (0.458) | (0.748) | (0.433) | (1.146) | (1.181) |
| Num. Witness | 0.000184 | 0.239*** | −0.00189 | 0.0288** | 0.103*** | 0.0179*** | 0.160*** | 0.0961*** |
|  | (0.00262) | (0.0266) | (0.00561) | (0.0104) | (0.0168) | (0.00503) | (0.0238) | (0.0116) |
| N | 18,997 | 18,997 | 18,997 | 18,997 | 18,997 | 18,997 | 18,997 | 18,997 |
| Adj. $R^2$ | 0.131 | 0.145 | 0.076 | 0.188 | 0.085 | 0.273 | 0.167 | 0.061 |
| Mean outcome var. | 0.9 | 9.7 | 1.6 | 1.9 | 6.9 | 1.5 | 7.8 | 4.3 |

Notes: *$p < 0.1$; **$p < 0.05$; ***$p < 0.01$. President, committee, and issue FEs are included. Standard errors are clustered at committee level.

## Appendix A

Table A9 *Divided government, President's issue priority, and bureaucrats as witnesses – House*

| Outcome = bureaucrat as witness (%) | (1) | (2) | (3) |
|---|---|---|---|
| Divided government | −2.153** | −0.292 | −1.304* |
| | (0.796) | (0.897) | (0.694) |
| Issue decile[a] | | 0.401** | |
| | | (0.169) | |
| Divided government × issue decile | | −0.384** | |
| | | (0.147) | |
| High salient issue[b] | | | 1.704** |
| | | | (0.687) |
| Divided government × high salient issue | | | −1.562** |
| | | | (0.683) |
| Controls | ☐ | ☐ | ☐ |
| N | 31,773 | 27,270 | 31,773 |
| Adj. $R^2$ | 0.275 | 0.277 | 0.275 |

*Notes:* $*p < 0.1$; $**p < 0.05$; $***p < 0.01$. President and committee FEs are included. Standard errors are clustered at the committee level. Hearing- and committee-level controls are included. a: President's issue priority measure based on the State of the Union speeches. It ranges from 1 to 10: 1 = least frequently mentioned issue, 10 = most frequently mentioned issue. b: 1 if *issue decile* ≥ 5 and 0 otherwise.

Table A10 *Divided government, President's issue priority, and bureaucrats as witnesses – Senate*

| Outcome = bureaucrat as witness (%) | (1) | (2) | (3) |
|---|---|---|---|
| Divided government | −2.836*** | −2.044** | −2.691*** |
| | (0.877) | (0.737) | (0.717) |
| Issue decile[a] | | 0.324* | |
| | | (0.166) | |
| Divided government × issue decile | | −0.147 | |
| | | (0.296) | |
| High salient issue[b] | | | 1.855** |
| | | | (0.783) |
| Divided government × high salient issue | | | −0.827 |
| | | | (1.368) |
| Controls | ☐ | ☐ | ☐ |
| N | 19,466 | 16,310 | 19,466 |
| Adj. $R^2$ | 0.279 | 0.286 | 0.280 |

*Notes:* $*p < 0.1$; $**p < 0.05$; $***p < 0.01$. President and committee FEs are included. Standard errors are clustered at the committee level. Hearing- and committee-level controls are included. a: President's issue priority measure based on the State of the Union speeches. It ranges from 1 to 10: 1 = least frequently mentioned issue, 10 = most frequently mentioned issue. b: 1 if *issue decile* ≥ 5 and 0 otherwise.

## A.5 Appendix for Chapter 7

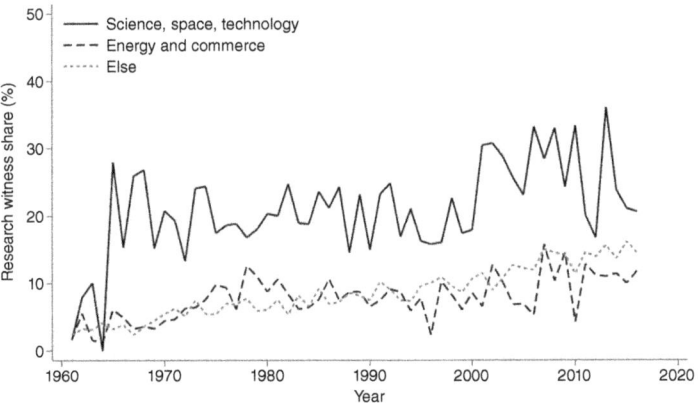

Figure A7 Research witness shares
Notes: It shows the share (%) of the research witnesses (witness from think tanks and universities) in three different types of committees in the House.

Table A11 *OTA elimination on the number of invited witness*

| Variable | Coef. | Std. Err. | t-stat | P-value | [95% conf. | interval] |
|---|---|---|---|---|---|---|
| Treated | −0.0183 | 0.6563 | −0.03 | 0.978 | −1.3833 | 1.3466 |
| 101th Congress | 0.0208 | 0.2794 | 0.07 | 0.941 | −0.5603 | 0.6020 |
| 102th Congress | −0.7329 | 0.4251 | −1.72 | 0.099 | −1.6169 | 0.1511 |
| 103th Congress | −0.9991 | 0.6318 | −1.58 | 0.129 | −2.3130 | 0.3148 |
| 104th Congress | 0.9819 | 0.5590 | 1.76 | 0.094 | −0.1806 | 2.1444 |
| 105th Congress | −1.6116 | 0.6859 | −2.35 | 0.029 | −3.0381 | −0.1851 |
| 106th Congress | −1.9415 | 0.6694 | −2.9 | 0.009 | −3.3337 | −0.5493 |
| treatedX101th Congress | −0.6811 | 0.4862 | −1.4 | 0.176 | −1.6922 | 0.3300 |
| treatedX102th Congress | −0.0100 | 0.5651 | −0.02 | 0.986 | −1.1852 | 1.1652 |
| treatedX103th Congress | −0.2014 | 0.8994 | −0.22 | 0.825 | −2.0718 | 1.6690 |
| treatedX104th Congress | −2.0086 | 0.6082 | −3.3 | 0.003 | −3.2734 | −0.7438 |
| treatedX105th Congress | −0.5624 | 0.7880 | −0.71 | 0.483 | −2.2012 | 1.0764 |
| treatedX106th Congress | −1.1619 | 0.7721 | −1.5 | 0.147 | −2.7676 | 0.4439 |
| Bill | 2.2112 | 0.4534 | 4.88 | 0 | 1.2684 | 3.1541 |
| Subcommittee | −1.1215 | 0.8328 | −1.35 | 0.192 | −2.8534 | 0.6104 |
| Number of committee member | −0.0154 | 0.0413 | −0.37 | 0.712 | −0.1014 | 0.0705 |

Notes: Number of observation is 10,179. Prob > F = 0.0000. Adj. $R^2$ = 0.0677. Issue fixed effects are included. Standard errors are clustered at the committee level.

Table A12 *OTA elimination on the invitation of research witness*

| Variable | Coef. | Std. Err. | t-stat | P-value | [95% conf. | interval] |
|---|---|---|---|---|---|---|
| Treated | 3.993364 | 2.7699 | 1.4400 | 0.1640 | −1.766887 | 9.753615 |
| 101th Congress | −0.3568618 | 0.4594 | −0.7800 | 0.4460 | −1.312171 | 0.5984473 |
| 102th Congress | 1.250601 | 0.9309 | 1.3400 | 0.1930 | −0.6853599 | 3.186562 |
| 103th Congress | −0.5356855 | 0.8278 | −0.6500 | 0.5250 | −2.257258 | 1.185887 |
| 104th Congress | 1.045746 | 0.9077 | 1.1500 | 0.2620 | −0.8420227 | 2.933514 |
| 105th Congress | 1.103274 | 0.9820 | 1.1200 | 0.2740 | −0.9388484 | 3.145397 |
| 106th Congress | 0.7270946 | 0.9801 | 0.7400 | 0.4660 | −1.31112 | 2.765309 |
| treatedX101th Congress | 0.0767433 | 0.5936 | 0.1300 | 0.8980 | −1.157769 | 1.311256 |
| treatedX102th Congress | 0.4090257 | 1.8902 | 0.2200 | 0.8310 | −3.521845 | 4.339896 |
| treatedX103th Congress | 0.6340882 | 1.0286 | 0.6200 | 0.5440 | −1.504983 | 2.773159 |
| treatedX104th Congress | −4.594514 | 0.6603 | −6.9600 | 0.0000 | −5.967743 | −3.221285 |
| treatedX105th Congress | −1.748871 | 0.8168 | −2.1400 | 0.0440 | −3.447461 | −0.0502822 |
| treatedX106th Congress | −3.706158 | 0.9647 | −3.8400 | 0.0010 | −5.712429 | −1.699888 |
| Bill | −1.811747 | 0.5606 | −3.2300 | 0.0040 | −2.977584 | −0.6459086 |
| Subcommittee | −2.064094 | 1.5808 | −1.3100 | 0.2060 | −5.351648 | 1.22346 |
| Number of committee member | 0.0176605 | 0.0659 | 0.2700 | 0.7910 | −0.1193818 | 0.1547028 |

*Notes*: Number of observation is 10,172. Prob > F = 0.0000. Adj. $R^2$ = 0.0787. Issue fixed effects are included. Standard errors are clustered at the committee level.

# References

Aberbach, Joel D. 1990. *Keeping a Watchful Eye: The Politics of Congressional Oversight*. Brookings Institution Press.

Albert, Kyle. 2013. "An Analysis of Labor Union Participation in U.S. Congressional Hearings." *Sociological Forum* 28 (3): 574–596.

Andersen, Simon Calmar, and Donald Moynihan. 2016. "Bureaucratic Investments in Expertise: Evidence from a Randomized Controlled Field Trial." *Journal of Politics* 78 (4): 1032–1044.

Arnold, Douglas. 1990. *The Logic of Congressional Action*. Yale University Press.

Austen-Smith, David. 1990a. "Credible Debate Equilibria." *Social Choice and Welfare* 7: 75–93.

Austen-Smith, David. 1990b. "Information Transmission in Debate." *American Journal of Political Science* 34 (1): 124–152.

Austen-Smith, David. 1993. "Information and Influence: Lobbying for Agendas and Votes." *American Journal of Political Science* 37 (3): 799–833.

Austen-Smith, David, and William H. Riker. 1987. "Asymmetric Information and the Coherence of Legislation." *American Political Science Review* 81 (3): 897–918.

Austen-Smith, David, and William H. Riker. 1990. "Asymmetric Information and the Coherence of Legislation: A Correction." *American Political Science Review* 84 (1): 243–245.

Awad, Emiel. 2020. "Persuasive Lobbying with Allied Legislators." *American Journal of Political Science* 64 (4): 938–951.

Awad, Emiel, and Clement Minaudier. 2024. "Friendly Lobbying under Time Pressure." *American Journal of Political Science* 68 (2): 529–543.

Ballard, Andrew O., and James M. Curry. 2021. "Minority Party Capacity in Congress." *American Political Science Review* 115 (4): 1388–1405.

Ban, Pamela, Daniel Moskowitz, and James M. Snyder. 2021. "Leadership Power in Congress, 1890–2014: Evidence from PAC Contributions and Newspaper Coverage." *Working Paper*, April 14, 2016 (https://papers.ssrn.com/sol3/papers.cfm?abstract_id=2765092).

Banks, Jeffrey S., and Barry R. Weingast. 1992. "The Political Control of Bureaucracies under Asymmetric Information." *American Journal of Political Science* 36 (2): 509–524.

Baumgartner, Frank R., and Beth Leech. 1998. *Basic Interests: The Importance of Groups in Politics and in Political Science*. Princeton University Press.

# References

Baumgartner, Frank R., and Bryan D. Jones. 1993. *Agendas and Instability in American Politics*. University of Chicago Press.

Baumgartner, Frank R., and Bryan D. Jones. 2015. *The Politics of Information: Problem Definition and the Course of Public Policy in America*. University of Chicago Press.

Baumgartner, Frank R., Jeffrey M. Berry, Marie Hojnacki, Beth Leech, and David Kimball. 2002. "Organized Interests and Issue Definition in Policy Debates." In *Interest Group Politics*, 6th ed., ed. Allan Cigler and Burdett Loomis. CQ Press.

Baumgartner, Frank R., Jeffrey M. Berry, Marie Hojnacki, David Kimball, and Beth Leech. 2009. *Lobbying and Policy Change*. University of Chicago Press.

Bellodi, Luca. 2023. "A Dynamic Measure of Bureaucratic Reputation: New Data for New Theory." *American Journal of Political Science* 67 (4): 880–897.

Bendor, John, Ami Glazer, and Thomas Hammond. 2001. "Theories of Delegation." *Annual Review of Political Science* 4: 235–269.

Bendor, Jonathan, Serge Taylor, and Roland van Gaalen. 1985. "Bureaucratic Expertise versus Legislative Authority: A Model of Deception and Monitoring in Budgeting." *American Political Science Review* 79 (4): 1041–1060.

Bendor, Jonathan, Serge Taylor, and Roland Van Gaalen. 1987. "Politicians, Bureaucrats, and Asymmetric Information." *American Journal of Political Science* 31 (4): 796–828.

Bertelli, Anthony, and David Lewis. 2013. "Policy Influence, Agency-Specific Expertise, and Exit in the Federal Service." *Journal of Public Administration Research and Theory* 23 (2): 233–245.

Bianco, William. 1997. "Reliable Source or Usual Suspects? Cue-taking, Information Transmission, and Legislative Committees." *Journal of Politics* 59 (3): 913–924.

Bimber, Bruce. 1991. "Information as a Factor in Congressional Politics." *Legislative Studies Quarterly* 16 (4): 585–605.

Bimber, Bruce. 1996. *The Politics of Expertise in Congress: The Rise and Fall of the Office of Technology Assessment*. State University of New York Press.

Binder, Sarah. 2015. "The Dysfunctional Congress." *American Review of Political Science* 18 (1): 85–101.

Blair, Peter. 2013. *Congress's Own Think Tank: Learning from the Legacy of the Office of Technology Assessment (1972–1995)*. Palgrave Macmillan.

Bolton, Alexander, and Sharece Thrower. 2021. *Checks in the Balance: Legislative Capacity and the Dynamics of Executive Power*. Princeton University Press.

Bonica, Adam. 2016. "Database on Ideology, Money in Politics, and Elections: Public Version 2.0." Stanford University Libraries (https://data.stanford.edu/dime).

Box-Steffensmeier, Janet, Dino Christenson, and Allison Craig. 2019. "Cue-Taking in Congress: Interest Group Signals from Dear Colleague Letters." *American Journal of Political Science* 63 (1): 163–180.

Box-Steffensmeier, Janet, Josh Ryan, and Anand Edward Sokhey. 2015. "Examining Legislative Cue-Taking in the US Senate." *Legislative Studies Quarterly* 40 (1): 13–53.

Bradley, R. 1980. "Motivations in Legislative Information Use." *Legislative Studies Quarterly* 5 (3): 393–405.

# References

Brasher, Holly. 2006. "Listening to Hearings." *American Politics Research* 34 (5): 583–604.

Broockman, David E. 2013. "Black Politicians Are More Intrinsically Motivated to Advance Blacks' Interests: A Field Experiment Manipulating Political Incentives." *American Journal of Political Science* 57 (3): 521–536.

Brownstein, Ronald. 2022. "The House GOP's Investigation Conundrum." *The Atlantic*, November 24 (www.theatlantic.com/politics/archive/2022/11/republican-house-majority-biden-investigations/672259/).

Burgat, Casey, and Charles Hunt. 2020. "How Committee Staffers Clear the Runway for Legislative Action in Congress." In *Congress Overwhelmed: The Decline in Congressional Capacity and Prospects for Reform*, ed. Timothy LaPira, Lee Drutman, and Kevin Kosar. University of Chicago Press.

Burstein, Paul. 1999. *Discrimination, Jobs, and Politics*. University of Chicago Press.

Burstein, Paul, and Elizabeth Hirsh. 2007. "Interest Organizations, Information, and Policy Innovation in the U.S. Congress." *Sociological Forum* 22 (2): 174–198.

Cameron, Charles, and B. Peter Rosendorff. 1993. "A Signaling Theory of Congressional Oversight." *Games and Economic Behaviors* 5 (1): 44–70.

Cameron, Charles, Cody Gray, Jonathan Kastellec, and Jee-Kwang Park. 2020. "From Textbook Pluralism to Modern Hyperpluralism." *Journal of Law and Courts* 8 (2): 301–332.

Cameron, Charles, and Jee-Kwang Park. 2007. "A Primer of the President's Program." In *Presidential Leadership: The Vortex of Power*, ed. Bert Rockman and Richard Waterman. Oxford University Press.

Carlson, David, and Jacob M. Montgomery. 2017. "A Pairwise Comparison Framework for Fast, Flexible, and Reliable Human Coding of Political Texts." *American Political Science Review* 111 (4): 835–843.

Carpenter, Daniel. 2001. *The Forging of Bureaucratic Autonomy: Reputations, Networks, and Policy Innovation in Executive Agencies, 1862–1928*. Princeton University Press.

Carpenter, Daniel P., Kevin M. Esterling, and David M. Lazer. 1998. "The Strength of Weak Ties in Lobbying Networks: Evidence from Health-Care Politics in the United States." *Journal of Theoretical Politics* 10 (4): 417–444.

Chin, Caitlin, Jackson Gode, Nicole Turner Lee, and Molly Reynolds. 2021. "With New House Rules, More Diversity in Technology Legislation and Hearings Is Possible." *Brookings* (www.brookings.edu/articles/with-new-house-rules-more-diversity-in-technology-legislation-and-hearings-is-possible/).

Clayton, Amanda, Diana O'Brien, and Jennifer Piscopo. 2019. "All Male Panels? Representation and Democratic Legitimacy." *American Journal of Political Science* 63 (1): 113–129.

Clinton, Joshua, Anthony Bertelli, Christian Grose, David Lewis, and David Nixon. 2012. "Separated Powers in the United States: The Ideology of Agencies, Presidents, and Congress." *American Journal of Political Science* 56 (2): 341–354.

Cohen, Jeffrey. 1995. "Presidential Rhetoric and the Public Agenda." *American Journal of Political Science* 39 (1): 87–107.

# References

Cox, Gary W., and Mathew D. McCubbins. 2005. *Setting the Agenda: Responsible Party Government in the U.S. House of Representatives*. Cambridge University Press.

Crosson, Jesse, Alexander Furnas, Timothy Lapira, and Casey Burgat. 2021. "Partisan Competition and the Decline in Legislative Capacity among Congressional Offices." *Legislative Studies Quarterly* 46 (3): 745–789.

CRS. 2006. "Hearings in the House of Representatives: A Guide for Preparation and Procedure." Updated June 13, 2006.

Curry, James. 2015. *Legislating in the Dark: Information and Power in the House of Representatives*. University of Chicago Press.

Curry, James. 2019. "Knowledge, Expertise, and Committee Power in the Contemporary Congress." *Legislative Studies Quarterly* 44 (2): 203–237.

Curry, James, and Leah Rosenstiel. 2023. "Unorthodox Lawmaking and the Value of Committee Assignments." Working Paper (https://drive.google.com/file/d/1Tj5lLfZoRgqyuCm5ONFp6oNsnvB2JBX-/view).

Davidson, Roger H., and Walter J. Oleszek. 1985. *Congress and Its Members*. CQ Press.

Davis, Christopher. 2015. "House Committee Hearings: Arranging Witnesses." *Congressional Research Service*.

Deering, Christopher, and Steven Smith. 1997. *Committees in Congress*, 3rd ed. CQ Press.

DeGregorio, Christine. 1994. "Professional Committee Staff as Policymaking Partners in the U.S. Congress." *Congress and the Presidency* 21 (1): 49–65.

Delevoye, Angele. 2020. "Ideology and Polarization in Congressional Hearings." Working Paper.

Dellis, Arnaud. 2023. "Legislative Informational Lobbying." *Journal of Economic Theory* 208: 105595.

Diermeier, Daniel, and Timothy Feddersen. 2000. "Information and Congressional Hearings." *American Journal of Political Science* 44 (1): 51–65.

Dodd, Lawrence C., and Richard L. Schott. 1979. *Congress and the Administrative State*. John Wiley & Sons.

Drutman, Lee. 2015. *The Business of America Is Lobbying: How Corporations Became Politicized and Politics Became More Corporate*. Oxford University Press.

Egan, Patrick, and Megan Mullin. 2017. "Climate Change: US Public Opinion." *Annual Review of Political Science* 20 (2): 209–227.

Ellis, Christopher, and Thomas Groll. 2020. "Strategic Legislative Subsidies: Informational Lobbying and the Cost of Policy." *American Political Science Review* 114 (1): 179–205.

Epstein, David, and Sharyn O'Halloran. 1999. *Delegating Powers: A Transactional Costs Politics Approach to Politics under the Separation of Power*. Cambridge University Press.

Esterling, Kevin. 2004. *The Political Economy of Expertise: Information and Efficiency*. The University of Michigan Press.

Esterling, Kevin. 2007. "Buying Expertise: Campaign Contributions and Attention to Policy Analysis in Congressional Committees." *American Political Science Review* 101 (1): 93–109.

# References

Evans, Diana. 1996. "Before the Roll Call: Interest Group Lobbying and Public Policy Outcomes in House Committees." *Political Research Quarterly* 49 (2): 287–304.

Feldman, Martha. 1989. *Order without Design: Information Production and Policymaking*. Stanford University Press.

Fenno, Richard F. 1973. *Congressmen in Committees*. Little, Brown & Co.

Flemming, Roy, Michael MacLeod, and Jeffrey Talbert. 1998. "Witnesses at the Confirmations? The Appearance of Organized Interests at Senate Hearings of Federal Judicial Appointments, 1945–1992." *Political Research Quarterly* 51 (3): 617–631.

Flock, Elizabeth. 2012. "Birth Control Hearing on Capitol Hill Had Mostly Male Panel of Witnesses (photo)." *The Washington Post*, February 16 (www.washingtonpost.com/blogs/blogpost/post/birth-control-hearing-on-capitol-hill-had-all-male-panel-of-witnesses/2012/02/16/gIQA6BM5HR_blog.html).

Fong, Christian. 2020. "Expertise, Networks, and Interpersonal Influence in Congress." *Journal of Politics* 82 (1): 269–284.

Foreman, Christopher. 1988. *Signals from the Hill: Congressional Oversight and the Challenge of Social Regulations*. Yale University Press.

Fouirnaies, Alexander, and Andrew Hall. 2018. "How Do Interest Groups Seek Access to Committees?" *American Journal of Political Science* 62 (1): 132–147.

Furnas, Alexander C., and Timothy M. LaPira. 2020. "Long-Term Trends in Congress's Brain Drain." www.newamerica.org/political-reform/reports/congressional-brain-drain/long-term-trends-in-congresss-brain-drain/. Accessed 2023-11-18.

Gailmard, Sean, and John Patty. 2012a. "Formal Models of Bureaucracy." *Annual Review of Political Science* 15: 353–377.

Gailmard, Sean, and John Patty. 2012b. *Learning While Governing: Information, Accountability, and Executive Branch Institutions*. University of Chicago Press.

Gamble, Katrina L. 2007. "Black Political Representation: An Examination of Legislative Activity within US House Committees." *Legislative Studies Quarterly* 32 (3): 421–447.

Gelman, Jeremy, Gilad Wilkenfeld, and E. Scott Adler. 2015. "The Opportunistic President: How US Presidents Determine Their Legislative Programs." *Legislative Studies Quarterly* 40 (3): 363–390.

Gilligan, Thomas W., and Keith Krehbiel. 1990. "Organization of Informative Committees by a Rational Legislature." *American Journal of Political Science* 34 (2): 531–564.

Gloseclose, Tim, and Nolan McCarty. 2001. "The Politics of Blame: Bargaining before an Audience." *American Journal of Political Science* 45 (1): 100–119.

Gormley, William. 1998. "Witnesses for the Revolution." *American Politics Quarterly* 26 (2): 1740195.

Gray, Virginia, and David Lowery. 2000. "Where Do Policy Ideas Come From? A Study of Minnesota Legislators and Staffers." *Journal of Public Administration Research and Theory* 10 (3): 573–597.

Green, Matthew, and Jeffrey Crouch. 2022. *Newt Gingrich: The Rise and Fall of a Party Entrepreneur*. University Press of Kansas.

# References

Grenzke, Janet. 1989. "PAC and the Congressional Supermarket: The Currency Is Complex." *American Journal of Political Science* 33 (1): 1–24.

Grier, Kevin, and Michael Munger. 1986. "The Impact of Legislator Attitudes on Interest-Group Campaign Contributions." *Journal of Labor Research* 7: 349–361.

Grier, Kevin, and Michael Munger. 1993. "Comparing Interest Group PAC Contributions to House and Senate Incumbents, 1980–1986." *Journal of Politics* 55 (3): 615–643.

Grose, Christian R. 2011. *Congress in Black and White: Race and Representation in Washington and at Home.* Cambridge University Press.

Grumbach, Jacob, Alexander Sahn, and Sarah Staszak. 2022. "Gender, Race, and Intersectionality in Campaign Finance." *Political Behavior* 44 (2): 319–340.

Hall, Richard L. 1987. "Participation and Purpose in Committee Decision Making." *American Political Science Review* 81 (1): 105–127.

Hall, Richard L., and Alan V. Deardorff. 2006. "Lobbying as Legislative Subsidy." *American Political Science Review* 100 (1): 69–84.

Hall, Richard L., and Frank Wayman. 1990. "Buying Time: Moneyed Interests and the Mobilization of Bias in Congressional Committee." *American Political Science Review* 84 (4): 797–820.

Hansen, John Mark. 1991. *Gaining Access: Congress and the Farm Lobby, 1919–1981.* University of Chicago Press.

Heitshusen, Valerie. 2017. "Senate Committee Hearings: Arranging Witnesses." *Congressional Research Service.*

Hertel-Fernandez, Alexander, Matto Mildenberger, and Leah Stokes. 2019. "Legislative Staff and Representation in Congress." *American Political Science Review* 113 (1): 1–18.

Hojnacki, Marie, and David Kimball. 1998. "Organized Interests and the Decision of Whom to Lobby in Congress." *American Political Science Review* 92 (4): 775–790.

Hojnacki, Marie, and David Kimball. 1999. "The Who and How of Organizations' Lobbying Strategies in Committee." *Journal of Politics* 61: 999–1024.

Huber, John, Charles Shipan, and Madelaine Pfahler. 2001. "Legislative and Statutory Control of Bureaucracy." *American Journal of Political Science* 45 (2): 330–345.

Huber, John, and Nolan McCarty. 2004. "Bureaucratic Capacity, Delegation, and Political Reform." *American Political Science Review* 98 (3): 369–384.

Huitt, Ralph K. 1954. "The Congressional Committee: A Case Study." *American Political Science Review* 48 (2): 340–365.

Johnson, Eddie Bernice. 2019. "Experts Needed: Options for Improved Science and Technology Advice for Congress." *U.S. House Committee on Science, Space, & Technology.*

Kim, In Song. 2018. "LobbyView: Firm-Level Lobbying & Congressional Bills Database." *MIT Working Paper* (http://web.mit.edu/insong/www/pdf/lobbyview.pdf).

Kingdon, John. 1981. *Congressmen's Voting Decisions.* Harper & Row.

Kingdon, John. 1989. *Congressmen's Voting Decisions.* 3rd ed. The University of Michigan Press.

Kingdon, John. 1995. *Agendas, Alternatives, and Public Policies.* HarperCollins.

## References

Kollman, Ken. 1997. "Inviting Friends to Lobby: Interest Groups, Ideological Bias, and Congressional Committees." *American Journal of Political Science* 41 (2): 519–544.

Kornberg, Maya. 2023. *Inside Congressional Committees: Function and Disfunction in the Legislative Process*. Columbia University Press.

Kosar, Kevin. 2020. "Legislative Branch Support Agencies: What They Are, What They Do, and Their Uneasy Position in Our System of Government." In *Congress Overwhelmed: The Decline in Congressional Capacity and Prospects for Reform*, ed. Lee Drutman, Timothy LaPira, and Kevin Kosar. University of Chicago Press.

Krause, George, and Anne Joseph O'Connell. 2016. "Experiential Learning and Presidential Management of the U.S. Federal Bureaucracy: Logic and Evidence from Agency Leadership Appointment." *American Journal of Political Science* 60 (4): 914–931.

Krehbiel, Keith. 1991. *Information and Legislative Organization*. The University of Michigan Press.

Kriner, Douglas, and Eric Schickler. 2016. *Investigating the President*. Princeton University Press.

Kriner, Douglas, and Liam Schwartz. 2008. "Divided Government and Congressional Investigations." *Legislative Studies Quarterly* 33 (2): 295–321.

Krook, Mona, and Diana O'Brien. 2012. "All the President's Men? The Appointment of Female Cabinet Ministers Worldwide." *Journal of Politics* 74 (3): 840–855.

LaPira, Timothy, and Herschel F. Thomas. 2016. "Congressional Analytical Capacity, Party Polarization, and the Political Economy of Revolving Door Lobbying." *Working Paper* (http://dx.doi.org/10.2139/ssrn.2827615).

LaPira, Timothy, and Herschel F. Thomas. 2017. *Revolving Door Lobbying: Public Service, Private Influence, and the Unequal Representation of Interests*. University Press of Kansas.

LaPira, Timothy, Kathleen Marchetti, and Herschel F. Thomas. 2020. "Gender Politics in the Lobbying Profession." *Politics & Gender* 16 (3): 816–844.

LaPira, Timothy, Lee Drutman, and Kevin R. Kosar. 2020. "Overwhelmed: An Introduction to Congress's Capacity Problem." In *Congress Overwhelmed: The Decline in Congressional Capacity and Prospects for Reform*. University of Chicago Press.

Lee, Frances. 2000. "Senate Representation and Coalition Building in Distributive Politics." *American Political Science Review* 94 (1): 59–72.

Lee, Frances. 2015. "How Party Polarization Affects Governance." *Annual Review of Political Science* 18: 261–282.

Lee, Frances. 2016. *Insecure Majorities: Congress and the Perpetual Campaign*. University of Chicago Press.

Lee, Frances, and Bruce Oppenheimer. 1999. *Sizing Up the Senate: The Unequal Consequences of Equal Representation*. University of Chicago Press.

Lewis, David. 2003. *President and the Politics of Agency Design: Political Insulation in the United States Government Bureaucracy, 1946–1997*. Stanford University Press.

Leyden, Kevin M. 1995. "Interest Group Resources and Testimony at Congressional Hearings." *Legislative Studies Quarterly* 20 (3): 431–439.

Lohmann, Susanne. 1995. "Information, Access, and Contributions." *Public Choice* 85 (3/4): 267–284.

Lorenz, Geoffrey. 2020. "Prioritized Interests: Diverse Lobbying Coalitions and Congressional Committee Agenda Setting." *Journal of Politics* 82 (1): 225–240.

Lowande, Kenneth. 2018. "Who Polices the Administrative State?" *American Political Science Review* 112 (4): 874–890.

Lowande, Kenneth, Melinda Ritchie, and Erinn Lauterbach. 2019. "Descriptive and Substantive Representation in Congress: Evidence from 80,000 Congressional Inquiries." *American Journal of Political Science* 63 (3): 644–659.

Malbin, Michael J. 1980. *Unelected Representatives: Congressional Staff and the Future of Representative Government*. Basic Books.

Matthews, Donald R. 1973. *U.S. Senators and Their World*. W. W. Norton & Company.

Matthews, Donald R., and James A. Stimson. 1975. *Yes and Nays: Normal Decision-Making in the U.S. House of Representatives*. Wiley.

Mayhew, David. 2005. *Divided We Govern: Party Control, Lawmaking, and Investigations, 1946–2002*. Yale University Press.

McCarty, Nolan. 2017. "The Regulation and Self-Regulation of a Complex Industry." *Journal of Politics* 79 (4): 1220–1236.

McCarty, Nolan. 2019a. *Polarization: What Everyone Needs to Know*. Oxford University Press.

McCarty, Nolan. 2019b. "Team Policy Production." *Working Paper* (https://papers.ssrn.com/sol3/papers.cfm?abstract_id=3505655).

McCubbins, Mathew D., Roger G. Noll, and Barry R. Weingast. 1987. "Administrative Procedures as Instruments of Political Control." *Journal of Law, Economics, and Organization* 3 (2): 243–277.

McCubbins, Mathew D., and Talbot Page. 1987. "A Theory of Congressional Delegation." In *Congress: Structure and Policy*, ed. Mathew McCubbins and Terry Sullivan. Cambridge University Press.

McCubbins, Mathew D., and Thomas Schwartz. 1984. "Congressional Oversight Overlooked: Police Patrols versus Fire Alarms." *American Journal of Political Science* 28 (1): 165–179.

McGann, James. 2020. "2019 Global Go to Think Tank Index Report." *Think Tank and Civil Societies Program*, University of Pennsylvania.

McGrath, Robert J. 2013. "Congressional Oversight Hearings and Policy Control." *Legislative Studies Quarterly* 38 (3): 349–376.

Mendelberg, Tali, Christopher Karpowitz, and Nicholas Goedert. 2014. "Does Descriptive Representation Facilitate Women's Distinctive Voice? How Gender Composition and Decision Rules Affect Deliberation." *American Journal of Political Science* 58 (2): 291–306.

Miller, Gary. 2005. "The Political Evolution of Principal-Agent Models." *Annual Review of Political Science* 8: 203–225.

Miller, Gary J., and Terry M. Moe. 1983. "Bureaucrats, Legislators, and the Size of Government." *American Political Science Review* 77 (2): 297–322.

Oleszek, Walter J. 1989. *Congressional Procedures and the Policy Process*. CQ Press.

Oleszek, Walter J. 2021. "Congressional Reform: A Perspective." *Congressional Research Service* R46933.

## References

Oreskes, Naomi, and Erik Conway. 2011. *Merchants of Doubt: How a Handful of Scientists Obscured the Truth on Issues from Tobacco Smoke to Climate Change*. Bloomsbury Publishing.

Ovide, Shira. 2020. "Congress Doesn't Get Big Tech: By Design." *The New York Times*, July 29 (www.nytimes.com/2020/07/29/technology/congress-big-tech.html).

Park, Ju Yeon. 2017. "A Lab Experiment on Committee Hearings: Preferences, Power, and a Quest for Information." *Legislative Studies Quarterly* 42 (1): 3–31.

Park, Ju Yeon. 2019. "Committee Chair's Majority Partisan Status and Its Effect on Information Transmission via Hearings." *Journal of Legislative Studies* 25 (4): 614–624.

Park, Ju Yeon. 2021. "When Do Politicians Grandstand? Measuring Message Politics in Committee Hearings." *Journal of Politics* 83 (1): 214–228.

Park, Ju Yeon. 2023. "Electoral Rewards for Political Grandstanding." *The Proceedings of the National Academy of Sciences* 120 (17): e2214697120.

Parrott, Michael. 2019. "What Role Do Interest Groups Play in House Committees? A View from Behind the Curtain." *PS: Political Science and Politics* 52 (2): 404–409.

Patty, John, and Ian Turner. 2021. "Ex Post Review and Expert Policymaking: When Does Oversight Reduce Accountability?" *Journal of Politics* 83 (1): 23–39.

Phinney, Robin. 2017. *Strange Bedfellows: Interest Group Coalitions, Diverse Partners, and Influence in American Social Policy*. Cambridge University Press.

Powell, Eleanor, and Justin Grimmer. 2016. "Money in Exile: Campaign Contributions and Committee Access." *Journal of Politics* 78 (4): 974–988.

Pressman, Jeremy. 2020. "Gender Imbalance in Expert Testimony at U.S. Senate Hearings." *The Forum* 18 (2): 197–205.

Quirk, Paul J. 2005. "Deliberation and Decision Making." In *The Legislative Branch*, ed. Paul J. Quirk and Sarah A. Binder. Oxford University Press.

Quirk, Paul J., and William Bendix. 2011. "Deliberation in Congress." In *The Oxford Handbook of the American Congress*, ed. George Edwards III, Frances E. Lee, and Eric Schickler. Oxford University Press.

Quirk, Paul J., William Bendix, and Andre Bachtiger. 2018. "Institutional Deliberation." In *The Oxford Handbook of Deliberative Democracy*, ed. Andre Bachtiger, John Dryzek, Jane Mansbridge, and Mark Warren. Oxford University Press.

Ratliff, Amisa, Jamie Neikrie, and Michael Beckel. 2022. "Fair Pay: Why Congress Needs to Invest in Junior Staff." Accessed November 18, 2023.

Richardson, Mark. 2019. "Politicization and Expertise: Exit, Effort, and Investment." *Journal of Politics* 81 (3): 878–891.

Richardson, Mark, Joshua Clinton, and David Lewis. 2018. "Elite Perceptions of Agency Ideology and Workforce Skill." *Journal of Politics* 80 (1): 303–308.

Ritchie, Melinda. 2018. "Back-Channel Representation: A Study of the Strategic Communication of Senators with the U.S. Department of Labor." *Journal of Politics* 80 (1): 240–253.

Ritchie, Melinda. 2023. *Backdoor Lawmaking: Evading Obstacles in the US Congress*. Oxford University Press.

Ritchie, Melinda, and Hye Young You. 2019. "Legislators as Lobbyists." *Legislative Studies Quarterly* 44 (1): 65–95.
Ritchie, Melinda, and Hye Young You. 2021. "Women's Advancement in Politics: Evidence from Congressional Staff." *Journal of Politics* 83 (2): 421–438.
Romer, Thomas, and James M. Snyder. 1994. "An Empirical Investigation of the Dynamics of PAC Contributions." *American Journal of Political Science* 38 (3): 745–769.
Romzek, Barbara, and Jennifer Utter. 1997. "Congressional Legislative Staff: Political Professionals or Clerks?" *American Journal of Political Science* 41 (4): 1251–1279.
Rudalevige, Andrew. 2002. *Managing the President's Program: Presidential Leadership and Legislative Policy Formulation*. Princeton University Press.
Sargent, John. 2020. "The Office of Technology Assessment: History, Authorities, Issues, and Options." *Congressional Research Service* R46327.
Schlozman, Daniel. 2015. *When Movements Anchor Parties: Electoral Alignments in American History*. Princeton University Press.
Schlozman, Kay Lehman, Philip Jones, Hye Young You, Tracy Burch, Sidney Verba, and Henry Brady. 2015. "Organizations and the Democratic Representation of Interests: What Does It Mean When Those Organizations Have No Members?" *Perspectives on Politics* 13 (4): 1017–1029.
Schlozman, Kay Lehman, Sidney Verba, and Henry Brady. 2012. *The Unheavenly Chorus: Unequal Political Voice and the Broken Promise of American Democracy*. Princeton University Press.
Schnakenberg, Keith. 2017. "Informational Lobbying and Legislative Voting." *American Journal of Political Science* 61 (1): 129–145.
Shepherd, Michael, and Hye Young You. 2020. "Exit Strategy: Career Concerns and Revolving Doors in Congress." *American Political Science Review* 114 (1): 270–284.
Shepsle, Kenneth, and Barry Weingast. 1987. "The Institutional Foundations of Committee Power." *American Political Science Review* 81 (1): 85–104.
Sinclair, Barbara. 1986. "The Role of Committees in Agenda Setting in the US Congress." *Legislative Studies Quarterly* 11 (1): 35–45.
Stewart III, Charles, and Jonathan Woon. 2017. "Congressional Committee Assignments, 103rd to 114th Congresses, 1993-2017."
Talbert, Jeffrey C., Bryan D. Jones, and Frank R. Baumgartner. 1995. "Nonlegislative Hearings and Policy Change in Congress." *American Journal of Political Science* 39 (2): 383–405.
Taylor, Dorceta. 2016. *The Rise of the American Conservation Movement: Power, Privilege, and Environmental Protection*. Duke University Press.
Truman, David B. 1951. *The Governmental Process*. Alfred A. Knopf, Inc.
Tudor, Grant, and Justin Warner. 2019. "Congress Should Revive the Office of Technology Assessment: Here's How to Do It." *Brookings Institute*, December 18 (www.brookings.edu/blog/fixgov/2019/12/18/congress-should-revive-the-office-of-technology-assessment-heres-how-to-do-it/).
Van Der Slik, Jack, and Thomas Stenger. 1977. "Citizen Witnesses before Congressional Committees." *Political Science Quarterly* 92 (3): 465–485.
Volden, Craig, and Alan Wiseman. 2014. *Legislative Effectiveness in the United States Congress*. Cambridge University Press.

## References

Warner, Justin, and Grant Tudor. 2019. "The Congressional Futures Office." *Harvard Kennedy School Belfer Center Paper* (www.belfercenter.org/publication/congressional-futures-office).

Weiner, Eric. 2007. "American Conscience Waking Up to Climate Change." *NPR*, July 7 (www.npr.org/2007/07/07/11787222/american-conscience-waking-up-to-climate-change).

Weingast, Barry R. 1984. "The Congressional-Bureaucratic System: A Principal Agent Perspective (with Applications to the SEC)." *Public Choice* 44: 147–191.

Weingast, Barry R. 1988. "The Industrial Organization of Congress; or, Why Legislatures, Like Firms, Are Not Organized as Markets." *Journal of Political Economy* 96 (1): 132–163.

Weingast, Barry R., and Mark Moran. 1983. "Bureaucratic Discretion or Congressional Control? Regulatory Policymaking by the Federal Trade Commission." *Journal of Political Economy* 91 (5): 765–800.

Wolfenberger, Donald. 2001. *Congress and the People: Deliberative Democracy on Trial*. Johns Hopkins University Press.

Wright, John R. 1985. "PACs, Contributions, and Roll Calls: An Organizational Perspective." *American Political Science Review* 79 (2): 400–414.

Wright, John R. 1996. *Interest Groups and Congress: Lobbying, Contributions, and Influence*. Allyn & Bacon.

Yackee, Jason Webb, and Susan Webb Yackee. 2006. "A Bias toward Business? Assessing Interest Group Influence on the U.S. Bureaucracy." *Journal of Politics* 68 (1): 128–139.

Zelizer, Adam. 2019. "Is Position-Taking Contagious? Evidence of Cue-Taking from Two Field Experiments in a State Legislature." *American Political Science Review* 113 (2): 340–352.

# Index

1994 Midterm election, 24, 90, 126

affiliation, 6, 10, 31–37, 42, 44, 46, 50, 51, 56, 57, 62, 64, 70, 76, 86, 112, 114
Affordable Care Act, 98
AFL-CIO, 35, 79
agenda-setting, 22, 106, 108
Alexander, Lamar, 1
Alumbaugh, Brad, 66
Amazon, 80, 145
American Association for the Advancement of Science, 122
American Bar Association, 35
American Chemical Society, 122
American Enterprise Institute, 107
American Farm Bureau, 35
American Hospital Association, 35
American Red Cross, 59, 60
amplifying effect, 125, 132
antitrust, 51
Armey, Dick, 127
Asian Pacific American Caucus, 29, 149
Axne, Cindy, 54, 55

Baylor Healthcare System, 59
bill, 5, 8, 20, 32, 62, 79–88, 92, 94–97, 99, 138, 141
Blair, Peter D., 122
Blumenthal, Richard, 5
Bogan, Vicki L., 54–56
Bradley–Terry model, 58
broadband, 51
Brock, Gary, 59
Brockton, 54
Brown, George, 131
bureaucracy, 36, 43, 46, 90, 98–103, 106
bureaucrat, 6, 8, 9, 22, 23, 27, 34, 42, 44, 46, 49, 50, 64, 65, 75, 76, 80, 87, 88, 95, 96, 99–103, 105–109, 111–114, 116–120, 141, 142, 144
Bush Tax Cut, 107
Bush, George W., 106, 107, 117
business group, 24, 31

campaign contribution, 13, 19, 23, 33, 36, 47, 68
career civil servant, 101
Carnegie Mellon University, 122
Citadel, 55
citation, 72–76
citizen, 6, 22, 25, 30, 34, 35, 44, 49, 50, 64–66, 76, 101, 102
climate change, 7, 71–73, 75, 76, 137, 140, 144–147
collective bargaining, 80
committee chair, 8, 13, 21, 23, 25–27, 38, 62–64, 81, 82, 84–86, 89, 90, 92, 94, 96, 99, 101, 106, 108, 126, 129, 142, 150
committee intent, 4, 21, 78, 84, 86, 89, 90, 92, 93, 97, 140, 141, 163, 165
committee median, 62
committee membership, 37
Committee on Agriculture, 45, 47, 82, 91, 92
Committee on Appropriations, 16, 26, 39, 40, 68, 91, 131
Committee on Armed Services, 44, 49, 50, 68, 91, 93, 109
Committee on Banking, 45, 54
Committee on Budget, 91, 129
Committee on Education and Labor, 91
Committee on Energy and Commerce, 26, 39, 40, 45, 59, 72, 83, 91, 125, 129, 132, 134
Committee on Finance, 25, 91

187

# Index

Committee on Financial Services, 54
Committee on Foreign Affairs, 44, 48, 68, 91, 109
Committee on Foreign Relations, 26, 48
Committee on Government Operations, 26, 44, 91
Committee on Health, Education, Labor and Pensions, 1, 40, 48, 98
Committee on Judiciary, 4, 91, 144, 145
Committee on Natural Resources, 40
Committee on Oversight and Reform, 12, 109
Committee on Rules, 91
Committee on Science, Space, and Technology, 68, 72, 92, 125, 129, 132, 134, 146
Committee on Small Business, 12, 45, 91, 92, 129, 132
Committee on Veterans' Affairs, 44
Committee on Ways and Means, 39, 59, 91, 106, 107
committee, constituent, 92, 93
Congressional Black Caucus, 29, 149
congressional briefing, 22
Congressional Budget Office, 9, 13, 101, 124
congressional capacity, 9, 10, 122, 124–126, 132, 135, 137, 138, 141, 142, 147, 148
congressional deliberation, 10, 141
congressional directories, 37
Congressional Hispanic Caucus, 29, 149
Congressional Information Service, 31
congressional official, 33
Congressional Research Service, 9, 13, 101, 123, 124, 126, 128, 129, 131, 139, 143, 148
congressional staff survey, 143
congressional support agencies, 9, 101, 123–125, 129, 137, 138, 147, 148
Congressional Tri-Caucus, 29, 30, 36, 149
conservative advocacy group, 24
contraceptive coverage, 47
Contract with America, 9, 124, 126, 127
Cornell University, 54
coronavirus, 1, 2, 144
corporation, 13, 33, 34, 42, 80, 88, 90
Correlates of War Project, 36
correspondence, 15, 22
COVID-19, 1, 2, 7, 138, 150

Darcy, Jo-Ellen, 66
Database on Ideology, Money in Politics, and Elections, 36

defense, 46, 94, 108, 110, 116
delegation, 99, 102–104
Department of Army, 66
Department of Commerce, 74
Department of Defense, 110
Department of Energy, 74, 75
Department of Justice, 144
Department of State, 110
Department of Veterans Affairs, 20
descriptive representation, 36
difference-in-differences, 10, 125, 133, 137
diversity, witness, 36, 51, 87, 88, 149, 167
divided government, 68, 69, 76, 100, 103–106, 108, 111–120, 144
domestic commerce, 46
donor, 13, 36, 59
Durban, Dick, 5
DW-NOMINATE, 37, 62, 86, 97

educational institution, 34
Ehlers, Vern, 123
electoral consequences, 88
Encyclopedia of Associations, 24, 30
Enders, John F., 128
energy, 129, 167
environment, 43, 94, 167
Environmental Defense Fund, 35
Environmental Protection Agency, 74, 110, 114, 147
executive agencies, 8, 9, 16, 20, 24, 80, 99–104, 106, 116, 127, 128, 142
executive branch, 8, 9, 20, 23, 28, 33, 34, 44, 98–101, 104–106, 108, 114, 119, 120, 127, 138, 141, 144
executive session, 32
expert witness, 43, 90, 92, 94, 95, 132, 141, 167
expertise, 2, 9, 10, 13, 14, 16, 18, 25, 82, 96, 102, 103, 106, 120, 124, 125, 127, 131, 135, 136, 141, 148, 151
ExxonMobil, 12

Facebook, 47, 145
family planning, 47
Farley, Michael, 59
Fauci, Anthony, 2
Fazio, Vic, 122, 138
Feinstein, Dianne, 145
filibuster, Senate, 105
fire-alarm oversight, 101, 102
floor median, 16, 62
Ford Motor Co., 35
foreign investment, 83, 84
foreign trade, 46

## Index

Foxx, Virginia, 80
Freedom of Information Act, 22

GameStop, 53, 54, 56
gatekeeper, 17, 82
gatekeeping, 19, 24
gender, 29–31, 36, 37, 47–49, 51, 62, 66, 68, 70, 149
Geophysical Research Letters, 73
Gill, Keith, 54–56
Gingrich, Newt, 124, 126
Global Investment in American Jobs Act of 2013, 83, 97
global warming, 12, 72, 73, 146, 147
Government Accountability Office, 90, 124
Government Publishing Office, 31, 57, 75
grandstanding, 16, 23, 57
greenhouse gas, 72, 73, 146
group witness, 83, 90–92, 94–96, 167

Hahn, Stephen, 2
Harkin, Tom, 98
Harper, Cynthia, 79
Harvard IV-4 dictionary, 57, 58
Hassett, Kevin A., 107
Hatch, Orrin, 145
HathiTrust Digital Library Project, 52
health-related organization, 34
hearing
   committee, 1–5, 10, 12, 14, 15, 20–24, 30, 31, 33, 36, 38, 49, 51, 60, 61, 68, 70, 76, 78, 87, 89, 90, 96, 99, 123, 141, 142, 147
   confirmation, 21, 30
   congressional, 10, 14, 15, 24, 27, 29–33, 36, 37, 42, 43, 47, 48, 50–52, 57, 73, 75, 99, 104, 108, 110, 144, 151
   investigative, 21, 23, 36, 104, 105, 119, 144
   legislative, 8, 20, 41–43, 78, 79
   non-legislative, 30, 82
   nonreferral, 8, 82, 84–89, 96
   oversight, 20–23, 36, 37, 40–44, 47, 48, 100, 104, 106, 144
   published, 6, 32
   referral, 8, 64, 82–94, 96
   transcript, 57
   unpublished, 32
   virtual, 150, 151
Herfindahl index, 86, 87, 89, 113–115
Holt, Rush, 122, 123, 125
House Office of Diversity and Inclusion, 51, 149
House Republican Conference, 127

Hunt, Catherine T., 122
Hutchinson, Cassidy, 21

immigration, 46
income inequality, 79, 80
independent agency, 109, 110
information
   analytical, 6–9, 56–60, 62, 64–66, 68–72, 75, 76, 78, 82, 84, 87, 89, 96, 99, 101, 113, 119, 125, 131, 135, 136, 140, 141, 144, 145
   asymmetric, 18
   expert, 17, 82, 87, 120, 124
   external, 4, 6, 8, 15, 141
   political, 8, 83, 84, 88, 140
   technical, 10, 16, 56, 123, 125, 126, 131, 138, 139, 142
information acquisition, 3, 15, 16, 100, 143, 144
information asymmetry, 17, 105
information flows, 4, 11, 15, 22, 140, 151
information provision, 12, 17, 19, 20, 66
information seeking, 18, 31
information transmission, 9, 15, 18, 120
information-seeking statement, 6, 57
informational advantage, 8, 13, 14, 18, 81, 99–101, 105, 106
Inouye, Daniel, 131
institutional trust, 47
intelligence, artificial, 5, 11, 51, 144, 148
interbranch relations, 99, 100, 106, 108, 111, 116, 118, 120, 141
interest group, 3–5, 13, 15, 18, 19, 22–25, 27, 30, 31, 33, 38, 42, 83, 88, 101, 103, 140, 141
internal capacity, 9, 28, 78, 124, 125, 131, 137, 143, 148
Internal Revenue Service, 59, 107
international affairs, 46, 94, 116, 117, 167
International Energy Agency, 75
international organization, 34, 36, 75
International Panel on Climate Change, 75, 145
investigation, 37, 80, 105, 144, 151
Issa, Darrell, 47

Jordan, Jim, 144
Journal of Climate Change, 73
Journal of Geophysical Research, 73, 74
judicial appointment, 30
jurisdiction, 30, 49, 68, 81, 82, 126, 129

Kadlec, Robert, 2

## Index

labor law firm, 79
labor law reform, 79, 80
labor movement, 79
labor union, 30, 31, 34, 35, 42, 46, 49, 79, 88, 90, 91, 95, 96, 116, 167
lawyer, 25, 34, 35, 44, 50, 164, 166, 169, 171
legislation, 2, 5, 8, 9, 12, 16, 20, 70, 80–84, 88, 89, 96, 99, 100, 104, 106, 120, 126, 138, 140, 141
legislative effectiveness score, 62–64
Legislative Reorganization Act in 1946, 126
legislative staff, 19, 143
legislative support agency, 34, 41, 139
legislative-executive relationship, 99
lobbying, 13, 18, 19, 33, 36, 38, 142, 143, 147
   coalition, 84
Lobbying Disclosure Act, 36
lobbyist, 9, 18, 19, 22, 30, 34–36, 44, 47, 50, 68, 124, 138, 142
LobbyView.org, 36

machine-readable dataset, 28
macroeconomics, 46, 94, 117, 167
majority, 14, 21, 68, 76, 78, 81, 101, 104, 112, 119, 120, 124, 129, 141, 142, 144, 146
   Democratic, 46, 69, 72, 98, 112, 116, 145–147, 162, 167–171
   party, 8, 9, 16, 25, 46, 69, 80, 81, 83, 91, 100, 104–106, 111, 112, 116, 119–121, 126, 127, 141, 144
   Republican, 9, 30, 46, 69, 72, 90, 98, 114, 124, 126, 127, 137, 147
Maloney, Carolyn, 47
Mann, Michael, 72, 73, 146, 147
markup, 91
Mass-based group, 88, 96
McCarthy, Kevin, 144
McLernon, Nancy L., 83
membership association, 35, 42, 44, 46, 76, 88, 90, 91, 95, 96, 167
membership organization, 33, 34, 42, 43, 50, 88
misinformation, 145
MIT, 35
Mosher, Charles, 127
Musk, Elon, 53

National Academy of Sciences, 122
National Aeronautics and Space Administration, 74
National Association for the Advancement of Colored People, 30
National Congress of American Indians, 35
National Oceanic and Atmospheric Administration, 74
National Organization for Women, 88
National Research Council, 74, 123
National Science Foundation, 128
national security, 32
native american, 34, 35, 44, 50, 76, 150
Natural Resources Defense Council, 43
Nature, 74
Nature Geoscience, 73
New York University, 122
Nobel Prize in Physiology or Medicine, 128
nomination, 20, 21, 30, 31, 36, 40, 41, 44, 80
   hearing, 36, 37, 40–42, 44, 96
nonprofit organization, 33, 34, 49, 64, 65, 67, 75, 143

O'Neill, Paul, 107
Obama, Barack, 47, 98, 117
Office of Public Management, 36
Office of Technology Assessment, 9, 10, 90, 122–125, 127–139, 147, 148, 173, 174
opening statement, 26, 79, 83, 107
Organization for International Investment, 83
outside expert, 16, 29, 138
oversight, 11, 12, 20, 23, 28, 36, 37, 40, 41, 44, 54, 80, 96, 99–102, 104, 105, 144
   hearing, 20–23, 36, 37, 40–44, 47, 48, 100, 104, 106, 144
   police patrol, 101

parent category, 34, 35
partisan incentives, 3, 4, 7–9, 28, 140, 141, 147
party leaders, 9, 13, 18, 38, 126, 140–142
Paycheck Protection Program, 12, 28
Peha, Jon M., 122
Pelosi, Nancy, 29, 146, 149
Pennsylvania State University, 72, 146
pension plan, 59, 60
Pension Rights Center, 59
pesticides, 82
Planned Parenthood, 47
polarization, 3, 7, 16, 23, 38, 64, 141, 142, 146, 147
Policy Agenda Project, 32, 36, 62, 70, 94, 97, 108, 121

# Index

policy committees, 91–93, 96
policy development, 56, 78, 96, 141, 144, 145
policy implementation, 70, 99, 100, 103, 105, 120
policy uncertainty, 103
Political Action Committees, 13, 23
political appointees, 101, 147
political message, 16, 23, 56, 57
political motivation, 31
positive theory, 16, 17
preference alignment, 101, 103
president, issue priority, 172
president, policy agenda, 101, 108
presidential veto, 105, 120
press release, 29
prestige committee, 91
Princeton Plasma Physics Laboratory, 122
Princeton University, 122
principal–agent, 16, 101, 104
private interest organization, 33
procedural statement, 57, 58
ProQuest Congressional, 31, 32

question-and-answer period, 27, 82

rank-and-file, 13, 81
ranking member, 26, 29, 80, 131
Reddit, 53–55
referred bill, 82
religious organization, 34
Repealing the Job-Killing Health Care Law Act, 98
representation, 3, 30, 36, 42, 100, 149, 150
research, 22, 24, 25, 35, 43, 44, 46, 50, 54, 55, 60, 64, 68, 70, 72, 73, 75–77, 87, 88, 90, 101, 113–115, 119, 123–125, 129, 131–134
  staff, 30
  witness, 135, 136, 167, 173, 174
Resolution, 80, 126
risk aversion, 103
Robbins, Frederick C., 128
Robinhood, 53–55
Rosenfeld, Jake, 79
Rosenthal, Craig, 59

Schuchat, Anne, 2
Science, 73, 74
science, atmospheric, 72, 146
Sebelius, Kathleen, 98, 99
Secretary of Commerce, 83
Secretary of HHS, 98

Secretary of Treasury, 54, 107
Select Committee on Global Warming, 72, 146
Select Committee on the Modernization of Congress, 122, 138, 151
Senate Democratic Diversity Initiative, 51
seniority system, 90
Sierra Club, 43
Smith, Lamar S., 146
social media, 5, 54–56, 145
social welfare, 49, 94, 108, 167
staff compensation, 143
STAN model, 59
standing committee, 6, 32, 37, 39, 40, 45, 48, 49, 90, 104, 130, 133, 136, 137
State of the Union address, 101, 116–118, 121
state or local government, 33–35, 42, 46, 65, 76
stm R package, 70
strategic witness selection, 14
structural topic model, 70
subcommittee, 16, 25, 26, 36–38, 62–64, 78, 79, 83, 86, 90, 167, 169–171, 173, 174
Subcommittee Bill of Rights, 38, 90
Subcommittee on Commerce, Manufacturing, and Trade, 83, 97
Subcommittee on Consumer Protection and Commerce, 26
Subcommittee on Privacy, Technology, and the Law, 5, 11
subpoena power, 25
substitution effect, 115, 119
Supreme Court, 21, 30
Swarthmore College, 122

TD Ameritrade, 53
technology, 94, 123, 124, 128–130, 132, 138, 139, 148, 167
Technology Assessment Advisory Council, 128
Teich, Albert H., 122
Terry, Lee, 83
testimony, 3, 6, 7, 9, 12, 21, 26, 28, 36–39, 49, 54–57, 60–62, 64, 66, 69–77, 79–81, 84, 89, 96, 98–100, 106, 107, 123, 125, 138, 146, 147, 157
  witness, 3–7, 14, 22, 23, 39, 56–59, 61–71, 124, 162
The Legislative Reorganization Act of 1970, 90

## Index

think tank, 6, 9, 34, 35, 43, 46, 64, 73–76, 79, 87, 88, 96, 101, 113, 116, 120, 123, 125, 127, 131–136, 142, 150, 167, 173
Thomas, Bill, 107
tobacco, 30, 161
trade association, 34, 35, 42, 44, 50, 75, 76, 88, 90, 91, 95, 96, 116, 142, 150, 167
trading, 53–56
transaction cost, 105
Truth in Testimony Disclosure Form, 26, 27
tweet, 53
Twitter, 54
type of information, 7, 10, 56, 76, 83, 140, 151
type of witnesses, 25, 29, 30, 44, 75, 78, 88, 146, 150, 151

underrepresentation, 47
unified government, 69, 70, 76, 105, 106, 108, 111, 112, 118, 120, 121, 141
union membership, 30
unit of analysis, 57, 112, 116
United Nations Environment Programme, 75, 145
university, 34, 35, 46, 73, 76, 96, 113, 116, 120, 125, 131, 133, 134, 173
University of California, Berkeley, 123
US Catholic Conference, 35

Velazquez, Nydia, 12
Veterans Benefits Administration, 20
Veterans of Foreign Wars, 35

WallStreetBets, 53–55
Walmart, 80
Washington Representatives Directory, 36
Washington University in St. Louis, 79
Waters, Maxine, 54, 55
Weller, Thomas H., 128
White House, 21, 23, 99, 100, 127, 144
Wilderness Society, 43
Wilson, Federica S., 79
Wilson, Woodrow, 4, 14
witness, 1–10, 12, 14, 15, 20–26, 28–51, 53–58, 60–62, 64, 65, 68–76, 78–84, 86–96, 98–101, 106, 108–116, 118–120, 122, 125, 131–138, 140–142, 145–147, 149–151, 153–156, 162, 167, 172, 173
    invitation, 3–6, 8, 15, 21, 24, 28, 81, 89, 92, 93, 97, 111, 115, 120, 131, 133, 140, 163, 165, 168, 170
World Bank, 35
World Meteorological Organization, 75, 145

Yellen, Janet, 54
YouTube, 54

Zuckerberg, Mark, 145

Milton Keynes UK
Ingram Content Group UK Ltd.
UKHW020342281124
451683UK00002B/31